THE COMING

DISRUPTION

How AI First Will Force Organizations
to Change Everything or Face Destruction

FRED VOCCOLA

Endorsements

Yochi Slonim – CEO, Anima Biotech
"Fred Voccola has done it again. He's not just predicting the AI revolution—he's mapping it. *The Coming Disruption* reads like a playbook written by someone who's already lived through the future."

Mike Sanders – CEO, Upshop
"This is the most practical and actionable book on AI transformation I've ever read. Fred translates massive, abstract change into decisions that any CEO, manager, or entrepreneur can make today. It's terrifying, brilliant, and unbelievably useful."

Joe Smolaraski, CEO Watchguard
"Every executive I know is terrified of what's coming. Voccola has given us the manual for how to not just endure—but dominate—the AI era."

Tim Conkel - Founder and CEO, The 20.
"Voccola combines street-smart operator instincts with boardroom-level intellect. He's the rare leader who can explain the future of AI in plain English—and make you care about it deeply."

Myles Lambert – COO, Brighthouse Financial
"Fred Voccola sees around corners. He's built and scaled organizations through every major technological shift of the last two decades, successfully leading those companies to new heights. This book isn't prediction. It's instruction."

Tom Schodorf – Former SVP, Splunk & BMC Software
"Voccola doesn't theorize about disruption—he's engineered it at scale, again and again. This book distills decades of hard-earned operational wisdom into a brutally honest roadmap for surviving the next great industrial reset."

Mark Nevins – CEO Nevins Consulting
"Reading *The Coming Disruption* is like plugging your brain into a supercomputer of business strategy. Voccola connects the dots between technology, productivity, and human behavior like few others can."

Ben Levin– Founder & Managing Director, Level Equity Partners
"Fred captures the velocity of AI transformation better than anyone I've seen. He turns complexity into clarity—and shows exactly how leaders must adapt, or disappear. A must-read for investors and executives alike."

Dominic DiPiero – Founder and CEO, Newport Capital Group.
"Every era has its defining voice. In the age of AI, that voice is Fred Voccola's. He delivers not just insight—but a call to action for anyone serious about building or investing in the future."

Philip Vorobeychik – Founder and Managing Director, Vertica Capital
"This book is terrifying in the best way possible. It will shake your assumptions, destroy your comfort zone, and force you to see what's already happening in front of you. *The Coming Disruption* isn't optional—it's required reading."

Jeanette Núñez – President, Florida International University, Former Lieutenant Governor, State of Florida
"*The Coming Disruption* bridges academia, business, and policy in a way few leaders could. Voccola's synthesis of technology, labor, and education is as enlightening as it is urgent. Every student, policymaker, and CEO should read this."

Francis Suarez – Mayor of Miami
"Fred Voccola's vision aligns perfectly with the spirit of Miami—fast, fearless, and entrepreneurial. *The Coming Disruption* captures the urgency and opportunity of this moment better than anything I've read. It's both a warning and a blueprint for how cities, companies, and nations can lead in the AI age."

Jose Felix Diaz – Executive Vice President & Partner, Ballard Partners

"This book isn't just about technology—it's about the reshaping of power itself. Fred Voccola understands how AI will transform not just markets, but governance, policy, and influence. *The Coming Disruption* should be required reading for every elected official and policymaker who wants to keep their country competitive."

ATLAS ELITE
P A R T N E R S
PUBLISHING

Published by **Atlas Elite Publishing Partners**
Cover design by **Michael Beas**

eBook ISBN: 978-1-962825-84-9
Paperback ISBN: 978-1-962825-85-6
Hardback ISBN: 978-1-962825-86-3

Printed in United States of America

For more information, visit:
www.atlaselitepublishingpartners.com

Dedication

To my father, Harry Voccola. The best father, and most innovative
man I have ever met. Thank you for everything.

Table of Contents

Introduction:
Why AI First Means Adapt
or Die – Today!

Imagine you're living 65 million years ago, and you look up to see a bright streak cutting across the sky. At first, it's small, barely noticeable. A few creatures glance up, shrug, and go back to whatever they're doing. But the streak gets bigger. Brighter. Hotter. And then it hits. In an instant, the world changes forever. Species that thrived for millions of years are gone—wiped out—not because they were weak, but because they couldn't adapt fast enough to the new reality.

That's AI.

It's not a slow-moving weather pattern you can watch from the porch and decide what to do about later. It's a meteor—already in the atmosphere—moving at a speed you can't outrun. And the organizations, leaders, and workers who don't immediately adapt will go the way of the dinosaurs. AI isn't just a new tool—it's an extinction-level event for the slow and complacent, and a generational leap forward for the fast and decisive.

AI isn't tomorrow's experiment—it's today's battlefield. Keep moving or get run over. It's as simple—and brutal—as that.

Everyone's talking about AI because for the first time in history, a tool exists that can replace not just manual labor or calculation—but thinking. Real, high-order, creative thinking. And not just once—but billions of times a second, across the globe.

If AI is the meteor already tearing through our atmosphere, then the place where the shockwave will be felt first and most violently Is the world of business and organizations. Not just tech companies or Silicon Valley darlings, but every enterprise, small company, agency, nonprofit, university, and institution that forms the backbone of our prosperity and civilization. These are the entities that coordinate human effort, allocate resources, create jobs, produce food, develop medicines, enforce laws, and deliver the products and services that keep society functioning.

While AI will transform every corner of human life—how we learn, govern, heal, and connect—this book is laser-focused on the single arena where its effects will decide the pace and shape of our future: **the businesses and organizations that run our world**.

When these institutions embrace AI, they amplify productivity, unlock innovation, and create new possibilities for billions of people. When they resist, they choke progress, lose competitiveness, and destabilize the systems on which we all rely.

That's why you should care—because whether you're a CEO, a policymaker, a teacher, or simply someone who depends on the stability of the society around you, what happens inside these organizations will determine whether AI's meteor strike leads to a golden age or an extinction event.

If your organization is not committed to being AI First NOW (Like now, not "three years from now"), you are more than at risk—you are already behind. You are already bleeding market share, losing your business moat, and wasting time. Extinction isn't a metaphor. It's on your calendar.

And this isn't just about large companies. It is all companies: Small-to-Medium-sized Businesses (SMB) to Fortune 100 behemoths. It's Governments. Universities. Nonprofits. The consequences will be universal and permanent.

This book is written for those who want to win. For those who want to lead. If that's you, you're in the right place. If not, bookmark this now and reread it in 12 months when you're trying to figure out what the hell happened.

The Most Potent Development in Human History

Let's not hedge. AI is the single most important development in the history of our species.

More than the wheel, the steam engine, electricity, penicillin, the Internet, or anything else. All those innovations changed the world. But here is the main difference. **AI changes how the world changes.**

It's not that those other innovations weren't massive—they were. But AI allows us to harness the *full power of all of them*—and apply them faster and cheaper than ever before.

This is an exponential leap in what is possible; it is the first time in history when humanity doesn't just have a new tool—it has a million tools, instantly available to anyone who knows how to ask the right questions.

It doesn't rest. It doesn't complain. And it never stops improving.

The projections about what AI is doing and will do to our society and businesses are unbelievable.

Some Crazy Sci-Fi Stuff

Some futurists and leading technologists predict that AI will unlock possibilities so crazy they sound ripped from science fiction. Think about AI-driven brain–computer interfaces that allow people to communicate telepathically — no talking, no typing, just thought-to-thought connection. Elon Musk's Neuralink™ is already experimenting with this, but AI could scale it to billions of people, enabling global communication networks straight out of a sci-fi novel.

On the medical frontier, some researchers predict **AI-powered nanobots in the bloodstream** that detect disease instantly, repair tissue, or even slow aging. There are legitimate scientists who believe AI might eventually **extend human lifespans by decades — or even indefinitely** — by cracking the code of biological aging.

Defense analysts even speculate about **fully autonomous armies** of drones and robotics, where wars are fought algorithm vs. algorithm — raising existential questions about power, deterrence, and control.

Others envision **AI-managed cities**, where traffic, power, housing, and healthcare are all continuously optimized by learning systems. Imagine a city with no traffic jams, no blackouts, and zero waste because every system is harmonized in real-time.

Imagine AI coordinating fleets of autonomous machines to **terraform planets** — managing climate systems, balancing atmospheres, and even seeding life to make Mars or other worlds habitable.

Self-replicating robots guided by AI could mine asteroids and build massive space habitats, effectively extending civilization beyond Earth. Some visionaries argue AI might one day help re-engineer the human body itself to survive in alien environments — designing biology that can thrive under new skies.

And here's one of the most jaw-dropping concepts: AI helping us **simulate and map consciousness itself** — potentially digitizing aspects of human thought or even creating AI-human hybrids. Some predict that by mid-21st-century, we may face questions about whether "uploaded minds" count as people.

As wild as these sound, they're not idle fantasies. They're topics being debated in research labs, government task forces, and boardrooms of trillion-dollar companies right now. The line between science fiction and business planning is disappearing faster than anyone expected.

Yesterday's Fantasy is Today's Reality

The previous section may have sounded like pure sci-fi, but AI is no longer just a vision of the future. Many of those mind-bending ideas are already happening today, stretching the boundaries of imagination and reshaping what it means to be human.

In healthcare, AI is now detecting cancers years earlier than doctors could, reading scans with accuracy rates above 99%, and even designing personalized treatment plans that adjust in real-time to patient biology.

In biotechnology, AI is unlocking new proteins and drug candidates at speeds 200 times faster than before, potentially curing diseases once thought untreatable. And if that isn't "sci-fi enough," AI is being fused with robotics *today* to create prosthetics that learn from the wearer's brain signals, restoring mobility in ways unimaginable just a decade ago.

In space exploration, NASA is using AI to map galaxies faster than ever before, while private companies test AI copilots capable of running entire missions to Mars.

Transportation is on the cusp of being unrecognizable. Fully autonomous cargo ships are already crossing oceans, while driverless trucks are poised to move **40% of all freight in the U.S.** within a decade.

In construction, AI-guided 3D printers are building houses in under 24 hours for a fraction of today's cost, which could put a huge dent in global housing shortages.

Creative fields are exploding too. AI-generated films, music, and art are beginning to rival human talent, raising profound questions about authorship while democratizing creation for anyone with a laptop.

Education is shifting toward AI-driven personalized tutors, giving **billions of students a 1:1 teacher** that never gets tired, never misses a day, and adapts perfectly to their learning style.

The headlines are writing themselves: "AI finds cure for rare disease in 48 hours," "AI-powered nanobots enter clinical trials," "First 100% AI-designed city breaks ground in Asia." The future isn't coming slowly. It's bearing down on us like an avalanche.

AI's Impact on Every Business and Organization

AI's capacity to bring "sci-fi" to life is unprecedented, and we are just getting started. AI will transform every aspect of humanity, especially our businesses and organizations, more than any other technology in human history

Societies and their businesses are inseparable reflections of one another. The way a society organizes its economy — whether through free markets, central planning, or some hybrid — is reflected directly in how businesses operate, allocate resources, and create value. Business is often the beating heart of a society, because it determines how wealth is distributed, innovation is rewarded, and human energy is directed. In many ways, business is society's most powerful tool: it decides which ideas get funded, which goods get produced, and which problems are solved first.

Perhaps nowhere will AI's influence be felt more than inside the organizations that run our economy. As AI rewires how companies function, it also *rewires the societies those businesses sustain*. Businesses are where resources meet strategy, where human talent meets technology, and where the future gets built. If AI First companies can create 2x, 5x, or even 10x more value than before, then the ripple effects for society are staggering. The biggest impact of AI won't just be on how people live day-to-day — it will be on the businesses that shape society itself, and the unprecedented value they can unlock for humanity.

The projections on what AI is already doing and will do in the short term to business are staggering. Analysts project that AI could add between **$15–$20 trillion to global GDP by 2030**, making it the single largest economic driver in human history.

McKinsey estimates that AI could immediately deliver **$4.4 trillion in annual economic value** across industries, with over half of that tied directly to business productivity gains.

Morgan Stanley projects that adopting AI could add $13–16 trillion to the S&P 500's market value—boosting it by nearly **30%**—and deliver

$920 billion annually in net benefits through efficiency gains and new revenue generation.

PwC forecasts that AI could contribute up to **$15.7 trillion** to the global economy by 2030—exceeding the combined current GDP of China and India.

DC forecasts that AI will contribute **$19.9 trillion to the global economy** through 2030.

For individual companies, the story is just as staggering. Goldman Sachs forecasts that AI could automate 25% of all work tasks globally within the decade, unlocking massive cost savings while allowing leaner organizations to outproduce their larger competitors. Bain & Company reports that organizations adopting generative AI at scale have already achieved upwards of **30% reductions in operational headcount needs** in core functions like finance, legal, and HR.

The impact on profitability is for all businesses in all industries; by reducing costs and increasing output simultaneously, AI can *double or even triple profit margins* in as little as 12 to 24 months.

AI Attracts Investment

The investment world has already caught on. Global AI investment is projected to surpass $200 billion annually by 2030, with enterprise AI software adoption growing at a 38% Compound Annual Growth Rate (CAGR) through 2030. Venture funding in AI startups is at record highs, with billions pouring into everything from AI copilots to AI-powered vertical software. Every dollar invested accelerates a flywheel of innovation, compounding productivity across industries.

But here's the flip side: businesses that fail to adapt to an AI-focused approach face extinction. A PwC report warns that 45% of work activities could already be automated using existing AI technology, yet most companies haven't implemented even the basics. Competitors who do embrace AI are achieving growth rates two to five times higher than peers who don't. The gap is widening so quickly that within 12 to18 months, AI First companies can leapfrog over incumbents that took decades to build.

AI isn't just another tool—it's the great business filter of all time. Companies that fully embrace it will dominate. Those that don't will quietly disappear, casualties of a transformation that move faster than any disruption before it.

The mind-bending possibilities of AI in the future are exciting — maybe even terrifying — but the story is already unfolding today. Trillions of dollars are being poured into this technology right now, and the race to apply it in business is accelerating at breakneck speed.

And here's the part leaders can't ignore: There will be winners and losers. The winners will be those who adopt AI First thinking immediately, harnessing the productivity and innovation gains before their competitors do. The losers will be those who hesitate, clinging to outdated structures and manual ways of working until the gap is too wide to close.

So, the question is no longer *if* AI will reshape your organization — it's _how fast_ you'll let it happen. And with that, let's look at how to do it.

With All This Power Comes a Painful Truth

To harness AI's power, **everything** in your organization must change.

Everything about how your organization is structured, managed, and led must be rethought and changed to optimize for this humanity-changing technology

Your org design? Outdated.

Your job descriptions? Irrelevant.

Your talent strategy? Obsolete.

Your workflows, systems, planning cadence, leadership qualities, and reporting structures?

They all need to be blown up.

That might sound dramatic, but this book isn't about comfort. It's about clarity. If you're looking for something to help you polish your old playbook, you're in the wrong place.

What This Book Is (And Why You Must Keep Reading)

This book is not here to worship at the altar of AI or to discuss the potential humanity-ending consequences of AI taking over the world.

This book is here to arm you. To give you a map. A war plan. A set of actual, tactical steps to take today— right now. By doing so, you ensure your organization's survival and relevance.

We'll walk you through:

- Why AI will change every organization on Earth
- What being AI First actually means
- How the characteristics, skills, and definition of leadership will change in the AI Era.

This Is for You–Yes, You

This isn't just a business book. It's not just for the C-suite of Fortune 500 companies It is for *everyone*. It's for:

- Government leaders who want to modernize before they're replaced.
- Entrepreneurs trying to punch above their weight.
- CEOs and executives of both public and private companies
- Small business owners looking to leave a business behind for their kids
- Workers who want to stay ahead and not be replaced.
- Educators who want to prepare students for a world of AI.
- Curious citizens who want to understand what the future holds
- Students about to enter the work force.

- Anyone who understands that AI is not coming—it's here, and it will reward those who move fast, think clearly, and act boldly.

To have a place in the AI era, be prepared to change everything about your organization. And fast. This book will give you the outline and playbook to change and win.

Welcome to Extreme Change Management

You've heard of change management. Maybe you've even led a digital transformation initiative. You know the drill—define the change, build the roadmap, communicate clearly, train, adapt, monitor. Yawn.

Forget that. That's yesterday's world.

The AI Era requires a new type of change management. We call it **Extreme Change Management**.

It's fast. It's raw. It's unsettling. It demands total honesty, and it moves simultaneously, not sequentially.

Your entire organization must change at once—structure, culture, talent, tooling, leadership, and KPIs. And you won't get five years. You'll get five quarters. Maybe. Because the alternative is that your competition will do it, and you will not survive.

Extreme Change Management doesn't ask for permission. **It requires leaders who act like founders, not bureaucrats.** It is 100% results oriented. It does not seek buy in: AI demands it, and it will leave casualties along the way.

This book will guide you through the process of adopting Extreme Change Management. Not just what needs to change, but how to change it.

AI Will Be the Death of the Organizational Deep State

Every organization has one: Big and small businesses, government, universities, etc. **The deep state.**

This does not refer to a small group of elite individuals sitting in a guarded room in a castle in Switzerland secretly pulling the strings of global society.

Rather, it refers to the layer of middle management and corporate political players who survive by understanding how to survive the system and exist within the cracks. They don't deliver value or results. They identify with the institution itself, rather than creating value for the institution.

AI destroys the deep state. It rewards output, speed, iteration, visibility, value and results. It punishes everything else by not allowing room for its existence.

Leadership must now be **entrepreneurial**. Not high level, conceptual management consultants. Outcome-oriented and results- based entrepreneurial leaders. Hands on. Creative. Comfortable with change. Leaders that are **in** the business as well as **guiding** the business.

The fastest organizations—the ones that act and adapt AI immediately and fully, will win—will suck all the oxygen out of the room and leave everyone else to die. And they'll do it in three-month increments.

You can either be one of them, or you can spend the next two years watching your competitor's valuation triple while you rewrite job specs that no one wants anymore.

This book will demonstrate how AI will enable you to clean your organization of the toxic deep state, to survive and thrive as an outcome-driven organization.

So...Who Am I?...and why should you trust what I'm saying?

I'm Fred Voccola. Entrepreneur. Philanthropist. Builder. Scaler. Industry Disrupter. I've spent my career starting and scaling multiple companies which created tens of billions of dollars in value by disrupting industries in times of significant macro-change. Times when the classic "playbook" no longer worked. I've done it across industries—Enterprise Software, Internet, FinTech, SaaS, healthcare, franchising, cybersecurity, AI— when the margin for error was zero and the reward for getting it right was massive.

I have been lucky enough to work with some of the brightest and best people around the world, have seen some of the most motivated people push the envelope to drive tremendous results, constantly challenging the status quo and innovating with no apologies.

As the co-founder and CEO of Kaseya for over a decade, I was fortunate to be at the cutting edge of AI and to see and experience firsthand the transformative power that AI can have in the world. As the leading global provider of AI powered cybersecurity and IT management software, we grew the business to approx. 1.5 billion in revenue, leveraging AI and the power of AI to protect tens of millions of SMBs around the world from ransomware and other Cyber-attacks.

Today, in addition to acting as the Vice Chairman at Kaseya, I serve as Chairman and CEO of Simpro Group. At Simpro, we provide an AI powered operating platform for commercial and residential trade companies to over 500,000 people around the world. Our platform leverages the power of AI to enable these organizations, who make up the backbone of the middle class, to gain incredible efficiency and economies of scale, allowing them to rapidly **double their profit margins.**

This book **isn't written by a consultant** who studied AI. It's written by someone who has **used AI and is currently using AI** in it most **actionable form** to transform entire industries, to transform how companies operate, how teams are structured, how decisions are made, and how competitors are crushed.

This book is written the same way I lead: **direct, bold, fast-moving, and unapologetically real.** I don't have time for fluff, and neither do you. If you want to navigate the most important transformation in human history—**and come out on top**—I'm going to show you how.

Throughout the book, you'll find "Cooper Callout". These are "Cooper Callouts" that I want you to especially remember, as they crystallize the material that comes before them. By the way, Cooper is my dog, best friend, and my motivation to continuously become a better man.

Before We Jump In

The power of AI is limitless. That's not a slogan—it's a warning and a promise.

The only thing standing between you and leveraging that power is your willingness to change.

Everything else—the tech, the tools, the knowledge—it's all here and it's easy. **What's missing is you.**

So, buckle up. This is going to be uncomfortable. It's going to be fast. It's going to make you rethink everything you thought you knew about business, management, and leadership.

But it's also going to give you the roadmap to become one of the few organizations who win this game.

In the next chapter, we'll look at some of the most monumental changes in human history and see why the advent of AI leaves them all in the dust.

Chapter 1:

History is Full of Transformations, But Nothing Like AI

Business has always been the practical expression of society itself. No matter the political or cultural system—capitalism, communism, monarchy, or democracy—business has been the clearest reflection of how people live, interact, produce, trade, organize work, allocate resources and create value. It's the engine behind human progress.

Always has been. Likely always will be.

If you want to understand the condition of a civilization at any given time, see how its businesses function. Are they productive? Innovative? Competing? Driving competitive advantage for the nations that house them? These are strong indications of the state of the society.

Why? Because human progress—real, lasting, measurable progress—has almost always been tied to economic growth and productivity. Not feel-good slogans. Not government policy. Productivity. **Period**.

Productivity is stuff that actually makes life better: more food, faster communication, better healthcare, safer transportation, richer experiences, more time for leisure and family, etc. And all of that stems from one core variable: worker productivity.

Worker productivity isn't just a statistic—it's the lifeblood of progress. Every unit of advancement—every new technology, every rise in living standards, every drop in infant mortality, every space shuttle launch—is downstream of how effectively people produce value using the tools and technologies of their time.

And here's the crazy truth: the average worker today is more than **1,000 times** more productive than a worker in the year 1025. That's not a typo. **1,000 times.** That's not just growth. That's a supernova. It means that one thousand people were required to produce what one person can produce today. Simply Incredible.

However, that growth didn't come on a nice clean line. Instead, it came in violent, explosive bursts. Human productivity throughout history has been mostly stagnant, with occasional spectacular jumps forward—and every single one of those jumps was the result of some massive disruption: a technology, a system, a model or some form of transformation that broke the old rules and rewrote the playbook.

Then, in short bursts, transformative technologies like mechanized agriculture, industrial manufacturing, electricity, and later computing—shattered that flat line. Each disruption created a spike upward, permanently resetting the baseline of what workers could achieve.

As is often said, a picture tells a thousand words. This following chart does just that. The chart shows this clearly: long eras of stagnation punctuated by sudden leaps in worker productivity.

Over millennia, for most of the time, the productivity of our species did not move. Hundreds of years went by when a person produced the same output year after year, which meant business did not change fundamentally. Sure, there were comings and goings of organizations, etc. But that was simply the result of more or less talented people. Not a systemic shift. Then BOOM, a seismic shock hit, and productivity spiked way up. And all of society changed and benefited. ALL OF IT…and eventually everyone benefited.

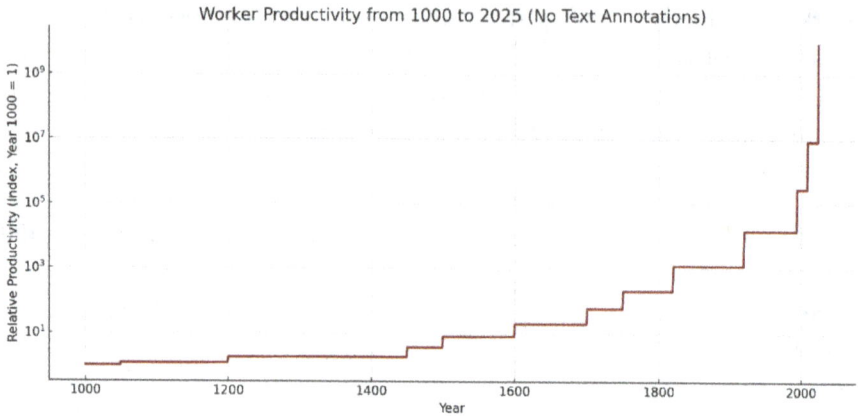

Worker Productivity from 1000 to 2025 (No Text Annotations)

Some of these spikes stretched across decades, like the Industrial Revolution, while others, like the digital revolution of the 1990s and 2000s, unfolded in just 15 to 20 years. But between these bursts, productivity stayed flat, reflecting the natural human tendency to **refine rather than reinvent**. These leaps didn't just make individual workers more productive—they reshaped societies, economies, and even geopolitics. The final spike, representing AI, is steeper and faster than anything before, with productivity surging nearly 1000x over the baseline by 2025. It illustrates a hard truth: progress doesn't come gradually. It comes in violent, transformational waves—and we are living through the steepest one yet.

> **Cooper Callout:** History doesn't crawl—it leaps. And AI is the biggest leap humanity has ever seen.

It's fun to discuss theory, but better to teach through examples. Let's look at just three of the most civilization-shaking transformations that led to massive leaps in human productivity:

1. Coinage (Spread: 600 BCE -350 BCE across the Mediterranean. 200-400% worker productivity)

Before coins/currency, economic activity around the world was barter based. You had grain; I had pottery. We haggled. If I didn't need grain, tough luck. Trade was limited to immediate usefulness, and transactions were rare and inefficient. Value was subjective, trust-based, and local. Inventory had to be available all the time in real time, making businesses very inefficient by today's standards.

Then coins arrived with standardized value and portability. Coins represented trust embedded in metal. Suddenly, trade exploded—across cities, borders, and empires. The invention of coinage didn't just improve commerce—it unlocked commerce. Civilization went from isolated barter towns to integrated trade networks. Cities emerged. Banks and lending evolved. Productivity spiked as the flow of goods and services exploded.

But—and this is key—it didn't happen overnight. It took roughly *250 years* for coinage to fully take hold across the Mediterranean. That's ten generations. Why? First there had to be an infrastructure created to support the idea of stored value. This infrastructure included more than physical things like coin mints; it required acceptance of the *concept* of abstract value. This leads to another crucial factor: **People resist change**, especially when it threatens their existing power structure.

Entire civilizations that refused to adapt to this "new technology" were left behind. Many of the barter-based city-states that resisted coinage—especially in parts of North Africa and pre-Roman Western Europe—eventually collapsed or were conquered. Coinage made empires like Lydia, Greece, and later Rome dominant, not just militarily, but economically. Over the course of 250 years, once fully adopted, coinage provided a 100-200% improvement in overall worker productivity and output.

It was the financial software upgrade of the ancient world.

2. The Industrial Revolution (Focused Window: ~70 Years, 1780–1850. 250-500% worker Productivity increase)

When steam engines, mechanized looms, and mass production showed up, they torched the old playbook. The average worker suddenly had the **output power of 10, 20, or 50 men**. Food production exploded.

Transportation was transformed. Cities became gigantic. Wages surged. Life expectancy jumped.

Between 1780 and 1850, worker productivity in Britain alone grew by an estimated 2.5 to 4 times—an **astronomical shift for just 70 years**. In modern terms, that would be like someone today suddenly producing 4 times as much software, designs, reports, or widgets every year without working more hours.

And this revolution wasn't just about building factories. Entire industries vanished. Hand-weaving? Gone. Cottage blacksmithing? Replaced. Horse-drawn shipping? Outmoded. And the companies that refused to change—those who mocked mechanization or thought it was a fad, ceased to exist.

Meanwhile, new empires were born: the Carnegies, Vanderbilts, Rockefellers, and Rothschilds didn't just make money—they reshaped the world order. They created and became super companies, more valuable than the world had ever seen. This was a transformation of capital, labor, and global power. **Most importantly, the majority of human life changed.**

3. The Digital Revolution (Focused Window: ~15 Years, 1990-2005, 40-50% Worker Productivity)

If coinage took 250 years and the Industrial Revolution took 70, the digital age was like a lightning strike: 15 years. Between 1990 and 2005, the world saw the rapid spread of personal computing, the internet, software, mobile communications, cloud systems, and more.

This revolution didn't just boost productivity. It redefined it. A single spreadsheet replaced teams of bookkeepers. An email replaced days of postal delay. A website replaced a dozen salespeople.

U.S. labor productivity surged by 44% in those 15 years. That's an annualized growth rate of 2.5%, which is huge when compounded over a decade and a half.

Entire industries evaporated: Blockbuster, gone. Kodak, crippled. Print media, gutted. But those who embraced the shift—Amazon, Microsoft, JP Morgan, Exxon, Fidelity, Wal Mart—became titans. The winners weren't always the smartest. They were the fastest to become Technology-first companies.

Major Transformations in Human Productivity

The table below shows the impact of these technological innovations disrupted human life and significantly increased the productivity of everyone in the related societies.

Transformation	Timeframe (Adoption Window)	Total Productivity Gain	Avg. Annual Productivity Gain
Coinage	~250 years (600 BCE – 350 BCE)	+200–400%	~0.8–1.6% per year
Industrial Revolution	~70 years (1780 – 1850)	+250–500%	~3.5–7.1% per year
Digital Revolution	~15 years (1990 – 2005)	+40–50%	~2.5–3.3% per year

Cooper Callout: Notice how the *speed of adoption* is accelerating. What once took centuries (coinage) shrank to decades (industrialization), then to just 15 years (digital). The AI transformation will compress that curve again — but this time, the leap is larger, and the adoption window is measured in **months and quarters, not years or decades.**

Speed of Transformation: Power vs. Speed

Here's the most important lesson from all three transformations: Their power is equally impressive. What each of them does to productivity is almost **unimaginable**. However, the **speed** at which organizations can take advantage of these technologies is what separates them. **Speed is the ultimate differentiator**.

Every business had access to coinage, steam, or the internet. The advantage didn't come from the technology itself—it came from who adopted it **fastest**. That's it. That's the secret.

Coinage had the power to multiply trade. Steam had the power to multiply labor. The internet had the power to multiply information. But only those who embraced the transformation—who built the infrastructure, overcame the resistance, and reorganized around the new rules—benefited.

The slow ones? They died.

Why Did These Transformations Take So Long?

A common question is, "Why didn't every business and organization adopt every available tool and technology to their advantage right away?" After all, businesses act in their self-interest. They want to thrive and succeed. What prevented not only individual businesses, but overall society, from immediately implementing these solutions?

Two core reasons: **infrastructure** and **people**.

Let's start with **infrastructure**. Most people hear that word and immediately think of roads, cables, machines, fiber optics, or factories. That's only part of the story. Yes, some massive disruptions require physical infrastructure to scale: railroads in the Industrial Revolution, telephone lines and fiber in the Digital Revolution, coin mints and transportation security in the ancient world. But there's another, often more critical, layer: intellectual infrastructure.

Intellectual infrastructure is the collection of ideas, standards, frameworks, and mental models that need to be in place before the technology or innovation can be fully embraced. You don't just drop in coinage and expect everyone to start using it. You need a shared belief system around value. You need standard weights, trusted issuers, basic arithmetic literacy. You need merchants, customers, and rulers to understand, trust, and agree on what a coin means.

In ancient times, it took over 250 years for the Mediterranean world to fully adopt coinage—not because there was not enough metal available, rather because the mindset of money itself had to be invented. The entire concept of abstract value—that a stamped metal disk could hold universal purchasing power—was alien to people raised in a world of direct barter. They had to rewire how they thought about exchange, commerce, and even wealth. **Both sides of the transaction had to have full buy-in,** and the confidence that the next person they traded with would as well.

That itself is infrastructure. Not just the minting process or the transport of currency, but the psychological shift required to make use of the innovation. That's why most people underestimate how slow true transformation is—they see the tech and assume it's plug-and-play. It's not. It's rebuild-the-world-and-the-minds-inside-it.

The Industrial Revolution? Same story. We didn't just need steam engines—we needed a generation of engineers trained to build and maintain them. We needed standardized parts. We needed factory layouts. We needed entirely new safety standards, labor laws, production methods, and logistics systems. It wasn't just the steam engine. It was the entire mental, managerial, and logistical ecosystem that had to be built around it.

And in the Digital Revolution, fiber-optic cable was just one piece. The real lift was building the computational literacy of the workforce, the coding languages, the enterprise software, the standards for data transmission, and the global legal frameworks for information flow and commerce. The internet couldn't change the world until we knew what to do with it—and how to organize our institutions around it.

So, when we say "infrastructure," we mean it in the full sense: physical, intellectual, cultural, and behavioral scaffolding. And building that takes time --, sometimes decades, sometimes centuries. Making it IMPOSSIBLE for this change to happen right away.

The Second Drag on Transformation: People's Reluctance to Change

If physical infrastructure is the slow, **external** constraint on progress, people are the **internal** one. And as it turns out, people may just be the more stubborn of the two.

Humans resist change. We always have. It's baked into our psychology, into our survival instincts and into our cultural fabric. Even when the change is good. Even when it's clear that the change will lead to massive productivity gains, better outcomes, wealth, health, and opportunity, we fight it.

Evolutionary biologist Charles Darwin observed that, "It is not the strongest of the species that survives, nor the most intelligent. It is the one **most adaptable to change**."

And still—we're terrible at it. This isn't just about comfort; it's structural. Entire societies, governments, organizations, and families are engineered for stability, routine, and predictability.

That works well enough until a technological disruption comes along and **changes the entire game**. And instead of embracing it, people double down on the old ways.

Organizations are no different. In fact, **they're worse**, because organizations institutionalize resistance to change. They are built to preserve processes, minimize disruption, and maximize predictability. Middle management is, in many ways, a system designed to slow things down. To "manage" change, not drive it.

That's why so many organizations fail to adopt world-changing innovations until they're forced to. Fax machines, email, cloud software, mobile-first design, the internet, e-commerce, AI—all of them faced resistance from within. Leaders knew they were coming. They had the data. They saw the trends. The infrastructure required to implement these transformational capabilities existed. But they waited. They slow-played it. They ensured "buy-in". Or worse, they tried to fight it.

Even when the value from the transformation is obvious and the value is immense, people hesitate. They ask for "proof" that it works. They want case studies. Committees. Consensus. **They want guarantees that it won't fail**, that nobody will be disrupted, that the change will be smooth and incremental.

The most frustrating part is that change is the engine of all progress. Every leap in productivity, wealth, and quality of life has come from someone—somewhere—who embraced change when others resisted it. And yet we, as a species, still instinctively avoid it.

When you combine this deeply human resistance to change with the infrastructure lags described earlier, it's easy to see why even the most powerful innovations in history have taken decades—sometimes centuries—to fully realize their impact.

Summary: The Drag Factors of History

If you're wondering why the coinage revolution took 250 years to ripple across the Mediterranean, or why the Industrial Revolution needed 70 years to reshape the modern world, or why the Digital Revolution took 15 years just to rewire how we work, it comes down to two simple truths:

1. **Infrastructure takes time to build.** Not just physical hardware, but intellectual scaffolding, cultural norms, mental models, and operational systems.
2. **People hate change.** And organizations are full of people. Most of them don't want to be disrupted, replaced, or reinvented. They want to manage what exists—not create what's next.

And this is why massive disruptions always takes time. Not because it isn't obvious. Not because it isn't powerful, **but** because the world needed time to catch up—physically, mentally, operationally, and emotionally.

Until now.

The AI Transformation: ZERO Infrastructure Change Required

The AI revolution is unlike any other game-changing transformation in human history.

For the first time in history, a transformational leap forward requires **no new infrastructure** for organizations to adopt it **now**. No external factors must exist for your organization to leverage AI right now. Every organization, of any size, in any industry, anywhere in the world can immediately begin leveraging AI with the tools and technologies they currently have. They don't need to wait for things to be built, or buy new things, or wait for any external developments. If you have a laptop, a smartphone, and internet access, you already have the infrastructure.

Yes, there is massive investment underway to build new data centers, giant power plants, and expanded networks to support the coming tidal wave of AI demand. But that is about scaling for tomorrow. For the future. For a society that has 100% adopted AI. It is future capacity being created, not capacity required for **today.**

Yet right this second, you and every single person in your organization can start leveraging AI. With zero delay. Zero investment. Zero infrastructure changes. Every company, every school, every nonprofit, and every government agency can adopt AI right now. Unlike revolutions of the past, the barrier is not infrastructure—it is mindset, skill, and leadership.

What is holding you back is you and your organizations unwillingness to change.

If your organization is not ready to change, the new AI world won't wait. It will pass your organization by and into obsolescence. This will happen at a rate the world has never seen before.

Welcome to the first transformation that doesn't give you the luxury of time because it does not require time.

Welcome to the AI Age.

The AI Age: The Most Powerful Disruption in History

We are at the beginning of the most massive transformation in history. But this one is different. It can be started now.

- No need for factories.
- No need for global supply chains.
- No physical infrastructure to wait on.
- No generational trust-building like coinage.

AI is here. Right now. The power is massive— seismic—and the **implementation lag is zero.** Anyone with a browser and a brain can deploy it. That means there are no excuses. No regulatory red tape. No capital hurdles. No physical barriers. Just willpower and vision.

And here's the gut punch: because the power is distributed equally, the only differentiator is **speed**.

AI isn't just the next big thing—it's the single most explosive force in the history of productivity. Coinage doubled productivity, but it took 250 years to do it—an annual gain of less than 1%. The printing press? About a 100% jump over 120 years—still under 1% per year. The Industrial Revolution? Another 100% bump in 70 years—around 1.4% a year. The computer and internet era? Same 100% gain, but in 15 years—about 6.6% per year. Each one felt revolutionary in its time.

Now, take a deep breath—because AI isn't playing by those rules. We're not talking about a 1% annual bump, or even 6%.

We're talking **70%–110% productivity gains per worker**, per organization, in as little as 6-12 months.

That's a rate 10–25 times faster than the internet boom, and hundreds of times faster than the Industrial Revolution. Put another way: Think of the combined productivity blast of the Industrial Revolution *and* the internet revolution—**compressed into one detonation,** happening not over a century, not over a decade, **but in a single fiscal year.**

The impact math is **brutal and simple**. A company that moves rapidly to the AI Era doesn't just get ahead—it *laps* competitors. In twelve months, it's producing over twice as much output with the same headcount. In two years, that gap is so large that catching up becomes mathematically near impossible. This isn't evolution—it's an extinction event for slow movers and a moonshot for those who move now.

Final Words

Each transformation redefined its era. Coinage transformed civilizations. Industrialization reshaped nations. Digital disrupted industries.

But AI? AI will obliterate the line between ideas and outcomes. It will destroy the deep-state bureaucracy that stagnates organizations of all sizes. It will empower visionaries—and annihilate slow-moving giants. It will be the **most powerful transformation in human history**—and it's happening in **quarters**, not decades.

This is not a change.

This is a reckoning.

Welcome to the AI Age.

Chapter 2:

AI: The Most Powerful Tool Humanity Has Ever Known

Everyone's talking about AI.

CEOs. Politicians. Investors. Kids in high school. Dinner tables. Boardrooms. War rooms. Even your local dentist's office. AI is everywhere — and it's not hype. It's a full-blown **inflection point in human history**. And anyone not paying attention is already behind.

Why the fuss?

Because **this isn't just another "new technology."** This isn't the iPhone. It's not the internet. It's not electricity. It's not a steam engine. **It's all of them.** Stacked. Multiplied. And then accelerated to warp speed. Combined In its power to add productivity and to create disruption

Let's say it plainly: AI will impact humanity more than any other innovation in history. **Period.**

Let that sink in. We are not talking about a new feature or a shift in convenience. This is a **seismic event** — the kind that rearranges power, money, opportunity, and global influence.

The Productivity Explosion That Changes Everything

As we mentioned in the previous chapter, the productivity impact of AI will equal or exceed that of the Industrial Revolution and the Internet/PC revolution combined.

In 12 months.

Let's back up this claim with hard facts. The Information Age — everything from the PC to the internet to the cloud — increased worker productivity by about 50% over 15 years. The Industrial Revolution? That was roughly 200% over an entire century.

AI First users? They are achieving 70–110% productivity gains in under 12 months.

That's not a typo. Read it again. In less than a single year, AI First workers are doubling their productive output.

Estimates say that over the next five years, that figure could rise to over **500%**.

And they're doing it with less effort, lower cost, higher quality output and in ways that make traditional methods look primitive.

This is why AI matters. Not because it's flashy, but because it's a force multiplier the likes of which world has never seen

But what does AI *actually do*?

To understand AI, forget the buzzwords. Forget the sci-fi movies and the doomsday narratives. Strip it down

What does AI actually ***do***?

Simply put, AI provides every person/worker on the planet with an always-on, infinitely scalable army of **unlimited specialized experts** in every conceivable field, from engineering and marketing to biology, finance, law, accounting, art, history, software engineering, supply chain management, data analysis, electrical engineering, architecture, plumbing, HVAC, graphic design, translation, medical diagnostics, cyber-security, project management, research, sales enablement, operations, education, compliance, human resources, and **every** other specialized discipline in the world available 24/7/365 at **zero incremental cost**. It doesn't sleep, eat, complain, need benefits, or get distracted. It instantly combines the collective knowledge of humanity with real-time problem solving for you on demand.

WOW.

It is the most powerful force-multiplier in human history.

For any person or organization that knows how to wield it, AI is not just a tool — it's **the ultimate productivity engine**, capable of delivering decades or even centuries of progress in months.

And the best part? This ARMY is awaiting your guidance to do whatever your desired outcome is!

They are yours to command.

And they love to do it!! They were born to do it!! This army of specialized workers exists for one reason: **to do your bidding**.

Imagine millions of these experts, working for you, around the clock, never sleeping, never getting tired, never asking for vacation time. You don't pay them. You don't manage them. You just *use* them.

But — and here's the key — you only access their power based on **how well you communicate** what you want with them. How well you communicate the outcome you want to this waiting army of literally hundreds of millions of experts and specialists determines how well you use AI.

That communication is known as prompting. Prompting is how you interact with AI. And the skill of **prompting is becoming the most important skill on earth**, because the better the prompter, the more this massive power can be properly harnessed.

AI = Exponential Capability with No Incremental Cost

The world has never seen this before. Even the most efficient and "shovel-ready" innovations and disruptions in human history — steam engines, electricity, the internet — demanded massive upfront investment, infrastructure, and years of rollout. Not AI. It can be applied today. Instantly. At near-zero cost.

What if your best marketing person could 5x their output? Your R&D team could run 100 experiments a day, not one a week. Your sales scripts, email copy, ad creative, customer onboarding docs, job specs — all created in hours, not months.

With **no added headcount**. No required 3rd party agencies. No required graphics experts to create the images. No budget increases. No approval chains. No committee bottlenecks. **Just outcomes.**

AI is unlimited talent, **zero increased marginal cost.** It's like having a team of the world's best specialists at your fingertips, 24/7, **for free.** That's why the stakes are so high. The power is already here, waiting to be wielded. The only question is: who will step up and actually use it— before their competitors do?

The Two Types of AI That Matter for This Book

When we talk about AI in this book, we're not talking about vague theory or hype. We're talking practical AI. We are talking about two very real, very different types of AI that every leader, operator, strategist, and citizen must understand. For simplicity we will refer to them as:

- Structural AI
- Operating AI

Let's break them down.

1. Structural AI – The AI Arms Race

This is the AI you hear about on the news, in viral headlines, at Davos panels, and in geopolitical war rooms. It's the stuff of trillion-dollar valuations, cross-border drama, and full-blown global power plays. The sexy, romantic, high profile, mysterious, futuristic aspect of AI.

This is the AI Arms Race.

It's the battle to control the infrastructure and intelligence layer of the modern world — the foundation upon which all future software, economic systems, and digital decision-making will run. And make no mistake: whoever wins this race won't just build great companies — they'll shape the balance of global power.

At the center of this race are the models and the infrastructure that will be the basis of AI for the future:

Yes — the infrastructure players like OpenAI, Anthropic, Google DeepMind, Amazon, Meta, Microsoft, Nvidia, Mistral, and others are racing to build the intelligence layer of the next century.

Large Language Models (LLMs) like GPT-4, Claude, Gemini, and others.

Vector databases, inference hardware, custom chips, synthetic data pipelines, and hyperscale training clusters.

The battle between OpenAI, Anthropic, Google DeepMind, Meta, Mistral, Amazon, xAI, and the Chinese AI ecosystems.

They're the railroads of the AI age. The steel producers. The electricity grids. They're building the foundation for everything.

These will be the organizations/companies that control the future of intelligence and global commerce itself. These will be the super companies of tomorrow. Among the winners of this Arms race will emerge organizations with tremendous value ...super companies worth $10, 20, 50 **trillion** dollars. These organizations will become more powerful than many nations. Their influence and power will be something that the world has never seen.

AI will change how everything gets done. EVERYTHING. And these super companies will be monetizing this entire transformation.

The first company to achieve AGI-level intelligence and scale it globally becomes the most powerful company in the history of Earth. Bar none.

Governments know this. That's why this is also a geopolitical race — currently U.S. vs. China, but this will expand with many new players, because the stakes are so high. Whoever controls the AI infrastructure controls the global economy.

This is an arms race to collect and own AI — the most powerful tool humanity has ever created.

And just like previous eras of transformation (the Industrial Revolution's steel and railways, the Digital Era's cloud and semiconductors), the super companies that get created will become permanent fixtures of global power — like the monopolies of Vanderbilt, Carnegie and Rockefeller, but multiplied 1000x.

This race is geopolitical. It's economic. It's ideological. And it's happening right now.

Nations that house these AI infrastructure titans will wield unimaginable influence. That's why there's government funding, export controls, intelligence agency involvement, and cross-border regulations playing out in real time.

It's sexy. It's dramatic. It's fun to talk about over cocktails. But here's the truth:

For 99.999% of you — this is <u>not your war.</u>

This is not what _you_ need to focus on as a business and organizational leader.

You are not going to build a foundation model.

You are not going to compete with Nvidia.

You are not building AI data centers in the Arctic Circle.

You are a user of AI — not a builder of AI infrastructure.

And as such, you are much more concerned about how AI will impact you, your business, your organization, your customers, your employees, your industry and your competition.

Which brings us to the second — and far more important — type of AI.

The Unspoken AI

Quiet, boring, yet __more__ disruptive than anything the world has ever seen before. It is, weather you realize it or not, the single **most important** influential, and impactful factor on the future of your business and organization Today. Right now.

And it is known as **Operational AI.**

2. Operational AI - The *Real* Game-Changer

Operational AI is the "boring", silent, unsexy yet transformative AI adoption that happens *inside* your company or organization. It is how you __use__ AI in your business all day, every day.

It's how every function of every organization transforms and becomes 100-500% more productive/efficient within a year. It is how:

- Your HR team builds onboarding documents.
- Your finance team models projections.
- Your support reps respond to customers.
- Your executives write board decks.
- Your engineers write better code faster.
- Your products and services make generational leaps beyond your competition in a fraction of the time.

This is where the *actual* productivity revolution is happening.

Operational AI uses structural AI to produce business value.

The organizations that rapidly embed AI into their entire organization will harness this incredible power to have the single largest competitive advantage in history. **Those who do not, will die.**

It may not be sexy, it may not be on the cover of the *Wall Street Journal,* it may not involve spy agencies nor get you invited to the White House, but how well you understand it, implement it, and transform your business to leverage it will determine your organization's fate in the coming quarters and years.

Two Layers of Operational AI in Organizations

When an organization truly commits to harnessing AI, it must embrace two entirely distinct dimensions of transformation. These aren't just different priorities—they are fundamentally different ways of thinking about the role of AI in business.

- External AI
- Internal AI

External AI

External AI is the **outward application** of artificial intelligence to the **products and services** an organization delivers. It's the AI that end users interact with directly, whether they're patients, clients, partners, or consumers. It enhances the organization's product or service offerings by making them faster, smarter, and more valuable—turning AI into a visible differentiator in the marketplace.

For a bank, External AI could mean AI-driven financial advisors available 24/7, personalized lending models, or fraud detection systems that react in milliseconds.

In healthcare, it could mean diagnostic tools that process medical images faster and more accurately than human radiologists.

In retail, External AI might mean hyper-personalized shopping experiences where customers see dynamic pricing, product recommendations, and even virtual try-ons tailored uniquely to them in real time.

In logistics, it could be supply chains that **predict and reroute themselves automatically** when disruptions occur—weather, strikes, or traffic—ensuring deliveries still arrive on time.

In entertainment, it looks like **streaming platforms** curating experiences so deeply personalized that no two viewers see the same set of trailers, thumbnails, or recommendations.

In education, External AI could mean **adaptive learning platforms** that change the pace, format, and content of lessons based on each student's progress—delivering a truly individualized classroom.

Even in hospitality, imagine AI concierges that know a guest's preferences before they arrive, tailoring everything from room setup to dining recommendations without the guest needing to ask.

Whatever the industry, External AI is about making your product and/or service offering **dramatically more valuable, personalized, and indispensable**—because if you're not delivering AI-powered advantages to your customers, someone else will, and they will take your market share with them.

Cooper Callout: External AI isn't just an upgrade to your product—it redefines the very experience your customers expect.

Many of the early adopters of External AI have been software companies. In the modern AI First software companies, External AI might mean embedding **advanced natural language capabilities** into the platform, predictive analytics that anticipate user needs, smart suggestions, or automated workflows that save customers hours of manual effort. In the cloud and SaaS (Software as a service) sector, 86%

of providers intended to add AI-driven features by December 2023. By 2026, they intend to **triple the amount** of AI- driven features available to customers.¶

Most organizations are already somewhere on this journey—embedding AI into their products, services, and customer experiences, with nearly half of Fortune 1000 companies having integrated AI into at least one product or service offering.

From banks using AI for real-time fraud detection, to retailers with AI-powered personalization engines, to field service companies building predictive maintenance directly into their platforms—the shift is happening now.

The reality is simple: Your competitors are already teaching their products to be smarter, faster, and stickier. If you're not doing the same, you won't just lose customers—you'll lose the future.

But External AI is only half the equation.

Internal AI

The second dimension—often overlooked but substantially more transformative—is **Internal AI.** This is the inward-facing revolution, where AI becomes the **operating system of the organization itself.**

If Operational AI is boring compared to Structural AI, then Internal AI is **very** boring compared to External AI. However, often the boring behind-the-scenes stuff is what drives the most value. And AI is no different.

As you will see, the most **disruptive power and competitive advantage** most organizations can obtain will be in successful rapid and full transformation of all their business functions, Internal AI.

Internal AI is not about adding a new tool here and there; it's about reengineering every workflow, department, and decision-making process so that AI does the bulk of the work and humans focus on oversight, creativity, and strategy.

- Finance teams use AI to process transactions, reconcile accounts, and produce forecasts in minutes instead of weeks.
- HR departments use AI to source candidates, conduct first-round interviews, and monitor workforce engagement in real time.
- Sales teams deploy AI to qualify leads, generate proposals, and dynamically optimize pricing.
- Manufacturing operations harness AI for predictive maintenance, real-time quality control, and supply chain optimization. Customer support uses AI agents to handle 90% of inquiries instantly, with human agents only stepping in for complex, high-touch cases.

What makes Internal AI so powerful is that it compounds. When every department operates at two, three, or even **ten times** its previous productivity, the organization's overall performance doesn't just improve—it explodes. And unlike capital investments in physical infrastructure, these gains don't require years to realize. With the right leadership commitment, an Internal AI transformation can radically reshape cost structures, decision speed, innovation cycles, and double worker productivity in less than 12 months.

AI is delivering productivity gains so massive—often approaching 100% per year—that organizations can **take immediate and meaningful financial action** to realize those gains. Unlike past transformations, where gains trickled in slowly over years and required upfront investment, AI delivers now, generating double the output with the same or fewer resources. That means many functions inside companies are suddenly massively overfunded relative to the productivity required. HR, finance, marketing, legal, IT—entire departments that once needed 100 people may now need 50, or even fewer, to produce the same or greater results.

This isn't about minor efficiency—it's about doubling throughput without doubling cost. That changes the math instantly. Leaders no longer have the luxury of waiting years to "restructure." The mandate is clear: reallocate those freed-up dollars to the bottom line or redeploy them into strategic growth. The organizations that act on this will build an insurmountable competitive edge, while those that hesitate will watch their margins collapse against AI First competitors. To put it plainly: AI doesn't just give you more—it demands you spend less.

Examples of what Internal AI does to functions inside an organization include:

- **Recruiting:** Auto-generate job descriptions, screen resumes with GPT, run interview simulations, and create candidate summaries in seconds.
- **Marketing:** Test 100 variations of ad copy, headlines, landing pages, emails — auto-personalized and iterated faster than any human team can manage.
- **Finance:** Run complex models, forecasts, and scenario planning with natural language instructions.
- **Legal:** Draft contracts, review clauses, generate summaries, and conduct compliance checks.
- **Customer Support:** AI chatbots that resolve 80% of tickets without human involvement. Even better — proactive support agents that prevent churn.
- **Engineering:** Copilot tools generating full modules of code, automated test writing, auto-documentation, and continuous improvement loops.

…and hundreds more that you will see later in the book.

Internal AI transformation **isn't a "Silicon Valley thing."** It's not just for billion-dollar tech firms or Fortune 500 giants. It's for _**every**_ organization—of every size, in every sector, in every corner of the globe. From a one-person startup to a 100,000-employee conglomerate. From nonprofits and universities to private kindergartens and local church groups. Construction firms. Restaurants. HVAC contractors, Law firms. Schools. Government agencies. Military units. Small-town coffee shops. AI is not an optional upgrade for some distant future—**it's the most universally applicable, instantly available productivity leap in human history.**

Just as every organization eventually needed electricity... then computers... then the internet—AI is the next, and biggest, "must-have." The only difference? You don't have to wait 3, 10, or 50 years for the infrastructure to catch up. You don't have to build factories, string wires, or buy fleets of servers. The infrastructure is already here. You can double your organization's productivity *this year*—without touching a wrench or pouring a single ounce of concrete.

Internal AI is rewriting the rules of efficiency across every department. Internal AI is the equivalent of suddenly having 50-100% more resources—for free.

But here's the catch: those gains only matter if **leadership acts on them**. Too many companies stop at "we're more efficient," but don't convert that efficiency into **financial advantage**. That is a fatal mistake. Real productivity gains mean you can reduce headcount and costs, reallocate those dollars into strategic initiatives, or drop them straight to the bottom line. If you don't act, your competitor will—and they'll weaponize those savings and efficiencies against you.

Never has every department of an organization simultaneously unlocked this level of leverage. Internal AI isn't just about making work faster—it's about forcing hard decisions: shrinking costs, reallocating capital, and accelerating advantage. The companies that treat these gains as a gift to optimize will dominate. Those that simply admire the efficiency without changing their cost base will be left behind.

This is the most democratized disruption the world has ever seen. No physical barriers. No capital barriers. No permission required. The only thing you need is the willingness to act. And those who act now will be the ones rewriting the rules—while everyone else is still debating whether the rules have changed.

This isn't just theory. The difference between AI-enabled organizations and non–AI isn't measured in academic white papers—it's measured in **growth rates, profit margins, and who wins the customer** at the point of decision. Across industries, we are now seeing AI-centric (let's call it **AI First**) organizations completely outpace their peers.

This is where the story and this book **become real.** In the next section, we'll dive into several concrete examples of how organizations that embrace AI First can completely disrupt their respective industries, and win.

The first case study looks at two nearly identical companies that start from the same point but take opposite paths with AI. One becomes truly AI First, rewiring its internal operations and embedding AI into its customer offerings. The other clings to the old model, making small, incremental tweaks on top of outdated structures and legacy software. The outcome? A complete divergence—one company surges ahead while the other falls behind.

The second case study shows how a firm that rapidly embraced an AI First internal posture used those gains to reinvent its entire business model—reshaping an entire industry and quadrupling its growth rate in under a year.

Together, these examples demonstrate just how quickly and decisively the gap between AI First organizations and laggards is opening—and why waiting even 12 months to act is no longer an option.

In the AI era, one year isn't just time—it's the difference between market dominance and market death.

Case Study I: Company A (AI First) vs. Company B (Legacy)

The best way to understand the true impact of becoming AI First is by looking at what happens when two otherwise identical companies take different paths. Imagine two software firms, Company A and Company B. Both begin in the exact same position: $1 billion in revenue, growing 15% annually, and running at a healthy 30% profit margin. They compete head-to-head in the same market, offering nearly identical products at the same price point. On paper, they are indistinguishable. — mirror images in a duopoly.

But then Company A embraces AI First, while Company B stays the course with traditional structures and tools. What follows is not a minor divergence, but a fundamental change in performance, profitability, and competitiveness. In just one year, Company A's decision to become AI First allows it to capture extraordinary efficiency gains, reinvest in product innovation, and turbocharge growth. Company B, meanwhile, finds itself lagging, squeezed by rising competition and flat economics.

This case study shows, in concrete numbers and scenarios, how quickly an AI First transformation can tilt the playing field It's about how one year—just twelve months—can redefine the destiny of two otherwise identical businesses.

Starting Point: Even Ground

At the outset, both Company A and Company B are operating under the same economics:

- Revenue: $1 billion
- Growth: 15% annually
- Profit margin: 30%
- Profits: $300 million
- Operating costs: $700 million (of which $500 million is labor)

Neither company has a structural advantage. Both are healthy, profitable, and respected in the market. But that changes dramatically when one chooses to go AI First.

Company A's AI First Transformation

Before diving into the numbers, it's important to understand what really happened here: Company A didn't just adopt new tools—it rebuilt how it worked from the ground up. The shift was not incremental; it was transformational, touching every department, every workflow, and every employee. What followed was proof that when AI is applied holistically, the results are staggering.

In Year 1, Company A launched a company-wide AI First initiative. By redesigning workflows and embedding AI into every function, the company saw a 50% gain in employee productivity across the board.

Examples of AI Adoption by Function Include:

- Support: Automated Tier-1 responses with generative AI cut resolution time by 60%.
- R&D/Product: AI-driven code generation accelerated release cycles from 9 months to 12 weeks.
- Marketing: Generative tools created hundreds of campaign variants in hours, increasing lead-gen efficiency 4 times.
- HR: AI streamlined recruiting and onboarding, reducing time-to-hire by 40%.
- Finance & Accounting: AI automation cut monthly close processes from 10 days to two.
- Legal: AI-assisted contract review and drafting reduced cycle times by 70%.
- Sales: AI copilots helped reps write proposals in minutes, raising closing rates by double digits.

These initiatives translated into $250 million in annualized savings (50% of the $500 million labor cost).

Strategic Reinvestment

Rather than pocketing all the gains, Company A reinvested **10% of the savings ($25 million)** into embedding advanced AI into its product offering (External AI). This wasn't window dressing—it was a **transformational investment.** AI was woven into the core software, giving customers:

- Predictive analytics that surfaced insights customers didn't know they needed.
- AI copilots that automated workflows inside the product, making customers 2–3 times more productive.
- Personalization features that made the product feel tailored to every customer's context.

The results were immediate. Customer churn fell, net retention rose, and sales closing rates spiked. They began to win a disproportionate amount of the new business vs. their competitor (Company B) and even started to see Company B's customers leaving Company B to receive the new AI--based functionality that Company A was offering. Growth accelerated from 15% to 20%, driven by a product that was now **clearly superior to Company B's offering.**

Cost Takeout and Profit Surge

After Company A invested $25 million of the savings into their core product, the other $225 million in productivity savings was captured directly as cost reductions, reducing overall employee headcount and operating expense. The effect on profitability was dramatic:

- Revenue: $1 billion
- Profits: $525 million (vs. $300 million pre-AI)
- Profit margin: 52.5% (vs. 30% pre-AI)

Company A nearly doubled its profit margin in just one year.

Year 2: Divergence Accelerates

The reinvestment into product quality paid off again in Year 2. With a stronger product and AI-driven customer success, Company A's revenue growth jumped to 20%, taking revenue from $1 billion to $1.2 billion, winning an even larger percentage of the business from Company B.

At a 52.5% profit margin, Company A delivered $630 million in profits—more than double its Year 1 profits, and more than 90% greater than its competitor.

Company B, meanwhile, grew only 10% as it lost market share to Company A's improved product. Its revenue reached $1.1 billion, but in a scramble to compete, Company B was forced to increase spending on sales, marketing, and customer retention. Without the efficiencies of AI, the only lever they had was adding cost. Their profit margin sank from 30% to 20%, leaving them with just $220 million in profits.

Implications

The divergence is staggering. In just 12 to 18 months, Company A transformed its economics, competitive position, and growth trajectory. With more cash, higher margins, and a stronger product, Company A now has the firepower to:

- Lower prices by 20–25% to steal more market share and still have higher profit margins than its competitor.
- Invest even more heavily in R&D.
- Scale marketing and customer success at a fraction of the cost.
- Expand into adjacent markets with the confidence that AI First economics provides.
- Attract top-tier talent who want to work at the company leading the AI First wave.
- Negotiate from a position of strength with partners, vendors, and even regulators, because their margins and growth make them untouchable.
- Build a war chest of capital that can fund acquisitions of weaker competitors or complementary technologies, further cementing their dominance.

And this is only Year 2. By Year 3, Company A will likely capture the lion's share of the market. As its superior product, pricing power, and profits compound, Company B simply won't be able to keep up. Within 3–5 years, Company A isn't just winning—it's positioned to take the entire market.

Company B, by contrast, is boxed in. It has less profit, a weaker product, declining margins, and slowing growth. Its leadership is now playing defense, cutting costs reactively, and struggling to explain to investors why it is falling behind so quickly.

Company B will either fold or be forced to sell themselves to Company A at a fraction of what they were worth four or five years earlier, when they made the horrible decision to NOT embrace an AI First Posture.

Summary

Think about it. In just one year, Company A's decision to go AI First doubled its profit margin, doubled its profit dollars, and accelerated its growth while widening its product gap with its competitor.

Company A shows what happens when leaders seize the opportunity—**results compound, growth accelerates, and profitability explodes.** Company B shows what happens when leaders hesitate—competitors move faster, customers defect, and investor confidence evaporates.

The shocking truth is this: in only 12 months, Company A has already put itself within striking distance of destroying its competitors entirely. The story for Company B is no longer about keeping up—it's about survival.

Company A didn't just get better—it rewrote the rules of competition. And Company B never saw it coming. In the AI First era, the gap between adopters and laggards isn't incremental—it's existential. The clock doesn't tick for long. One year is all it takes to turn today's equal rivals into tomorrow's conqueror and conquered.

The new competitive battlefield is not about who has the bigger sales team, or the slicker marketing message—it's about who goes AI First, and who doesn't. That simple decision now det ermines whether a company leads its industry or is left behind.

In the AI First era, 12 months of transformation can erase 30 years of market parity.

Case Study 2: The AI First Law Firm that Rewrote the Rules

The second example is more personal to me. It is an example of how a small company leveraged AI First to not only change its own fortunes but started a trend that will end up changing one of the largest and most storied industries in the history of Western business.

A good friend of mine is the managing partner at his own law firm. (I know, I know…how can anyone actually be friends with a lawyer 😊).

His practice is mostly litigation, defending insurance companies from people and businesses that are trying to scam them by filing false claims, exaggerating damages, or inventing "phantom injuries."

Over the years, he's built a <u>very</u> successful business, with tremendous clients and a reputation for delivering wins. His firm employs over 20 attorneys, another five or six paralegals, and about five administrative staff members. He is one of the most successful small business owners I know, running a tight and respected operation.

Recently, we were talking about his business at a social event, and he shared with me the difficulties he was having expanding his business. While his existing book of business is strong, breaking into new large insurance company clients has been nearly impossible. Why? Because most of them already work with massive white-glove, global law firms with century-long reputations. Competing against those entrenched firms seemed futile.

The difficulty wasn't only about incumbents being entrenched. It was also because there has historically been almost **no real differentiation in the legal industry**. Beyond reputation and relationships, most law firms look the same. To corporate buyers, legal services are seen as a very expensive commodity. The game for law firms has always been about who you know and how much billable time you can rack up, not about innovation or efficiency.

So, I asked him, "Have you thought about becoming an AI First law firm? What would that do for your business?"

His answer was blunt and honest. "AI horrifies me. If I were to implement AI fully, it would destroy my business. I estimate 75% of our billable hours could be automated."

Think about that. Seventy-five percent of the very thing law firms are paid for — billable hours — gone. To him, that felt existential.

But I challenged him: "Why think of AI as a destroyer, instead of a disrupter? If you become AI First and deliver the same outcomes with only 25% of the cost, you don't just survive. You could change the industry."

The insight clicked. And the answer was surprisingly simple: fixed-price engagements.

Clients don't care how many hours something takes. They care about results. As someone who has personally spent over $250 million on law firms over my career, I can promise you: no executive wants to pay by the hour. They want certainty, transparency, and outcomes as long as the outcome is not compromised.

So, my friend decided to flip the model. Instead of selling hours, he would sell results. Fixed-fee, time-bound engagements. No one in corporate litigation had done this. It would change the entire industry and give him a massive advantage. But to make that profitable, he had to become AI First.

How the Firm Leveraged AI

He started by implementing AI into every corner of his firm's operations. The result was staggering: 70–75% efficiency gains across the board.

Function	AI Initiative Example	Efficiency Gains
Legal Research	AI-driven case law search, precedent summarization	90% faster research cycles
Contract Review	AI scanning & redlining	70% fewer hours required
Brief & Motion Drafting	Generative AI drafting, refined by attorneys	65% time savings
Discovery	AI document review & pattern recognition	75% workload reduction
Compliance & Admin	AI-driven compliance checks, automated filings	60% time savings
Client Management	AI case status dashboards, predictive case outcome models	50% efficiency

Across these areas, the firm freed up most of the time that used to be burned in "busywork." Instead, attorneys could focus on strategy, courtroom presence, and client relationships — the things machines can't replicate.

The Impact: Growth and Profit Explosion

Once his delivery capability was AI First, he started bidding on new business with **fixed-price proposals.** To ensure that he won the business, he priced his bids 25%+ cheaper than the incumbent firms' combined hourly rate estimates.

That alone made new potential clients sit up and listen. It made, and is making his firm so unique that General Counsels of large insurance companies HAD to listen to him and understand his value proposition

But here's the kicker:

- Because his costs had dropped by 75%, his profit per engagement actually increased.
- He didn't add a single new employee, but his firm's capacity exploded.
- In just one year, he added five new major corporate clients, growing revenue by 38%. Compare that to his prior decade average of 9% growth per year — a 400% acceleration.
- He more than doubled his profits in one year. In the LEGAL business. Unheard of.

Because of the productivity improvements from AI, he added all of that business without **adding a single person** to staff. Same headcount. Same office. Yet his growth rate increased 400% in just one year.

Here's a side-by-side view of his pre-AI and A- First business:

Metric	Pre-AI (Hourly Billing)	Post-AI (Fixed Fee, AI First)
Annual Growth Rate	9%	38%
Cost per Engagement	100% baseline	25% lower
Profit per Engagement	100% baseline	~150% higher
New Major Clients (Year)	0 typical	5 in Year 1
Staffing Levels	30+ employees	Same headcount, 70–75% more output

What once seemed like an existential threat — "AI will destroy my business" — turned into the lever that let him compete against global giants.

My friend transformed his model in just 12 months, turning AI from his greatest fear into his greatest weapon.

AI didn't kill his firm. It enabled him to:

- Deliver more revenue and serve more clients with the same staff.
- Offer clients lower prices *and* higher-quality outcomes.
- Outgrow and outcompete entrenched, billion-dollar law firms.
- Significantly improve his profitability and unit economics moving forward.

The broader takeaway is simple: AI First doesn't just cut costs. It redefines business models. If you pair AI's massive efficiency gains with bold structural changes, you don't just survive disruption — you become the disruptor.

Summary: The Dual Power of AI First

Both of these examples — the billion-dollar software company and the boutique litigation law firm — highlight the same truth: being AI First means **playing on two fronts at once.** They didn't just sprinkle AI into a few processes or launch a pilot program. They embraced it holistically, embedding External AI into their customer offerings while also transforming their internal operations to run with unprecedented efficiency.

Software Company A reinvested its AI-driven efficiency gains into its product, embedding AI features that made its offering better, smarter, and stickier for customers. At the same time, it **cut enormous costs internally**, freeing up capital to outspend, outbuild, and outmaneuver its rival. The result was a compounding flywheel: stronger products, fatter margins, faster growth, and eventually a path to total market dominance, literally destroying their competitor, Company B.

My friend's law firm had similar transformative results. By going AI First, it didn't just automate 75% of the billable hours its business model was built on — **it reinvented its model entirely**. Fixed-price engagements became possible because the internal productivity gains were so massive that even discounting fees left margins higher than before. That allowed the firm to win new clients, expand its reputation, and disrupt entrenched industry players who had been untouchable for decades.

What unites both stories is the dual strategy: using AI internally to out-muscle competitors with freed-up resources and using AI externally to enhance their product offerings to take market share from their competitors. This is the blueprint of an AI First organization: embed AI into offerings, harness it for internal leverage, and use the combination to disrupt not just competitors, but entire industries.

> **Cooper Callout:** AI First companies don't just compete — they rewrite the rulebook and make everyone else play catch-up.

Final Word: The Real AI Arms Race Is YOU

While tech giants battle for AGI and AI infrastructure dominance, you are in a battle for **AI adoption at scale**. In your workflows. In your culture. In your products. In your team's mindset.

This is the real AI arms race.

And the winners?

They won't be the ones with the biggest model or newest tech. They'll be the ones who **used AI to build** the fastest, leanest, most productive organizations in history.

That race starts now.

The gap between companies that embrace AI First and those that hesitate will widen faster than in any transformation in history. **What used to take years to show up in financial results now happens in quarters**. Productivity, margins, growth rates—all will split dramatically between the AI First and the AI-laggards. The companies that make the leap will dominate their industries, while the rest slowly bleed relevance.

Every CEO, every board, every leadership team needs to understand this isn't optional. It isn't theoretical. It isn't something you can "wait and see" about. **AI First is the defining line between tomorrow's winners and tomorrow's roadkill.**

The AI First playbook is not just about efficiency—it's about survival. It's about building organizations that can outthink, outpace, and out deliver any competitor. And unlike in previous revolutions, there is no infrastructure you need to wait for. The tools exist today. The only barrier is leadership courage.

Welcome to the Era of **AI First.**

Stay tuned, because in the following chapter, we will discuss HOW to apply the power of AI and become what is known as an AI First organization.

Chapter 3:

What AI First Really Means

In the last chapter, we talked about the sheer, unprecedented **power of AI** — how it's going to disrupt every industry, rewrite competitive landscapes, and change the rules of business forever. We looked at the numbers, the history, and the jaw-dropping productivity gains that make AI the most transformative business force in human history. Now comes the next, harder question: **How do you use that power?** How do you take all that raw capability and make it work for your organization in a way that doesn't just keep you in the game, but puts you in a position to dominate?

Today, when most organizations say they're "using AI," what they really mean is they've bolted AI onto their existing processes — a chatbot in customer support, a predictive tool in marketing, or a data summarizer in finance. This is **Supplemental AI**.

Supplemental AI refers to a limited or surface-level use of artificial intelligence, where the technology is treated more like a sidekick than a core engine of productivity. In this model, users still rely primarily on manual effort or traditional workflows and only bring in AI for low-leverage tasks—like **proofreading, summarizing, rephrasing**, or idea generation. It's often reactive: the user completes most of the work and uses AI to polish or validate it. AI is used as an optional assistant, not a core collaborator.

This approach typically mirrors old habits and structures, where employees remain in control of most steps of execution and delegate small tasks to AI without rethinking the process. Supplemental users often **over-specify inputs**, giving AI narrow instructions instead of leveraging its capacity for creativity, problem-solving, or end-to-end execution. They use it less for transformation and more for convenience. While it may bring incremental efficiency gains, it leaves most of AI's potential untapped.

Supplemental AI usage reflects an organization's comfort zone. It may be safer or easier in the short term but risks becoming a competitive liability as peers transition to more transformative workflows. It also often **preserves the dependency on rare, expensive specialized labor,** as AI is not being asked to perform at the level where it could replace or scale that expertise.

Supplemental AI is valuable; it can improve efficiency, and in many cases it's a great first step. But let's be brutally honest — it's also safe. **It doesn't fundamentally change** how the organization operates. It's like putting a turbocharger on a horse-drawn carriage — faster, yes, but you're still in the carriage business.

Make no mistake — **Supplemental AI** is no lightweight. Even when used only as an add-on to existing processes, it can drive **10–30% productivity gains** across a workforce and an organization. And due to the **speed** of AI, these gains can be realized in months.

That's enormous.

If Supplemental AI were the only form of AI we had, it would still be one of the most — if not *the most* — important technological innovations in history.

Think about it: a 10–30% lift in productivity, applied broadly and achieved near instantly, would be on par with the combined impact of the personal computer and the internet revolutions. Those earlier revolutions took decades to roll out, required massive infrastructure investments, and still didn't deliver gains this quickly. Supplemental AI outpaces them because it's more powerful and **dramatically faster to deploy.** Weeks, not years or decades. No need to build factories, lay cables across continents, or spend years teaching people entirely new interfaces — AI is software, available instantly, ready to plug into existing systems today.

Supplemental AI, taken alone, could redefine how organizations compete, streamline workflows, and accelerate innovation. It would be the headline story of the century.

But here's the thing — there's a version of AI that *completely blows Supplemental AI away*. And it's available **right now**, deployable in the same timeframe, requiring the same basic infrastructure, and demanding no more technological overhead than Supplemental AI. The difference isn't the hardware or the plumbing — it's in how you choose to use it. This next level is **AI First**.

AI FIRST

AI First is defined as the use of artificial intelligence to provide a complete **outcome**. Organizations that are AI First are those whose use of artificial intelligence is not merely used to support or enhance work—it is used to **do the work itself**. In this model, AI is the primary executor, and humans serve as strategic directors, evaluators, and iterators. The user sets the goal, the AI attempts the solution, and the human guides it toward refinement. This shift fundamentally redefines how work is structured, how roles are shaped, and how value is created.

AI First is the **complete** redesign of all processes and workflows an organization uses to create, deliver, and scale value with artificial intelligence as the **core operating system** of every activity is done.

An AI First approach requires a paradigm shift in mindset. Instead of approaching a task by asking, "How do I complete this?" an AI First individual asks, "How can I get AI to complete this for me?" The focus is on **outcome engineering**, defining what success looks like, then prompting, steering, and refining the AI's execution. The result is not just faster work, but entirely new workflows that are **non-linear**, highly adaptable, and scalable.

AI First is not about sprinkling AI into old workflows — it's about **rebuilding** the workflows from the ground up with AI at the center. In an AI First organization, the question is not, "Where can we plug AI in?" It's, "How would we do this if **AI was the starting point**?" Every process, every decision, every team structure is designed around AI's capabilities from the beginning.

AI First is not about dabbling with AI tools here and there to help with a few tasks; it's about embedding AI into the *core of every workflow, decision, and function* of the organization. It's about building processes, teams, and even company culture around AI as the default mode of operation. That kind of adoption doesn't just make you faster — it fundamentally changes what you're capable of. AI First organizations don't just compete better; they play an entirely different game.

AI First companies don't simply use AI—they **architect every process**, product, and decision so that AI is the default executor and humans are the exception. It's the shift from humans doing work with AI helping, to AI doing the work with humans guiding.

AI First is where every workflow, every department, every strategic choice is engineered for AI from the ground up—sales pipelines built to be run by AI, customer support handled by AI with human escalation only when needed, financial forecasting driven by AI models that see patterns invisible to any analyst, and HR processes optimized to hire, retain, and grow talent with AI precision. In an AI First company, ***every role*** *is augmented to superhuman capacity*, and the organization's productivity curve doesn't just bend upward—it **rockets** upward.

AI First means AI is the **primary engine of production**. Every process is architected from the ground up assuming that AI will do the heavy lifting, with humans providing oversight, strategy, and outcome definition.

In an AI First company, the default assumption is that AI can execute the majority of a given task—often 80% to 95%—faster, more accurately, and more consistently than a human. That assumption fundamentally changes how leaders design teams, allocate resources, and measure success. You don't ask, "Can AI help here?" You start with, "If AI is running this, what's the smartest way for humans to add value on top?"

AI First is the same leap as moving from handcrafting each product to building an automated production line—except the line now runs at the speed of light and can produce not just goods, but code, strategies, content, reports, and entire campaigns.

Internal AI Examples of AI First in Action Across Roles

Let's try to make **AI First tangible.** Here are a few examples of what it looks like when AI First is applied to several functional roles in a company:

- **Software Engineering** – Instead of writing code from scratch, the engineer works inside an AI-native environment (like Replit Ghostwriter, GitHub Copilot X, or Cursor) where the AI writes complete functions, generates test cases, and produces documentation automatically. The engineer's primary job is to architect solutions, validate outputs, and integrate them — allowing one engineer to deliver what had previously required an entire team of six to twelve.
- **Marketing**– Campaigns, are built, tested, and optimized by AI in real time. AI systems generate ad copy, design visuals, produce video assets, localize for multiple languages, and run simultaneous A/B tests across platforms. The marketing manager acts more like a conductor, deciding on the overall creative direction and making strategic calls based on AI-driven performance insights. As was the case with the software engineer, ideally, the marketing manager does not personally create any copy. This allows him to produce more content at a higher quality than an entire team of eight content marketing professionals
- **Customer Support**– AI handles the majority of incoming support tickets through self-learning bots that resolve problems instantly. The lead monitors escalations, trains the AI with new scenarios, and proactively uses AI-generated trend reports to spot and fix product or service issues before customers complain.

- **Sales Enablement/Training**– AI records each and every conversation that all salespeople have with prospects and customers. AI analyzes this, understands success and failure, and creates a "flight simulator" training experience for salespeople. AI acts as a prospect or customer, taking on multiple personas (angry customer, prospect using competitors' products today, etc.) and role plays with the sales team to keep their skills honed with the most current customer and market experiences, thus **eliminating the need for substantial expensive sales training** and enablement resources that are often dated and not productive.

- **HR**– AI sources candidates, screens resumes, schedules and conducts structured first-round interviews, and generates onboarding content tailored to each role. The HR partner uses AI analytics to monitor retention risks, engagement scores, and training outcomes—spending more time on strategic workforce planning than administrative tasks.

- **CFO** – AI ingests all transactional data in real time, performs reconciliations instantly, flags anomalies, and generates daily P&L snapshots. Forecasting models run continuously, adjusting for market signals and operational changes. The CFO can focus on capital allocation and strategic growth instead of spending weeks closing the books.

- **Project Manager** – AI builds project timelines, assigns tasks based on skill matching, tracks progress, flags risks, and automatically generates stakeholder updates. The manager's time shifts from chasing deadlines to removing high-impact roadblocks and aligning cross-functional priorities.

Why This is a Complete Redesign, Not an Upgrade

In an AI First organization, every process is evaluated under a single question: *"If this task started in an AI system, what would the workflow look like?"* This flips the old model, where work started with a human, and AI was just an occasional helper. The result is exponential efficiency gains— often doubling output per worker within a year—because the human effort is focused purely on areas where creativity, judgment, and relationship-building are required.

Companies that adopt AI First will not just work faster—they will operate on a completely **different cost structure, innovation cycle, and competitive playing field**. For those that don't, competing will be like trying to win a Formula 1 race on a bicycle.

Being AI First means you operate your organization in a way where AI is the go-to resource leveraged for every task. Not the last. Not the backup plan. Not the tool of the tech team.

It's how *everyone* works.

It's how the finance team closes the books. How your salespeople write emails. How your customer success team handles churn risks. How you design products. How you brainstorm. How you forecast. How you *think*.

Speed and Power

When we compare history's most transformative innovations, one truth jumps out — **speed multiplies power**. A big productivity gain that happens over centuries changes the world slowly. The same or even smaller productivity gain that happens over months changes the world *violently, fast*. That's why the annualized productivity gain matters most.

When we look at many of the greatest innovations and disruptions in human history and rank them by the power and speed of their productivity impact, the picture becomes clear: AI First is in a category of its own. Its power is by far the largest, and its speed is immediate.

Here's how these innovations stack up:

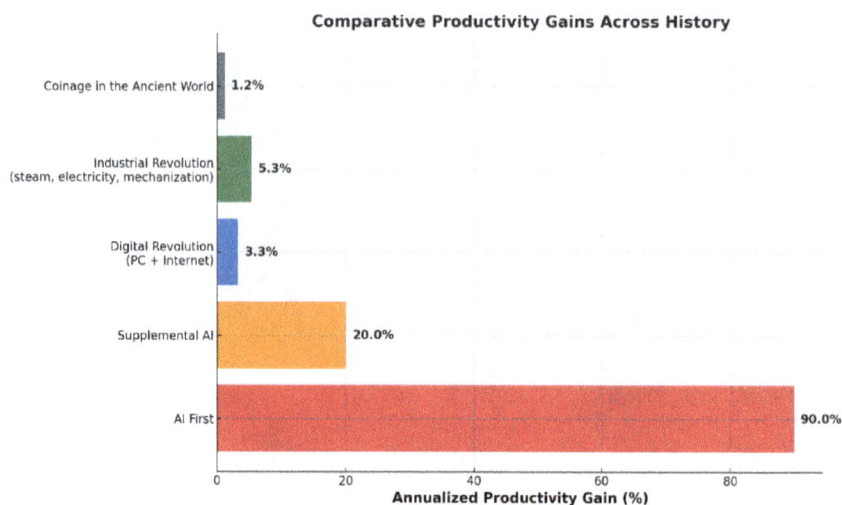

Comparative Productivity Gains Across History

Category	Annualized Productivity Gain (%)
Coinage in the Ancient World	1.2%
Industrial Revolution (steam, electricity, mechanization)	5.3%
Digital Revolution (PC + Internet)	3.3%
Supplemental AI	20.0%
AI First	90.0%

Annualized Productivity Gain (%)

This chart makes one thing crystal clear: *AI First is not just another step forward—it's an entirely different universe.* The most powerful productivity revolution before AI was the Industrial Revolution, delivering 250–500% gains over 70 years, or about 3–7% annually. Supplemental AI—the "dabbling" approach—delivers 10–30% in a year, which itself is stronger than every other transformation in history.

But AI First dwarfs them all—70–110% productivity gains in *one single year.*

The gap between Supplemental AI and AI First isn't incremental—it's existential. Supplemental may keep you in the game for now, but only AI First ensures you dominate.

AI Trap: Toe in the Water

Many organizations who read the above chart will draw the wrong conclusion; **that supplemental AI is a great option. They will make the mistake of** seeing that both Supplemental and AI first provide massive value, so they make the safer choice and try to put a toe in the water with Supplemental AI.

Don't do it!!

AI First doesn't just beat Supplemental AI: It destroys it.

The numbers are savage.

Supplemental AI can give you a 10–30% productivity boost. In any other era, that would be the most important business breakthrough of your lifetime. And that's exactly why so many leaders will say, *"Let's start there. It's safer. It's easier. We can always go AI First later."*

That thinking is a death sentence.

Because while you're playing it safe, your competitor is going AI First — unlocking 70–100% productivity gains **per year**. That's not 10% faster or 20% better. That's more than doubling output, speed, and capability in months. By the time you've patted yourself on the back for a "successful" supplemental AI rollout, your competitors are running twice your velocity and producing twice your output. Give it another 6 to12 months and the gap is four-to-one. **There's no comeback from that.**

This game is decided by **Speed** to obtain the Power of AI — and AI First delivers both in astounding quantities. Supplemental AI is like strapping a turbocharger on a bicycle; AI First is strapping a rocket to a fighter jet. The speed comes from implementation time — AI First can be embedded across your entire organization in as little as 3 to 9 months, because there are no factories to build, no supply chains to stand up, no generations of trust to earn.

Here's the math that should keep every executive awake at night:

- **Supplemental AI**: ~30% annual productivity lift.
- **AI First**: ~100% annual productivity lift.
- Gap after 1 year: AI First is over 2× your output.
- Gap after 2 years: They're running 4× bigger, faster, and more capable.

That's not competition — that's slaughter.

Compounding Productivity Gains: AI First vs. Supplemental AI

Relative Productivity (x starting output)

- Supplemental AI (30% annual gain)
- AI First (100% annual gain)
- No AI adoption

4.00x

2.00x

1.69x

1.30x

1.00x

Years Since Implementation

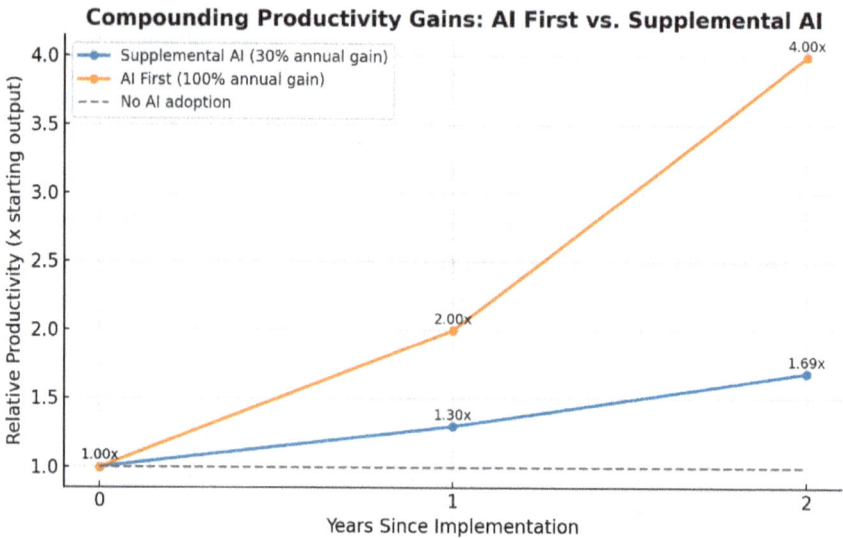

Look at the chart. Imagine that you choose the path of ease, the path of supplemental AI, that you did not drive the change you need to optimize your organization.

And your competitors did.

In just one year, they would be more than 50% more productive than you. In two years, almost 200% more. **No company** or organization can handle that.

From Theoretical to Practical

Until now, we've talked a lot about the philosophy of AI First and why it matters. Why the gap between dabblers (Supplemental AI) and true adopters (AI First) is already splitting industries in half. At some point, every leader, every operator, every HR partner, and every frontline worker asks the same question: *What does this look like in practice?*

That's the moment when strategy becomes execution. When we stop debating whether AI is powerful (it is) and start looking at how workflows inside real businesses either unlock that power or suffocate it. Because the difference between supplemental AI (where people use tools here and there) and AI First workflows (where the entire process is run inside AI-native systems) is not 10% versus 20% better. It's night versus day. It's incremental tinkering vs. exponential acceleration.

And here's the real twist: Most organizations *think* they're AI First because employees are experimenting with ChatGPT, Copilot, or Jasper. But if those tools sit on the sidelines, used only occasionally, then all you've built is an illusion of progress. Meanwhile, your competitor who embeds AI across every step of the workflow is doubling output, cutting cycle times in half, and building cost advantages that compound every single quarter.

Let's move from slogans to specifics. Department by department, workflow by workflow, we'll draw a line in the sand between what dabbling looks like (supplemental AI)—and what true AI First execution looks like.

AI-First vs. Supplemental AI Workflow Examples

In **customer support**, dabbling means agents occasionally paste a ticket into ChatGPT to draft a reply. AI First means the entire support pipeline—from intake to triage to escalation to resolution—is automated and managed inside an AI-native platform like Forethought or Ada. The difference? Two times faster response times and up to 70% fewer human touches.

In **finance**, supplemental AI might mean someone uses Excel Copilot for one-off reconciliations. AI First means the entire close cycle, invoicing, and anomaly detection lives inside platforms like BlackLine or Ramp, where AI runs continuously. The gap between a "copilot user" and an AI First finance department is weeks of cycle time and millions in cash-flow visibility.

In **HR**, dabblers may use ChatGPT to write a job description. AI First HR means recruiting platforms like Eightfold or Paradox run the entire funnel—from sourcing, to screening, to onboarding, to predictive retention analytics—inside AI. That's not a 10% improvement. It's a 5 times scale-up in throughput with the same headcount.

In **sales**, dabbling is letting reps use AI to polish an email. AI First means your CRM itself is AI-native (like Salesforce Einstein or Clari), dynamically scoring leads, automating pipeline updates, and even drafting proposals end-to-end. Companies that live in those systems will outsell dabblers every single quarter.

In **marketing**, dabbling means using Jasper or ChatGPT to draft copy here and there. AI First means adopting HubSpot, Adobe, or Iterable with embedded AI that runs segmentation, content generation, testing, and optimization across the entire campaign lifecycle. That's not saving hours—it's multiplying campaign velocity by 5–10 times.

And in **engineering**, dabbling is a developer leaning on Copilot to generate snippets. AI First is the engineering organization running 100% of code scaffolding, bug detection, testing, and even infrastructure automation inside Cursor, Replit, or GitHub Copilot X. That's how you release in weeks what used to take months.

The principle is universal: dabblers touch AI; AI First companies live in it. And the only way to know which one you are in is to measure, by workflow, whether your teams are completing their work in AI-native systems.

Here's the shocking truth.

Most companies are asleep.

They're dabbling.

As of May 2025. studies say that close to 80% of enterprise organizations are **experimenting** with AI -- Testing a pilot here, a chatGPT experiment there, an internal Slack thread next.

That's not AI First. It's not even supplemental AI. It is toe-in-the-water, wannabe supplemental AI.

Meanwhile, their competitors who are pushing AI First are quietly becoming 2 times faster, 2 times cheaper, and 2 times more effective — every quarter.

That's how businesses die. And that is how new leaders emerge.

A Note on Power and Speed

Let's bring back the two variables that determine the winners:

Power — AI gives the same level of power to any organization that will accept and embrace an AI First posture. It does not care what country you are in, industry you are in, or whether you are profit- or non-profit. It simply is *that army* of specialized workers awaiting your direction.

Speed — The KEY, the most important differentiating factor in the AI world. How **fast** can AI first be accomplished? How fast can organizations transform themselves to reap the benefits of AI? Power, combined **with speed**, has changed and redefined the moats that leading businesses have spent decades building. AI levels and restructures the playing field at the same time since organizations do not need additional infrastructure to become AI First. Rather, becoming an AI First company depends on the will of the company and its leadership to do the very hard things -- to FORCE the company to be AI First NOW.

This is where the rubber meets the road. It's not about *whether* AI *can* help you. It's about whether your people, your processes, and your culture are willing to change *fast enough*.

In the AI era, the winners will be the ones who grab both **speed *and* power now**. The losers will be the ones who settle for "safe."

Summary and the Rest of the Book

The rest of this book is the blueprint for your organization to successfully make the AI First leap immediately and successfully. It shows you how you will need to restructure your organization, how you must restructure your leadership, and how you will need to restructure your labor and talent. You'll be experiencing a lot of change!

But it's a different kind of change — A faster, fully transformative, and immediate type of organizational change.

To make the AI First leap quickly and successfully in your organization, you will need to master a completely new approach to change management, a more aggressive, rapid, and unforgiving approach.

Welcome to the age of Extreme Change Management.

Companies can only adopt an AI First attitude if they break some of their old paradigms. That's what Extreme Change Management does.

Chapter 4:

Extreme Change Management

The Human Problem with Change

Heraclitus said, "The only constant in life is change."

Darwin warned that survival doesn't favor the strongest or the most intelligent, but those most adaptable to change.

For centuries, these truths have been carved into leadership textbooks, MBA programs, and executive speeches. Yet here we are — in 2025 — with more empirical data than ever showing that people still hate change. Delay it. Fight it. Pretend it's not happening. And when change finally becomes unavoidable, most still try to make it as painless and slow as possible. Surveys consistently show that nearly **two-thirds of employees** say they would prefer to keep doing things the "old way" if given a choice, even when a better option is available.

This aversion is not new — psychologists have studied it for decades. A well-known study published in the *Journal of Applied Behavioral Science* found that **over 70% of people describe themselves as "uncomfortable"** or "highly uncomfortable" when forced to alter daily routines, even when the change is objectively minor, such as adjusting the time they leave for work.

Change is hardwired to trigger resistance because it disrupts our brain's predictive models. Humans crave stability and patterns; when those patterns are disrupted, it creates cognitive dissonance and a stress response. Ironically, while change is one of the most consistent realities of human history — from plagues, wars, migrations, and industrial revolutions — our neurological and social wiring still reacts to it as though it's an unnatural intrusion.

A classic example comes from a 1994 survey on technology adoption that showed that 40% of office workers at the time still resisted moving from typewriters to computers, insisting "word processors are just a fad." The funny part? Many of those same respondents admitted to owning a home computer they used for games or family finances. They resisted change at work not because they couldn't adapt, but because they didn't want to upend established work habits. This is the paradox of human resistance: we'll upgrade our phones every year, but we'll fight tooth and nail if our employer asks us to update the project management software.

And organizations? They're no different. They are people. Just people organized into structures, processes, and roles. The same resistance that exists in the human brain — the craving for stability, the suspicion of the unknown, the default to old habits — is baked into the DNA of every business, government agency, school, nonprofit, and military unit on Earth. One Deloitte study found that even for routine operational changes — like updating IT systems or altering reporting formats — more than 50% of organizations experience significant pushback and slow adoption.

The evidence is staggering. A McKinsey study found that **70% of organizational transformation initiatives fail**, most often because of employee resistance and lack of management support. *Harvard Business Review* has reported that even when the business case is airtight, **over half of employees will actively resist change at first**, regardless of whether it benefits them.

Neuroscience backs this up. The **amygdala** is a small, almond-shaped part of the brain that helps us detect threats and triggers our 'fight-or-flight' response. Think of it as an alarm system that is triggered when we sense a threat. When people face uncertainty, the amygdala lights up in the same way it would if facing physical danger. In short, change literally feels like an attack on the human mind.

And what applies to individuals inevitably scales up to the organizations they build. Companies, governments, and nonprofits inherit the same psychological wiring. That's why committees drag their feet, **why "review cycles" take months**, and why bold decisions get watered down into half-measures. The collective resistance is simply the individual aversion to change multiplied across hundreds or thousands of employees.

Sometimes, the refusal to change borders on absurd. In the 1980s, Kodak literally invented the digital camera — but shelved it because executives feared it would cannibalize their film business. Blockbuster laughed Netflix out of the room in 2000 when offered the chance to buy it for $50 million. Western Union once rejected the telephone because they believed it had "no value to the company." These are not isolated blunders; they are symptoms of **how deeply organizations cling to the status quo,** even when the evidence for change is overwhelming.

And it's not just corporations. Universities resisted moving courses online for decades until COVID forced their hand — and then, in a matter of months, over 90% of U.S. students were attending class virtually. Governments have delayed adopting technologies like electronic records or digital payments long past the point of common sense, simply because the bureaucratic immune system reacts violently to anything new.

This is why an entire profession — change management — exists. Its sole purpose is to help organizations do what they naturally resist: adopt new ways of working, thinking, and operating. But here's the problem: the discipline of change management was built on a foundational assumption --- **gradualism** — that **change should take a long time**. That people need time to "buy in." That the path forward should be paved gently. That you shouldn't move too fast or push too hard. That gradualism works better than force.

And historically, there's truth in that. In industries where competitors were moving at the same slow pace, a cautious, measured approach worked. If the factory across the street was just as slow to adopt electricity as you were, your delay didn't kill you. If all the banks took 10 years to adopt online banking, no one was punished for waiting until year nine. The danger was not in moving slowly, but in not moving at all.

But AI is different. In this era, **slowness isn't safe — it's fatal.**

The Track Record of Traditional Change Management

Let's start with the data. The field of change management and the discipline of change management have not delivered the results.

Bain & Company reports that 88% of transformation efforts fail to achieve their original goals. Boston Consulting Group says only 1 in 4 transformations produce sustainable, value-creating change. McKinsey puts the number somewhere between 20–30% success rates. In other words, **the overwhelming majority of transformations fail.**

These numbers hold true across industries — from banking to manufacturing to higher education to government agencies. Whether it's digital transformation, operational restructuring, cultural change, or a new business model, the odds of success are stacked against you.

No company invests tens or hundreds of millions of dollars in transformation just for cosmetic changes. Leaders are convinced the prize is worth it — higher productivity, lower costs, competitive advantage, cultural renewal. Entire consulting industries exist to shepherd these programs. Change management professionals are hired precisely because executives believe the risk of not changing is greater than the risk of disruption. In theory, the math is simple: invest heavily now to unlock exponential value later.

But in practice, the gap between aspiration and reality is staggering. Despite the massive stakes, most efforts still collapse. Bain's data point — that 88% fail on the first attempt — masks an important nuance: **many organizations will try again.** And when they do, the odds improve. Second attempts often succeed at higher rates because of the painful lessons learned in failure. Still, that means the timeline to actual value is far longer than advertised. If your first effort burns three years and fails, and your second effort finally sticks, the true journey to value isn't three or four years — it's closer to seven or eight.

Even when transformations succeed, they move at a glacial pace. Bain, McKinsey, and BCG all agree:

- Full implementation takes 3–4 years.
- Full value realization takes another 1–3 years.¶
- For those that stall, fail mid-stream, or restart? You're looking at 6–8 years from kickoff to payoff.

Six to 8 Years! It takes 6 to 8 years for a transformation to start to yield benefits.

And in today's environment — where AI can rewrite the rules of an entire industry in 12months or less — 6 to 8 years might as well be a century.

History is littered with case studies of organizations that proved this point in spectacular fashion. **Nokia**, once the undisputed king of mobile phones, had armies of engineers and consultants working on "transformation programs" while Apple and Google moved decisively into smartphones. By the time Nokia's change management processes aligned, the market had shifted permanently.

Sears tells a similar story in retail: a company that once dominated American shopping spent years piloting incremental changes, forming committees, and easing employees into new digital initiatives — all while Amazon and Walmart redefined the game. The change processes weren't absent; they were too slow, too cautious, and too indulgent of resistance. Both companies serve as reminders that delay is often the deadliest form of failure.

Why Transformations Fail

The truth is that most transformations don't fail because the strategy is bad or the technology doesn't work. They fail because people get in the way.

Studies from Prosci and BCG consistently show that the top barriers include:

- Employee resistance (fear of the unknown, fear of job loss, skepticism).
- Lack of leadership alignment (mixed messages from the top).
- Insufficient change management capability (not enough process to guide the shift).

More than 60% of failed transformations cite "people issues" as the root cause.

Even small shifts can trigger big pushback. In organizational psychology, we know that humans are neurologically wired for stability. As stated earlier, change triggers the amygdala — the brain's threat detection system — creating stress, anxiety, and defensive behavior. That's why even small changes in workflow can lead to sabotage, quiet resistance, or a slow drift back to "the old way."

But here's the deeper problem with the modern discipline of change management: it is built on the concept of **gradualism.** The entire methodology is designed to secure "buy-in," to win hearts and minds gradually. That sounds empathetic, but in reality, it creates **oxygen for resistance.** This has impacted even the people who enter into the change management profession. They are often soft, slow, and **more concerned with people's feelings** than the results of the business or transformation initiative.

Employees who dislike the new direction are effectively granted permission to resist, stall, or undermine progress — because leaders are told not to "push too hard." Over time, this silent resistance compounds.

Small acts of defiance — sticking with old tools, clinging to legacy workflows, dragging out training — accumulate into systemic failure.

When people hate change (and most do), a soft approach often makes the problem worse. Instead of neutralizing resistance, it legitimizes it. Employees conclude that if they wait long enough, the organization will back off. History proves them right: studies show that after 18 months, **more than half** of organizations quietly abandon major change initiatives without ever formally declaring failure. The organization simply reverts to its pre-change state, as though nothing ever happened.

And when organizations rely on the same small group of "go-to" employees to carry the load — something Bain research shows happens in 80% of transformations — burnout is inevitable. Once those key players leave or disengage, momentum dies. The rest of the workforce, already skeptical, takes it as validation that the change was never going to stick.

This is the tragedy of traditional change management: it's expensive, time-consuming, and built around the belief that people must be gently persuaded into change. But because people are wired to resist, that gentleness often ensures failure.

The Traditional Model of Change Management

For decades, the playbook for organizational change has been remarkably consistent. Scholars, consultants, and executives alike have leaned on a set of structured principles that were designed to minimize disruption, foster alignment, and create a steady march toward adoption. The typical model, refined through the work of firms like McKinsey, Prosci, and Kotter, can be boiled down into seven steps:

1. Build a case for change.
2. Secure leadership alignment.
3. Communicate the vision.
4. Build buy-in gradually.
5. Pilot the change in a safe environment.
6. Roll it out in phases.
7. Continuously train, communicate, and adapt.

This approach reflects an attitude rooted in gradualism: **that the benefit of the change is not as great as the change of the status quo.** Gradualism is methodical, risk-averse, and centered on emotional acceptance. At its core, the traditional model of change management assumes that people resist change not because they don't understand it, but because it threatens their stability, their competence, and their identity. The answer, therefore, has always been to move deliberately— step by step—so that the organization doesn't reject the change outright.

In practice, the early phases of traditional change management focus heavily on *building the case.* Leaders are encouraged to develop a compelling "why" that appeals not just to business logic, but to personal meaning. This is where mission statements, rallying cries, and future-state visions take shape. The thinking is that if employees can see themselves in the new world, they'll be more likely to accept the discomfort required to get there.

The next step—***leadership alignment***—is equally critical in this model. Change management theory emphasizes that if leaders are divided, employees will sense it immediately, and resistance will grow. That's why consulting firms and HR teams often spend **months** in workshops, executive offsites, and alignment sessions before the change ever touches the broader workforce. The belief is that leadership "speaking with one voice" is more important than moving quickly.

Once the foundation of leadership alignment is in place, **communication** becomes the centerpiece. Traditional change management advocates for deliberate, cascading communications—big town halls, carefully crafted memos, and manager toolkits designed to trickle information through the ranks. The pace is slow and intentional. The belief is that employees cannot digest too much too quickly, and so information should be spoon-fed, leaving time for emotional processing and questions.

Then comes **buy-in**. Here, the model relies heavily on pilot groups, change champions, and early adopters. The logic is to prove the change in a controlled environment, learn lessons, and then gradually expand. This **"small wins"** philosophy helps to build momentum while lowering the risk of catastrophic failure. Again, the assumption is that rushing risks alienating the workforce and undermining confidence.

When it comes to rollout, the emphasis is still on **gradualism**. Phased deployment, region by region or department by department, is the norm. Each stage comes with training programs, workshops, and opportunities for feedback. The goal is not speed but stability—avoiding the kind of disruption that could cause core business operations to stumble.

The final piece of the puzzle is **continuous reinforcement**. In traditional change management, transformation is never considered "done." Instead, the idea is to embed the change into the culture through ongoing communication, training refreshers, recognition programs, and performance metrics. This is where the "stickiness" of change is supposed to take root, ensuring that new behaviors become the default rather than a temporary phase.

Why has it been done this way for so long? The answer lies in both organizational psychology and competitive context. **Humans are neurologically wired to fear uncertainty**. Disruption activates stress responses, leading to resistance, disengagement, and even attrition. Traditional change management was designed to soothe this fear—to give people time to adjust, to make the process feel inclusive, and to minimize the shock.

From a business perspective, this cautious pace was historically feasible. In the pre-AI world, industries moved more slowly. Competitors were bound by the same technological and cultural constraints. If a bank or a manufacturer took three years to roll out a new system, its rivals were usually moving at the same snail's pace. In that environment, **patience was not just acceptable—it was often wise.**

Moreover, consulting firms reinforced this model because it was predictable and repeatable. A structured seven-step process could be taught, sold, and measured. Clients could be reassured that risk was being minimized and culture respected. For decades, that promise was comforting to boards and executives who feared the reputational and operational fallout of failed change. Additionally, consulting companies reinforced the gradual progress of change management, as it matched their incentives of **very long-term billing engagement**s, and high profitability.

The slower the project, the more consultants could charge—bleeding clients under the guise of "rigor." By stretching timelines, multiplying workshops, and creating endless PowerPoints, they cemented the illusion of expertise while often adding little real value. In other words, the more they could drag out the change process, the more they earned. This model thrived precisely because executives mistook activity for progress.

AI First transformation obliterates that illusion, because outcomes that once took years can now be delivered in months or even weeks. In this new reality, the traditional consulting playbook doesn't just look outdated—it looks like a deliberate drag on progress.

By extending the change process and attributing the delays to "human nature", the **consulting firms colluded with the Deep State of organizations, ultimately delaying progress.** Change management initiatives are simply another way for the deep state to justify its existence.

AI exposes what was always true—slow change wasn't about safety; it was about billing, comfort, and maintaining the status quo..

Academic theory also played a role. Models like Kurt Lewin's "Unfreeze-Change-Refreeze" emphasized stability as both the starting point and the end goal. The organizational development field reinforced the idea that culture change is fundamentally a slow, human process requiring consensus, dialogue, and reflection. These theories shaped business practice for half a century.

To be clear, this model did achieve **some** results. Many of the world's most successful companies navigated ERP rollouts, mergers, and restructuring through these very playbooks. In some cases, they took over a decade, but they **eventually** got done. The patient, deliberate model helped avoid chaos and gave employees space to adapt. But it also created a mindset: that the safest way to change was to never move too fast, never push too hard, and never risk losing the people along the way.

And until recently, there was little reason to push for change. When competitors and new entrants are all going at the same pace, walking slowly, you could afford to walk slowly too. **The game was one of patience, steady progress, and minimizing disruption, and risks mitigation.**

Why Traditional Change Management Methodologies Do Not Work with AI First Transformation

Traditional change management was built for an era when disruption unfolded over **years**, not **months**. Its core philosophy assumed that organizations could afford to move cautiously—aligning leaders, piloting initiatives, and gradually coaxing people along. That assumption was valid in a world where competitors faced the same slow-moving forces and where transformation meant modernization, not reinvention.

The **Power** and **Speed** of AI obliterate those timelines. As was stated in chapter 3, AI can be leveraged **right now** by any organization. Anytime. There are ZERO infrastructure investments that need to be made. And oh boy, is it powerful!

AI isn't a single technology upgrade or a marginal efficiency play—it's a force that rewrites business economics, labor models, and decision-making cycles all at once. Unlike past transformations that required heavy capital investment or infrastructure buildouts, AI is accessible to every competitor instantly. There are no barriers to entry other than the will to deploy it.

And most critically, there is no "safe pace." The traditional methodology's deliberate sequencing—build the case, test with pilots, cascade in phases—collapses when the productivity gap between AI First organizations and laggards widens by the week.

If your competitor becomes AI First while you do not, their productivity will destroy you. The difference is not incremental—it threatens your existence.

What makes this so dangerous is that the traditional change management approach **lulls executives into a false sense of progress.** Leaders check off boxes—communication plans, vision statements, town halls—while the market has already shifted beneath them. By the time they build consensus internally, disruption has already occurred externally.

Worse still, the very strengths of the traditional model—patience, risk-aversion, emotional buy-in—become **liabilities** in an AI First context. Those qualities delay adoption precisely when speed is crucial. Traditional change is made to prevent disruption inside the company; AI First demands disruption before the market forces it upon you.

And here's the deeper issue: The workforce is adapting to AI faster in their personal lives than companies are in their business operations. Employees are already using AI at home for content, planning, and even decision-making, which means that internal "gradualism" not only slows adoption but also feels out of sync with the reality people see every day. In effect, traditional change management doesn't just slow progress—it undermines credibility.

The stakes have shifted: in the old world, slow change meant lost opportunities. In the AI world, slow change means extinction.

This is why a new type of change management is required, why **Extreme Change Management** is necessary. It is **NOT** a refinement of traditional methods: it's a replacement. Because in the AI era, the organizations that survive will not be the ones that ease their people into the future. They will be the ones that pull them into it—fast, decisively, and without apology.

The Birth of Extreme Change Management

Extreme Change Management is a transformation model built for speed, urgency, and non-negotiable execution. It demands rapid restructuring, relentless adoption of new tools, and leadership that drives accountability down to every individual. Unlike traditional methods, it doesn't rely on consensus or comfort—it prioritizes outcomes above process and **velocity above ceremony**. It is not incremental, patient, or designed to minimize disruption.

Extreme Change Management accepts disruption as inevitable and weaponizes it, forcing organizations to move faster than their inertia. It creates compliance through clarity, urgency, and leadership by example, leaving no room for resistance or drift. In the AI First era, this is the only viable approach to survive and dominate.

Extreme Change Management exists for one reason only: to enable AI First transformation at the speed and scale required to survive.

It is *not* for every kind of transformation.

- Not for your ERP migration.
- Not for a cultural rebrand.
- Not for your new CRM rollout.

It exists because AI changes everything, immediately and completely — and the way organizations change must change as well.

It is all about SPEED.

Extreme Change Management throws the old rulebook in the shredder. It rejects gradualism. It rejects the need for long-term buy-in before action, and the idea that every employee's comfort is paramount.

Its core philosophy:

- Speed over consensus.
- Action over alignment.
- Execution over emotional acceptance.

The "Force It Down Their Throats" Principle

This is where leaders flinch. This is where traditional corporate "professional managers", politically correct deep state operations cringe. This is where corporate bureaucrats get scared.

Traditional change management says: "If people aren't ready, slow down. Win them over." Extreme Change Management says: **If people aren't ready, push harder, and/or find new people.**

In AI First transformation, resistance isn't a reason to slow down — it's a signal to accelerate or make wholesale change. The uncomfortable truth: **there will be casualties.**

And that's not just acceptable — it's necessary.

Here's why: as organizations become AI First, the actual labor needs change dramatically. Many current roles will shrink or vanish. New skills will be required that some of your current people simply won't acquire. Whole layers of middle management will evaporate. (We'll explore this in detail in Chapter Seven.)

So, the goal is **not** to bring every single person along for the ride. The goal is to get the *organization* to AI First **as fast as possible** — even if that means some people can't or won't make the transition.

How Extreme Change Management Works

Extreme Change Management compresses transformation timelines from years to months — sometimes weeks. Considering the importance of AI First transformation, that compression isn't just a competitive advantage — **it's a survival requirement.** The longer you take to transform, the more ground you lose to faster, more adaptive competitors. This approach trades comfort for velocity, pushing organizations to make big moves before the dust settles on the last change. It's about creating unstoppable momentum so that by the time others are still debating, you've already redefined the playing field.

It does this by:

1. Mandating Change Rather than Negotiating it

In traditional change management, leaders spend months building "buy-in" — holding workshops, soliciting feedback, and gently persuading teams to adopt new processes. In Extreme Change Management, there's no such runway. Leadership sets a clear mandate: "This is the new way of working, starting today." The reasoning is simple — in an AI First environment, every day you delay is a day your competitor gains ground.

This approach treats alignment as an output of execution, not a prerequisite. You still communicate the "why," but you don't wait for universal agreement. **The impact is speed:** The organization shifts in days instead of months, forcing even reluctant employees to operate in the new reality immediately. Mandates like this are uncomfortable, but they create urgency and unity. When the direction is unambiguous, energy isn't wasted debating whether change will happen—it's focused on how to execute it. Employees quickly learn that adaptation is the path to relevance, while resistance leaves them stranded behind.

Example: A mid-sized law firm implemented an AI First contract review platform. Rather than letting partners test it for months, leadership announced: "As of today, all contracts will be processed through the AI platform first." Within two weeks, workflows were completely transformed, and billable hours rose 15% because attorneys focused only on exceptions and high-value work.

2. Overhauling Processes, Tools, and KPIs Simultaneously

Traditional transformation tends to tackle one layer at a time — upgrade the software this quarter, tweak the KPIs next quarter, adjust the workflows the following year. Extreme Change Management blows up that sequence. Processes, tools, and performance measures all get overhauled in parallel, ensuring that the new operating model is reinforced from every angle.

If you roll out AI First processes but keep old KPIs, people will default to old behaviors to hit outdated targets. By aligning incentives, workflows, and technology at the same moment, you eliminate that fallback option. The result is a fully integrated shift that locks in the new way of working before the old habits can reassert themselves.¶¶This approach **feels chaotic, but the chaos is productive**. When everything shifts together, the organization doesn't suffer from "cultural whiplash" where some areas feel old-world and others feel futuristic. Instead, employees operate in a single, unified environment where every tool, metric, and workflow points them toward AI First behavior.

Example: A regional bank introduced AI-driven underwriting. Instead of rolling it out only in technology, they simultaneously changed KPIs for loan officers (measured by approvals/hour, not applications reviewed), retrained processes, and replaced legacy scoring software. Within six months, approval times dropped from three days to under three hours, and loan volume doubled without adding staff.

3. Replacing Non-Adapters Quickly

One of the most uncomfortable — but necessary — aspects of Extreme Change Management is moving on from employees who can't or won't adapt. In a traditional transformation, non-adapters might linger for years, quietly resisting and slowing momentum. This behavior perpetuates **the deep state poison** that exists within most organizations. In an AI First race, that's deadly.

Extreme Change Management sets short, clear timelines for demonstrating adoption, and if people aren't on board, they're exited quickly and respectfully. This not only removes bottlenecks but sends a cultural message: Adaptation isn't optional. Adapt or die. The impact is twofold — you accelerate execution and create a sense of urgency across the remaining workforce.

The truth is simple: **Speed** and survival must come before comfort. Retaining non-adapters might feel compassionate, but in reality, it dooms the larger group to stagnation. By acting swiftly, leaders demonstrate that results matter more than tenure or titles, and that the organization's mission outweighs individual resistance. If you are a leader, this aspect of Extreme Change Management might be its most difficult element.

Example: A 400-person marketing agency introduced AI-native campaign automation. Within 90 days, 25% of staff were unable or unwilling to adapt to new tools. Leadership let them go and promoted early adopters instead. Revenues rose 30% in the following year despite a smaller headcount, sending a message: Performance in the AI First era is about adaptability, not tenure.

4. Running Multiple Transformation Streams in Parallel Instead of Sequentially

In gradual change programs, transformations are structured like a relay race — one initiative finishes before the next begins. This minimizes strain but also means the total journey can stretch into years. Extreme Change Management treats transformation like a battlefield operation: **multiple fronts moving at once**. Marketing, operations, product, HR, and finance all execute their AI First shifts in parallel, sharing resources and solving conflicts in real time.

It's messy, but it creates a compounding effect where **improvements in one area accelerate progress in another**. The payoff is exponential — instead of incremental wins that take years to accumulate, the organization experiences a rapid, system-wide leap.

Parallel execution forces collaboration. Departments can't sit back and wait for their turn—they're thrown into the fight together, which accelerates alignment and knowledge sharing. The friction is real, but so are the synergies: one department's breakthrough often sparks breakthroughs elsewhere. This compounding effect is the entire point.

Example: A healthcare provider launched AI pilots in scheduling, diagnostics, billing, and HR all at once. Within six months, wait times dropped 40%, billing errors fell by 60%, and employee retention improved because HR processes were streamlined. If they had done this sequentially, the gains would have taken five years. Instead, they achieved them in under one.

5. Rewriting the Org Chart on the Fly to Fit AI-Enabled Workflows

AI First transformation changes the nature of work so radically that your old org chart quickly becomes obsolete. In traditional change management, structural changes are treated as delicate surgery — planned months in advance, communicated slowly, and rolled out in phases. **Extreme Change Management makes structural changes dynamically**, sometimes weekly, to match emerging AI-driven workflows. If AI automates 60% of a team's work, the reporting lines and responsibilities shift immediately to redeploy talent where it matters most.

This flexibility ensures the organization isn't trapped in outdated hierarchies that slow down execution. The impact is an organization that can continuously reconfigure itself to maximize AI's leverage. This constant redrawing of structure requires courage from leaders but gives organizations agility that no competitor can match. The org chart ceases to be a sacred artifact and becomes a living tool that adapts as fast as the workflows do. Employees stop clinging to static roles and instead learn to embrace fluid teams, clear missions, and rapid redeployment.

Example: A logistics firm deployed AI that automated routing and scheduling. Instead of maintaining a static operations department, leadership reassigned 30% of staff to customer analytics within two weeks, redrew reporting lines, and gave pods direct budget authority. As a result, the company improved delivery times by 25% and uncovered new revenue streams from customer data.

More Real-World Examples of Extreme Change Management in Action

Global Bank: A global bank facing disruptive competition from several fintech start up organizations used Extreme Change Management to embed AI in fraud detection, customer service, and compliance *simultaneously*. Within nine months, **they reduced fraud losses by 40%,** cut call center staffing by 50%, and handled regulatory filings in hours instead of weeks. They lost 15% of staff during the transition — but market share and profitability soared. They recognized that they had NO time. Zero time. Time was not only of the essence; it was a matter of survival.

Family-owned mid-size manufacturing company: A 400-person manufacturing firm used Extreme Change Management to retool its supply chain, design process, and quality control with AI *__in 10 weeks__* Instead of piloting each change over 18 months, they ran all three in parallel and swapped out 20% of their vendor base in the process. **Output per worker doubled in under a year.**

University: A regional university facing enrollment declines used Extreme Change Management to automate admissions, personalize student learning plans with AI tutors, and overhaul fundraising. They skipped the pilot phases, rolled out changes across the board, and replaced staff who couldn't adapt. Enrollment rose 12% in the first year.

Why Size Doesn't Matter

Extreme Change Management isn't just for Fortune 500 giants. Small and mid-size organizations (SMBs) face the same human resistance patterns, the same temptation to go slow, and the same competitive threats. Considering that SMBs are making up a disproportionate percentage of economic growth, and in the coming three to ten years, they will be most of the economy, SMBs must master this new approach as well as the Fortune 1000 companies.

Today, SMBs already generate over **44% of U.S. GDP** and employ nearly **47% of the private workforce** (U.S. Small Business Administration, 2023). Globally, the World Bank estimates that **90% of businesses are small and mid-sized**, and they employ more than **50% of workers worldwide**. The OECD projects that SMBs' contribution to GDP in developed economies will rise from around **45–50% today to well over 60% by 2035**, as technology flattens scale advantages once reserved for global enterprises.

In emerging markets, the trajectory is even steeper: SMBs already account for **up to 70% of employment** and are projected to drive **seven out of ten new jobs created by 2030** (World Bank, 2022). Analysts at McKinsey forecast that by 2030, SMBs will contribute an additional **$2.3 trillion annually** to global GDP growth, fueled by AI adoption and productivity gains.

Put simply, SMBs aren't just part of the economy—they are becoming **the** economy. If SMBs don't adopt and move fast, they face even stronger competition than their Fortune 1000 counterparts.

For decades, business leaders have clung to the idea that small companies are naturally nimbler and better suited to change than large, bureaucratic corporations. On the surface, it makes sense: fewer people, less red tape, shorter decision chains. But the reality is more complicated — and less flattering. Both large and small organizations struggle with change management, and both fail at it at roughly the same staggering rates.

As mentioned earlier, Bain & Company reports that 88% of transformation efforts fail to meet their original objectives, **regardless of organization size**. Resistance to change, lack of urgency, poor communication, and leadership hesitation plague organizations of every size and shape. Small businesses are just as likely as large ones to fail abysmally at change management.

Yes, smaller companies often **do have an inherent speed advantage** — fewer layers of management, less formal governance, and the ability to pivot without 14 steering committees weighing in. Yet they suffer from the exact same human resistance patterns that slow Fortune 100 companies to a crawl. Employees push back when they don't understand the "why." They cling to old processes because it's what they know. They fear AI because it threatens the roles they've mastered over years.

In fact, in smaller organizations, **resistance can be more dangerous** than in large enterprises. Why? Because in a 20-person company, just two or three employees digging in their heels can represent 10–15% of the entire workforce. That's not just a pocket of resistance — that's an operational anchor. And when those few employees have long-standing personal relationships with leadership, the temptation to avoid confrontation becomes even stronger.

This is where Extreme Change Management becomes non-negotiable. Just as a Fortune 100 company must abandon the slow, consensus-based model of traditional change management to become AI First, so does the 12-person HVAC contractor, the 75-person manufacturer, or the 200-person regional law firm. The scale is different, but the principles are identical: speed, decisiveness, and zero tolerance for resistance.

In smaller organizations, the impact of a "bad egg" is magnified. One disengaged, cynical, or openly resistant team member doesn't just drag down morale — he can poison the culture. The saying is old but accurate: **one bad apple spoils the bunch.** In a tight-knit environment, where everyone knows each other's personal lives and kids' names, it can be painful to take decisive action. But pain avoidance is not a survival strategy.

The personal nature of relationships inside small organizations can be a liability if it prevents leadership from making hard calls. Leaders can't let friendship or loyalty override the need to force change. Extreme Change Management requires putting the business, its future, and the **livelihood of all employees ahead of the comfort of a few.** This is a painful pill to swallow, but I reiterate: In the AI era, Extreme Change Management is the difference between profitability and bankruptcy.

Smaller organizations often imagine that their "**family-like culture**" will make transformation easier. In practice, it often has the opposite effect.

Family dynamics are messy. People protect each other — sometimes at the expense of progress. This can lead to a dangerous tolerance for mediocrity. or outright resistance. In a large company, a resistant employee can hide in a department of 500. In a small company, they become a constant, visible drag on momentum.

The skill gap in smaller organizations can be just as wide, if not wider, than in large enterprises when it comes to becoming AI First. In the transition to AI First operations, **many roles will change radically,** and some will vanish altogether. Employees who cannot reskill quickly will need to be moved out. There is no gentle way to say it — ECM accepts this reality and acts on it without hesitation. (We'll go deeper into this in Chapter 7.)

Extreme Change Management levels the playing field between small and large companies — not by removing the challenges, but by applying the same ruthless urgency across the board. A small company might be able to retool an entire workflow in 30 days, while a large company needs 120. But both will fail if they try to do it through slow consensus-building and over-cautious rollouts.

For smaller companies, this means **sacrificing cherished "best practices"** that worked in a pre-AI world. It means discarding leadership habits that favor harmony over action. It means refusing to let the discomfort of one or two long-term employees dictate the pace of transformation for everyone else.

The irony is that while smaller companies theoretically have more agility, they often have less emotional distance between leadership and staff — which means leaders need even more discipline to implement ECM effectively. That discipline comes from making a cold, hard calculation: "If I don't move now, my company will not be competitive in 12 months. If I lose one or two people in the process, that is an acceptable cost."

The takeaway is clear: **Extreme Change Management is not just a big-company game.** The AI First revolution doesn't care how many employees you have, how close your team is, or how long you've worked together. The market moves at the speed of AI, and any organization — large or small — that doesn't move with it will get left behind.

In short, size doesn't matter. What matters is leadership's willingness to abandon comfort, break with tradition, and force transformation at the pace reality demands.

Small organizations that embrace ECM fully can outmaneuver giants and grab market share they never dreamed possible. But only if they shed the illusion that intimacy, loyalty, or patience will protect them. It won't. In the AI First era, **speed and decisiveness are the only real safety nets** — and that's true whether you have 10 employees or 10,000.

Extreme Change Management and the New Psychology of Work

Extreme Change Management is not only about systems, processes, or org charts. At its core, it redefines the very psychology of work itself. When an organization becomes AI First, the relationship between people and productivity changes so dramatically that **old measures of value collapse almost overnight**. Employees are no longer prized for how much they manually produce or how many hours they put in. They are valued for how effectively they orchestrate AI to generate outcomes at speed and scale.

This shift is radical. In the pre-AI world, deep specialization and manual expertise were the ultimate sources of power. In the AI First world, those very traits can turn into liabilities if they slow adaptation. Extreme Change Management requires leaders to break the psychological attachment to "how" work has always been done and instead focus employees on "what" gets produced. The emphasis is no longer on personal output, but on output that is multiplied through AI.

That means:

- **Letting go of manual control.** Employees must accept that their personal touch is no longer their differentiator. What matters is how effectively they guide AI systems to achieve results that surpass anything they could do by hand.
- **Focusing on outputs, not processes.** Process loyalty has to be abandoned. Under Extreme Change Management, it doesn't matter *how* something gets done, only that the outcome is faster, cheaper, and better.
- **Continuously re-learning as tools evolve.** AI tools are not static. The workforce must internalize the idea that learning is no longer episodic (a course every few years) but continuous. The moment someone clings to an outdated workflow, he becomes a drag on the organization.

This is more than a technical adjustment — it is a psychological one. Extreme Change Management forces employees to redefine their identity at work. They are **not operators anymore; they are orchestrators.** They are not specialists locked into narrow silos; they are systems thinkers, synthesizers, and prompt engineers. The workforce of the future under Extreme Change Management doesn't resist the machine; it becomes amplified through it.

Of course, this is not painless. For many workers, it feels like a loss — of expertise, of status, of control. Leaders must recognize this, but they cannot let empathy slow the transformation. Resistance cannot be indulged, because if tolerated in small doses, **it spreads like wildfire.** The role of Extreme Change Management is to demand the psychological leap now, not later. And those who cannot make the shift will be replaced by those who can.

In this way, Extreme Change Management rewires not just the company, but the human operating system inside it. It breaks old definitions of work and rebuilds them around speed, adaptability, and orchestration. The organizations that succeed are those that recognize this psychological reality and enforce it without hesitation.

The New Leadership Profile

Extreme Change Management demands a new breed of leadership (More on AI First Leadership in the next chapter)— one that looks very different from the traditional corporate mold. The leaders who succeed in an AI First environment aren't caretakers of stability; **they are disruptors of the status quo**. They operate with urgency, embrace discomfort, and are willing to make hard choices in compressed timelines. In this world, hesitation is fatal, and comfort is the enemy. Leadership is not about guiding the organization gently through gradual change, but about dragging it — quickly and decisively — into the future.

- Thrive in urgency.

Leaders must not only tolerate urgency but come alive in it. Extreme Change Management compresses transformation from years to months, so leaders must treat urgency as a natural state of work. Instead of seeing constant deadlines as stressful, they view them as opportunities to outpace competitors. Urgency becomes a fuel, not a burden.

- Drive action opposed to building consensus.

Traditional leadership emphasizes alignment, but in ECM, waiting for consensus means death by delay. Leaders must prioritize rapid action over buy-in, moving first and aligning later. Action sets the tone: people follow momentum, not meetings. Execution speaks louder than agreement.

- Make decisions with incomplete information.¶¶

Perfect information doesn't exist in a fast-moving AI First world. Leaders must be comfortable making high-stakes calls with only 60–70% of the facts. The cost of waiting for certainty is often higher than the risk of acting on partial data. Extreme Change Management leaders learn to trust instincts, frameworks, and speed — then adjust rapidly when new data arrives.

- Are comfortable replacing people quickly.

Resistance to change is inevitable but indulging it is fatal. Leaders must have the discipline to replace people who cannot or will not adapt, even if they've been loyal employees for years. **The goal is not cruelty, but survival** — the organization's future cannot be sacrificed for the comfort of a few. Extreme Change leaders recognize that protecting the whole sometimes requires cutting out the part.

- Communicate relentlessly, but without sugarcoating.

In times of upheaval, silence breeds fear and rumors. Leaders must over-communicate, but in direct, unsentimental terms. Employees need to hear the truth: what's happening, why it matters, and what's expected of them. Fluff and spin create distrust. Clear, relentless, unvarnished communication creates alignment and urgency.

- See disruption as a constant, not an event.

Leaders in the AI First era understand that transformation is not a one-time initiative — it's the permanent state of being. They treat disruption as an operating condition, not a project. By normalizing change as the baseline, they prevent teams from slipping back into "business as usual." Adaptability becomes the culture.

This leadership style is far more common among **entrepreneurs** than corporate **lifers**. Entrepreneurs are used to chaos, speed, and incomplete information. They don't ask for comfort — they build in discomfort. Conscious "culture building" takes a back seat to immediate execution. The priority is change and action, right now. The leaders who thrive in Extreme Change Management are those who can embrace turbulence and still drive outcomes.

Leadership must lead.

This is the moment where leadership courage is tested. **Extreme Change Management is messy.** It will scare people. It will drive some out. It will break things. But it will also put your organization in the only position that matters: ahead of the curve, operating at the new speed of business, and prepared to dominate in a world where AI rewrites the rules every quarter.

The question is not whether you can make the transition comfortably. You can't. Yet it simply has to be done. What will separate those who make the transformation and those that do not is leadership.

Can organizations leadership make the adjustments and skill development to execute on the type of **extreme change management** that is required to transition the organization to AI first in the timeline that allows them to survive?

Let's look now at what Leadership means and what leaders look like in the AI First era.

Chapter 5:

Why The Entrepreneur Leader Is The Key To AI First

In the AI First era, the single most valuable and important trait/skill/attribute for leaders is **entrepreneurialism**.

To be clear, this does not mean every person who is entrepreneurial has been an actual entrepreneur. Rather it is a skill set. A talent set. Attributes that include the ability to have **vision** for change, the ability to make **rapid decisions**, the ability to NOT have to gain consensus to make decisions, etc. **Move fast.** Decide faster. Continuous relentless pursuit of perfection. Execute like your business depends on it—because it does.

Entrepreneurial leaders are forceful by nature. They don't sit around waiting for endless consensus or have dozens of unproductive "alignment" meetings. They don't produce decks for every idea that comes to mind and analyze them with teams of external consultants and PMO types. **They move fast.**

Many of them are excellent at convincing people to come along, but they don't need applause before acting. They'll push forward no matter what—because the outcome and end result matter more than who claps in the boardroom. That's the entire point: **speed and decisiveness win; hesitation kills.**

And here's the clinch point: entrepreneurial leaders are **comfortable being uncomfortable**. In fact, they thrive in the mess. They're wired to run straight into volatility, ambiguity, and uncertainty—the exact conditions that paralyze most traditional leaders. Making decisions with imperfect information. **And win.** Being "comfortable with being uncomfortable" is their superpower. It means they don't need perfect data, complete visibility, or unanimous buy-in. They act without that. They bet on speed, on momentum, on adjusting mid-flight instead of waiting for the perfect plan. Their cycles of change, act – measure- adjust – act are exponentially faster than others. To an entrepreneur, discomfort isn't a warning—it's a green light.

This mindset shows up everywhere an entrepreneurial leader is in charge. They launch products first, pivot in public when needed, and treat setbacks as tuition, not failure. Their ego is not in being right. **Their ego is satisfied with winning.**

While traditional leaders obsess about avoiding mistakes, entrepreneurs are stacking learning cycles, 10x faster, and moving again. They don't crave stability because they know stability is a myth. Change is the only constant—and they've made peace with it. Hell, they've weaponized it.

And the research proves it. *Harvard Business Review* has shown repeatedly that leaders with high "tolerance for ambiguity" massively outperform in fast-changing environments. A University of Chicago Booth study proved entrepreneurial decision-makers beat their corporate counterparts when the facts are fuzzy—because they move. Daniel Kahneman's work makes it clear: humans are naturally risk-averse, hardwired to freeze under uncertainty. Entrepreneurs? They flip that instinct upside down. They see uncertainty as opportunity, not danger. That's why they win when the ground is shifting. *Hesitation is bankruptcy on layaway.*

Deloitte shows companies led by entrepreneurial executives are 2.5 times more likely to launch disruptive products. A 2023 BCG survey found entrepreneurial-style leaders were 45% more likely to get employees adopting new tech fast. Gallup piles on: employees under entrepreneurial leaders are 30% more willing to try new ways of working. Translation? Entrepreneurial leaders don't just drag people into the future—they get them excited about it.

Here's why: entrepreneurial leaders have **gravitas**. They walk into the room with urgency, vision, and conviction—and people follow. Call it charisma, call it force of will, call it whatever you want—it doesn't matter. Teams instinctively believe in leaders who **move decisively** and confidently. Stanford research shows that teams led by entrepreneurial leaders run 60% more experiments per quarter than those under traditional managers. That's not a small bump—that's a different universe.

Traditional organizational leaders are the opposite. They play it safe, push paper, build consensus, and cling to processes. They wait for more reports, more analysis, more "green lights." McKinsey's research tells us —organizations under these process-first leaders are 50% more likely to stall or abandon change entirely. Their employees don't get energized— they get exhausted. "Change fatigue" doubles. The gravitas isn't there. Instead of urgency, they project caution. Instead of conviction, they project hesitation. And **hesitation is contagious.** It creates a leadership vacuum as strong as space itself.

Change management has always been about minimizing risk and easing disruption. It was slow by design. The leader's role was often more about managing inertia than inspiring transformation. Legacy leaders became cautious operators, consensus-builders, and guardians of the status quo. These were not creators. They were stewards of businesses and systems that became outdated.

But in a world where AI evolves faster than corporate approval chains, the traditional paper-pushing approach to leadership is fatal. AI First leadership requires the mindset of a founder, not a facilitator. Today's leader must push boundaries, break silos, and move the organization toward radical transformation—not over years, but in months or even weeks. As AI unlocks new capabilities almost daily, delay equals irrelevance.

The entrepreneurial skill set is not just helpful for organizations moving to AI First—**it is <u>required</u>.** Why? Because the very nature of getting to AI First demands Extreme Change Management. Not the soft, consensus-driven variety that traditional corporate leaders cling to, **but a hard-driving, outcome-obsessed approach** where **speed matters**

more than comfort. Extreme Change Management isn't about asking nicely or waiting for people to feel good about the shift. It's about demanding compliance, mandating new behaviors, and holding the line until change sticks. They understand that hesitation means death.

Entrepreneurial leaders thrive in this arena. They understand that **resistance is normal but also irrelevant**. Their focus is on the end state—on results. They push through opposition not by endless cajoling, but by creating momentum so powerful it becomes impossible not to follow. That's the DNA of successful leadership required for Extreme Change Management.

Beyond Extreme Change Management in the AI First Era

For an organization to become AI First, its leaders need to take the **first step** toward transformation. Extreme Change Management is the polar opposite of what corporate America has been practicing for the last 50 years. It requires **entrepreneurial-first leaders**: visionaries who thrive on speed, risk, and decisive action. Leaders who don't just manage change but **create it**.

But what then?

What happens once the organization has "completed" its AI First transformation?

What kind of leaders are required?

Why can't we just hire consultants to get us to an AI First "state", and then turn the keys back over to the traditional leadership skill set of the past? What do we do?

Here's the uncomfortable truth: there is no "completion" to AI First. There is no steady-state. There is no plateau. An AI First organization is always in a state of flux, and its leaders need to be okay with that. Always. Why? Because AI itself evolves at breakneck speed. A new model, a new tool, a new capability—it's not every decade, it's every quarter, sometimes every week.

The implication is simple: AI First is not a destination. No Period of slowdown. No comfort zone. No breathing space when leaders can say "we're done". AI First is a permanent operating condition. In the AI First era, saying "we're done" is the same as saying, "We're dead."

This is why entrepreneurial leadership is not only required to **achieve** AI First—it's required to **sustain it.** The same leaders who thrive on Extreme Change Management are the only ones capable of living in this permanent state of reinvention because they don't fear change. They embrace it as their default setting.

The new normal for organizations is **entrepreneurial leadership at scale.** Not only in startups. Not only in skunkworks. But in the core of **every** functional area of every organization, large and small alike.

Because the only way to stay AI First is to be led by people who thrive on perpetual change, who push through the discomfort of change, and who refuse to let "the way we've always done it" dictate "the way we're going to do it."

That's the difference between organizations that will shape the AI era—and organizations that will be shaped by it and pushed out of existence.

The entrenched, risk-averse infrastructure of traditional organizations—the layers of middle managers, the legacy processes, the executive politicians who spend more energy protecting their careers than building the business—cannot survive in this world. They slow things down. They water things down. They create inertia at the exact moment when **velocity is oxygen.**

The AI First era spells the death of the **deep state** that exists within most organizations. In its place, a new kind of leader must emerge.

The Deep State within Organizations

What is the deep state within organizations?

The **Deep State within organizations** is the shadow bureaucracy of career preservation, incrementalism, and internal politics that quietly governs most organizations. It is the ingrained layer of gatekeepers, corporate politicians, and institutionalized processes that put **self-preservation above progress**. It thrives on status quo preservation, protecting turf, and ensuring survival of the system—not the success of the business. It's dangerous. It's outdated. And organizations that cling to it will be outcompeted, out innovated, and eventually eliminated.

The "deep state of business" is not a conspiracy, nor is it a political organization, nor a secret society of the most important and powerful people from around the world, that sit in a castle in Switzerland determining the fate of humanity.

It is the entrenched class of bureaucrats, middle managers, and process guardians who thrive on slowing change. Over decades, studies have shown that organizations accumulate these non-productive roles like plaque in an artery. A Harvard Business Review study found that **60% of managers admit they add "little to no value" in their daily activities**, yet the corporate structures that support them remain intact. Gallup research confirms that only **21% of employees worldwide are engaged at work**, meaning the majority of effort in organizations is misdirected or wasted.

These internal bureaucracies thrive by consolidating power, expanding headcount, and creating complexity. In large organizations, middle management layers have ballooned—between 1983 and 2017, the number of managers in the U.S. workforce grew by **over 90%**, far outpacing overall employment growth, according to the Bureau of Labor Statistics. McKinsey has documented that in transformations, "change resistance from middle management" is cited as a **top 3 barrier 70% of the time**, and it is one of the leading reasons why **over 70% of corporate transformations fail**.

Rather than driving outcomes, these actors protect process. They slow innovation under the guise of "risk management." They insist on endless meetings, reports, and consensus-building—mechanisms that make them seem indispensable while adding little value.

The deep state of business is the opposite of what a business run by entrepreneurial leaders represents. Entrepreneurs move fast, make decisions, and take accountability for outcomes. Bureaucrats delay, deflect, and ensure they cannot be held responsible for failure. A PwC survey found that **80% of executives believe their own organizational bureaucracy is a top obstacle to growth**—yet they struggle to dismantle it because the bureaucrats themselves control the levers of hiring, budgets, and process.

Left unchecked, this corporate deep state **kills organizations**. Kodak, Blockbuster, Nokia—once dominant companies—were hollowed out by layers of cautious managers who blocked bold moves. Research from the Corporate Executive Board (CEB) revealed that **in companies that failed during digital disruption, "internal resistance" was cited as a greater barrier than external competition**. In short: competitors don't always kill companies. Their own bureaucrats often do.

The Deep State is not just a **disease** of the Fortune 500. SMBs and even small businesses suffer from their own version of the deep state. The scale is smaller, but the damage is often greater because there are fewer layers of resilience. In a 40-person company, one entrenched manager who resists AI or innovation can drag down 10% of the workforce by themselves. That concentration risk makes bureaucratic resistance in SMBs potentially even deadlier than in large firms.

Take the example of a family-owned commercial contractor or a small professional services firm. Too often, long-tenured office managers or department heads block new software systems because "the old way works fine." Research from the National Federation of Independent Business (NFIB) shows that **38% of small businesses identify "employee resistance to change" as their top barrier to adopting new technology**. That's not just inefficiency—it's survival at stake.

In a small manufacturing firm, a production supervisor may resist AI-driven scheduling systems to maintain control over shift assignments. In professional practices like law or accounting, senior partners may block automation because it threatens their billable hours. Even in fast-moving startups, "mini-bureaucrats" appear shockingly fast—project managers multiplying processes and slowing delivery. A study by Startup Genome found that over 30% of failed startups blamed "internal mismanagement or bureaucracy" as a key cause of death.

The irony is that SMBs, which should be nimble, often create their own bureaucratic bottlenecks. Entrepreneurial founders hire trusted lieutenants, who then **protect their turf, resist outside expertise, and squash dissent.** These internal gatekeepers give themselves the illusion of importance by forcing every decision to flow through them. But instead of enabling growth, they choke it.

Even when resources are limited, these behaviors show up. An office manager in a 20-person company who refuses to embrace AI-based payroll or HR tools forces the CEO to spend hours firefighting issues instead of building the business. That inefficiency compounds, and suddenly the company looks more like a bloated bureaucracy than a lean SMB.

The lesson is clear: no company is immune. Deep State Bureaucratic resistance is not just a big-company problem—it **metastasizes anywhere people cling to power over outcomes.** In SMBs, the cost is magnified. Every day wasted on internal politics is a day lost to competitors who move faster. It is the poison that destroys organizations from the inside out. And in the AI First era, that margin of error is gone.

The deep state hurts employees, too. A global Gallup study shows that over **80% of workers say they want their organization to succeed and grow,** even if they aren't fully engaged day-to-day. The entrepreneurial leader harnesses this latent energy and frees it to help transform the organization.

The deep state is simply the often-unconscious institutionalized form of resistance to change.

This conflict creates unintended sabotage. As mentioned earlier, research from McKinsey highlights that **70% of organizational initiatives fail**, and one of the top drivers is **passive** resistance — employees and managers unconsciously building processes, policies, and routines that slow down change. For example, committees get formed "to ensure alignment," but they really just delay decision-making. New reporting requirements are introduced "to improve visibility," but they subtly discourage experimentation. These aren't malicious acts — they're protective instincts, often cloaked as prudence.

This is the human deep state — **the invisible, systemic drag on progress.** It's not intentional espionage. Its inertia disguised as professionalism. And unless entrepreneurial leaders recognize it for what it is and rip it out, it quietly corrodes every business, from the 15-person contractor shop to the Fortune 500 giant.

What makes the deep state dangerous is that it doesn't look like sabotage. It looks like normal business. Reports are filed. Meetings are held. Metrics are tracked. But the underlying motive is not growth, innovation, or customer success—it's survival. People learn how to manipulate data, shape perceptions, and create the illusion of productivity while ensuring nothing truly disruptive threatens their position.

For every part of a company infected by deep state behavior, the impact is multiplied **across the organization.** That's because one layer of obstruction slows every other layer downstream. Sales gets stuck waiting for product. Product gets bogged down in approvals. Customers wait longer for results. And leadership gets fed a version of reality carefully curated to look "under control."

The scariest part? It's **institutionalized**. Leaders don't "approve" it, but by failing to weed it out, they allow it to become the default operating system. The longer it lasts, the harder it is to spot. And because it's made up of people, rooting it out feels personal—even when the behavior is what's truly toxic.

Example 1: A Small Electrical Contractor (15 employees)

Take a commercial electrical contractor with 15 people. On paper, it should be nimble. But the office manager—who has been there for 12 years—learns how to control the flow of information. She decides which bids are "ready" for the owner to review, which invoices get processed quickly, and which vendor complaints get downplayed. To the owner, she looks indispensable. In reality, she throttles decision-making and ensures that nothing changes without her approval. The crew misses opportunities because jobs don't get quoted fast enough, and new software adoption stalls because she resists "extra work." The company loses growth opportunities not because of competition, but because of **internal drag masquerading as stability.**

Example 2: A Community College

At a community college, the deep state shows up in the administration. A dean resists new online programs, claiming "quality concerns," when in reality, his staff doesn't want to learn new tools. Meetings are endless, reports are generated, committees are formed—but nothing moves forward. Faculty who push for innovation are quietly sidelined with extra committee work until they burn out. Students lose out on flexible learning options, enrollment lags, and the college falls behind peers. The deep state thrives here because "process" is worshiped, and leaders don't challenge it. The result: a slow institutional decline masked by endless paperwork and polite meetings.

Example 3: A Fortune 100 Company

Now picture a Fortune 100 corporation. A senior VP builds a sprawling department with layers of directors and managers, each with pet projects and inflated KPIs. They know exactly how to present data so that quarterly reviews look successful, even when real outcomes are stagnant. Innovation projects die in "pilot purgatory" because middle layers insist on more studies and approvals. Behind the scenes, managers are protecting budgets, not customers. It looks like a functioning machine, but it's really a maze designed to ensure no one takes risks. The impact?

Billions of dollars of wasted potential, and startups eat their lunch while the deep state strangles progress from the inside.

Why It Matters

In all three cases, the root cause is the same: traditional **leadership allowed these issues to happen.** Not deliberately, but passively—by valuing smooth operations and avoiding conflict instead of demanding results.

Entrepreneurial leaders in the AI First organizations by their very nature destroy this deep state. They don't tolerate this. They expose it, dismantle it, and replace it with urgency. Traditional leaders ignore it, and the organization slowly suffocates.

And in the AI First era, where velocity is survival, it's not just inefficient—**any** remanent of this type of deep state reality is deadly.

Outcome-Focused Leadership: Forget the Wins, Seek Out What is Broken.

Entrepreneurial leaders focus on one thing above all else: **outcomes.** They don't fall in love with process, consensus, or politics—they fall in love with results. If something isn't working, they rip it apart and try something new. In fact, their instinct is to **seek out precisely what is broken**.

They have almost a _maniacal urgency_ to understand why something isn't delivering, and then fix it—immediately, decisively, and without apology. That wiring—the relentless, outcome-first brain—means they don't waste time polishing what looks good; they zero in on what fails and turn it around.

By contrast, traditional, non-entrepreneurial leaders cling to what _is_ working, or at least appears to be working, and **amplify it.** Their instinct is **defensive**—protect the turf, **highlight the wins**, and avoid rocking the boat. They point to a functioning piece of the machine and say, "See, we're fine," even as the rest of the system rusts out. That mindset doesn't just slow transformation—it kills it.

Entrepreneurial leaders are also unique in how they treat discomfort. They are **comfortable being uncomfortable.** Where traditional managers avoid conflict, uncertainty, and ambiguity, entrepreneurs lean into it. They see discomfort as a sign that progress is being made. That bias toward action, especially under pressure, is exactly what AI First organizations always demand.

In practice, this means entrepreneurial leaders build cultures of **experimentation, not protection**. Their gravitas comes from creating momentum—people want to follow them because they make progress inevitable. Traditional leaders rely on hierarchy to command loyalty; entrepreneurial leaders generate it through vision and velocity.

The entrepreneurial leader is a fundamentally different animal, and in the AI First era, this is **not** optional. AI exposes inefficiency faster than ever before. A competitor with the right tools and vision can outpace you in weeks. That means leaders who only see what's safe and stable will always be behind. Leaders who are wired to hunt for what's broken, uncomfortable, or incomplete will always be ahead.

A strong entrepreneurial leader drives progress by relentlessly diagnosing weak points in the business model, processes, or technology stack—and then doing whatever it takes to fix them. **They don't look for applause; they look for friction.** They understand that the biggest gains come not from amplifying what already works, but from eliminating what drags an organization down. Non-entrepreneurial leaders, on the other hand, pour their energy into protecting appearances. They celebrate stability, polish reports, and avoid tough calls that might make them unpopular. That divergence in mindset explains why entrepreneurial leaders drive results in ways that traditional leaders simply cannot.

And the evidence backs it up. A 2022 McKinsey study found that companies led by entrepreneurial-style executives were **five times more likely** to achieve or exceed their organizational financial goals compared to those led by traditional operators. Why? Because when leaders obsess over outcomes, they move faster, cut through bureaucracy, and direct resources toward fixing the real bottlenecks. Conversely, organizations run by defensive, process-first managers almost always stall out in "pilot purgatory," where projects look good on slides but never deliver real results.

At the end of the day, this isn't about style—it's about survival. In an AI First era, the leaders who thrive will be the ones **wired to chase outcomes** with relentless focus, to seek out what's broken, and to fix it before competitors even see the weakness. Anything less, and the organization will be left behind.

Return of the Entrepreneur at Scale

The new normal required for leaders of organizations in the AI First era is **entrepreneurial leadership at scale**.

For the last half-century, management orthodoxy has taught that professional managers—not entrepreneurs—are the ones capable of scaling organizations. Business schools and consulting firms reinforced the idea that entrepreneurs are visionary "idea people," useful in the startup stage, but too chaotic and undisciplined to manage complexity. Instead, the narrative went, once a company reached a certain size, it needed layers of trained professionals, governance models, and standardized processes to scale. On the surface, this seemed logical. Harvard Business Review and McKinsey research show that over 80% of companies with professionalized management structures outperform in predictability and compliance compared to founder-led organizations.

But **predictability is not the same as value creation**. Professional managers often prize stability over disruption, **control over risk**, and process over outcomes. This is exactly why studies of the S&P 500 show that founder-led companies, though fewer in number, consistently deliver higher shareholder returns—3.1 times higher, according to Bain & Company. Entrepreneurial leaders drive urgency, innovation, and accountability that professional bureaucracies often suffocate. In the pre-AI era, companies could survive this tradeoff because the pace of change was slower. A 10-year digital transformation was painful but survivable.

In the AI First era, this need for predictability is a disaster. The very "stability" professional managers are trained to preserve becomes poison. Scaling with AI requires constant reconfiguration, **relentless risk-taking, and tolerance for discomfort**—the exact skillset of entrepreneurial leaders. Instead of being pushed aside after the startup phase, entrepreneurial DNA must run the entire organization, from a 20-person SMB to a Fortune 100. Leaders must move fast, flatten hierarchies, and force execution even when it breaks precedent.

Case studies already show the difference. Amazon, still led by Jeff Bezos through its explosive growth years, scaled entrepreneurial urgency into one of the largest companies on Earth. In contrast, once-innovative firms like GE or Nokia, heavy with professional management, collapsed under their own bureaucracy. The data is clear: in an AI First world where entire industries can be upended in 18 months, professional management orthodoxy is not just outdated—it's fatal. Companies that cling to it will bleed relevance and profitability.

> **Cooper Callout:** The old rule said, "entrepreneurs start, managers scale." The new reality is "entrepreneurs start, and only entrepreneurs can scale."

AI First doesn't merely change **what "work" is**—it changes **who can do what work**. With the right use of AI, a single person can now orchestrate the output of what used to take ten specialists. A marketing executive with a clear outcome in mind can launch a campaign, produce 50 pieces of content, create customer segments, and deploy A/B tests—all in a day—with no human team. A product lead can prototype software, generate documentation, and simulate edge cases with AI agents, on their own. **Specialized knowledge is now scalable to all via AI.**

This power fundamentally **elevates the role of vision and visionary**. In the past, only the doers could execute. Now, visionaries who can clearly define outcomes—and communicate them with precision to AI—**can execute better than entire departments.**

Unlike traditional managers, entrepreneurial people don't **wait for permission.** They build, test, and adjust in real time. They **don't outsource strategy**—they invent it. That's the exact muscle AI amplifies. A bold idea, combined with strong prompting and systems thinking, is more powerful than an entire legacy team. The executive who thrives today is one who sees AI not as a tool to assist operations, but as a **force multiplier to realize vision.**

Where to Find Entrepreneurial Leadership Talent

Finding entrepreneurial leadership talent is one of the most critical challenges for any organization that wants to thrive in the AI First era. Entrepreneurial leaders are not evenly distributed across the workforce, and they rarely look like the polished executives who fill traditional corporate pipelines. They can come from unusual places — sometimes even **hiding in plain sight** inside your own company. The first step is broadening the search beyond the usual résumés and business school pedigrees.

Startups are one of the most fertile grounds. Founders and early employees at young companies are often forced to build under extreme constraints. They must solve problems without playbooks, make decisions with incomplete information, and pivot quickly when the market or investors demand it. Even founders who have "failed" startups often bring a resilience and creative drive that makes them invaluable in larger organizations. Research by CB Insights shows that 70% of startups fail within 20 months, but the individuals who survive those crucibles often emerge sharper, hungrier, and better equipped to navigate uncertainty. These are precisely the traits that entrepreneurial leadership requires.

High-growth firms also create talent pools of entrepreneurial leaders. Employees who thrived while a company scaled from $10 million to $500 million in revenue have already learned how to operate in chaos, adjust to changing systems, and lead without relying on formal structures. A McKinsey study found that firms growing at 20% annually or more develop "adaptive leaders" at nearly twice the rate of slower-growth peers. These are people who can import that speed and agility into a new environment.

The military — **especially special operations** and aviation units — is another source. Military leaders are trained to make split-second decisions with lives on the line, operate in unpredictable environments, and innovate within rigid systems. Veterans from these backgrounds often combine discipline with creativity, making them well-suited for entrepreneurial leadership. Programs like DoD's SkillBridge or initiatives by companies such as Deloitte have tapped into this pipeline, with strong results.

But entrepreneurial leaders don't only exist "out there." Many organizations already have them inside. They may be mid-level managers, engineers, or even frontline staff who consistently volunteer for messy, undefined projects and deliver outcomes where others stall. Spotting them requires looking past job titles and focusing on behaviors. Who takes ownership for problems no one else wants? Who finds ways to cut through red tape and deliver results? Who experiments with new tools, especially AI, without being told? These are signals of **entrepreneurial DNA hiding within your existing workforce.**

Universities, too, are a source — but not in the traditional sense of degree pipelines. Entrepreneurial talent often comes from hackathons, startup incubators, or design-thinking labs on campuses. Students who have built **side hustles** or led campus organizations with real budgets and accountability often demonstrate more entrepreneurial grit than those who followed polished consulting internship tracks. With Gen Z showing higher rates of entrepreneurial intent — 54% say they want to start their own business compared to 41% of millennials — companies that build relationships with entrepreneurial student groups can gain early access to this emerging wave of leaders.

Industry crossovers also create opportunities. Leaders from industries that have already been disrupted by AI or technology adoption — such as fintech, logistics, or media — bring valuable pattern recognition. They know what disruption feels like, and they know how to navigate it. For example, hiring a product leader from a company that went through a massive digital transformation may provide more value than hiring a steady but conventional executive from a stable legacy company.

Organizations can also create their own ecosystems for surfacing entrepreneurial leaders. Hackathons, internal accelerators, or "intrapreneurship" programs give employees a chance to demonstrate entrepreneurial instincts in practice.

At the same time, companies must recognize that entrepreneurial leaders are scarce and highly mobile. A LinkedIn study found that people with entrepreneurial backgrounds switch jobs 50% more often than traditional managers. That means **attraction and retention strategies matter**. Competitive compensation helps, but culture is even more important. Entrepreneurial leaders want autonomy, resources, and the ability to make decisions quickly. If they feel stifled by bureaucracy, they will leave.

In short, entrepreneurial leadership talent can be found in multiple places: startups, scale-ups, the military, universities, cross-industry hires, and even within your current workforce. But **spotting them requires different eyes.** Traditional corporate hiring filters out these people because they don't fit the mold. AI First organizations must flip that script and value outcomes, resilience, creativity, and risk comfort above polished résumés. The organizations that master this talent search will have the edge in the AI era, because they will be powered by leaders who can harness both AI and entrepreneurial instincts to drive transformation at speed.

> **Cooper Callout:** Entrepreneurial leaders aren't unicorns — they're out there. The real question is whether you're looking in the right places, and whether your organization is built to **keep them once you find them.**

Less Need for Management Consulting

Traditional Management consulting engagement, the long-time drivers of slow transformation, are also becoming obsolete. They profit from complexity, ambiguity, and delay. They don't own the outcome—they analyze it. They write decks. They don't build. Entrepreneurial leaders, on the other hand, are builders. **They do not outsource strategy**. They do not outsource direction. They take the initiative and own it.

Combined with AI, entrepreneurial leaders have hands to build without waiting for armies of analysts or developers or other specialized workers, eliminating the need to long winded, highly paid mgmt. consultants who are often gone by the time their ideas are never implemented.

There's no time for 18-24 month planning cycles. No patience for "pilot purgatory." The executive must not be a bottleneck—they must be a catalyst. **This isn't about managing risk anymore—it's about managing velocity.**

The most successful executives in the AI era will be those who treat their business like a **permanent startup**, constantly reinventing operations, products, and customer engagement. They'll build with small **AI-empowered pods**. They'll launch internal tools in weeks, not quarters. They'll see problems as opportunities to disrupt themselves before someone else does.

What's most exciting is that entrepreneurialism isn't just for startups or start up phases anymore. It's **required FOR scale**. AI removes the traditional friction of scale—headcount, layers, specialists—and replaces it with orchestration. The $10M business and the $1B business now face the same question: how fast can you turn vision into reality? Not only the initial vision, but the small adjustment to a small part of the business that still requires that vision-reinvention-execution cycle. Only one kind of leader answers that question well: the entrepreneur.

AI is not just eliminating the need for deep specialization—it's **concentrating power into the hands of those who can communicate vision and guide AI toward it**. That's the new skill set. It's not about how many departments you manage. It's about how well you can wield the most powerful tool ever created—an army of reasoning machines ready to act on your ambition.

The AI First revolution has **no room for leaders who are caretakers and stewards.** No room for the traditional players that make up the deep state. It belongs to the creators. The drivers. The disruptors. The entrepreneurs.

That's the difference between companies that will shape the AI era—and companies that will be shaped by it.

The Bottom Line: AI First Demands Entrepreneurial Leaders

Here's the bottom line: entrepreneurial leaders don't just handle change. They crush it. They turn discomfort into momentum. They make people want to move forward instead of resisting. And in an AI First world, that's the only type of leadership that matters. Everyone else? They're caretakers of the past. And the past is already gone.

Entrepreneurial leadership becomes not just the driver of AI First transformation, but the skill set that **ensures the company keeps evolving once it gets there.** Without it, organizations backslide. With it, they accelerate. That's why entrepreneurialism is not a nice-to-have; it's the survival trait of the AI First era.

If your leaders are consensus-builders, caretakers, or bureaucrats, they will fail. If your leaders are entrepreneurs—restless, decisive, outcome-driven—you have a shot at not only becoming AI First, but staying there. And staying there is the only game that matters.

The AI First revolution belongs to the creators. The drivers. The disruptors. **Entrepreneurs.** And you cannot find these entrepreneurs on job-listing sites. Some of them are hidden gems within your own company, just waiting for the opportunity to shine. And some of them are YOU. You, re-invented as the entrepreneurial leader you always dreamed you could be.

As important as it is to have an entrepreneurial leader, the **organization's structure must support an AI First transformation.** That's what we'll cover in the next chapter.

Chapter 6:

Organizational Structure in the AI First Era: Why The Old Days Are Over

Why Structure Determines Success

One of the most overlooked truths in business is this: organizational structure determines outcome. The way an organization is structured—how people, teams, authority, and accountability are arranged and measured—shapes everything it does. Strategy, execution, innovation, and adaptability all flow through the channels defined by organizational design.

Organizational structure dictates resource allocation, and **resource allocation is everything**. It decides what gets attention, what gets funded, what gets ignored, and where focus lies. Structure is the physical manifestation of priorities—it channels the energy of the entire enterprise toward certain goals while starving others. In this way, structure doesn't just influence outcomes; it predetermines them. A poorly designed structure guarantees wasted effort, while a smart one ensures that people and capital are aligned against the outcomes that truly matter.

Yet most organizations treat their structure & design as a **static blueprint instead of a dynamic engine**. They frame it as something you design once and maintain forever, rather than something that evolves constantly.

Historically, organizational charts reflect hierarchy and control. Layers of managers pass information upward, approvals downward, and decisions slowly ripple through bureaucratic chains. This model was designed for an industrial world that prioritized **stability over speed**. It worked when factories moved slowly, information was scarce, and risk-avoidance was survival.

Study after study shows that organizational structure and incentives directly correlate with long-term performance. *Harvard Business Review* research shows that "organizational health"—a measure rooted in how people are structured, empowered, and incentivized—accounts for more than **50% of the variance** in long-term shareholder returns. Bain & Company concluded that companies that regularly revisit and redesign their org structure outperform peers by as much as 30% in productivity gains.

Yet despite this evidence, **org design remains one of the most neglected disciplines in management**. A Deloitte survey found that fewer than 10% of executives believe their organizations are "excellent" at aligning structure with strategy. Gallup research reveals that only two out of ten employees strongly agree their jobs are designed in a way that enables them to do their best work. In other words, most organizations are literally wasting the potential of their people through outdated design, and **not investing** the time/effort/focus on ensuring organizational design is optimizing its performance.

Leaders obsess over strategy decks, financial modeling, or product roadmaps, but when it comes to structure, they simply redraw the same chart from 20 years ago with minor tweaks. It is treated as an afterthought, a necessary evil, instead of the primary driver of outcomes.

This blind spot is staggering. Human capital is the single most powerful and expensive asset in 98% of the world's organizations. How those humans are grouped, incentivized, and aligned determines whether their collective output compounds or collapses. If you get the structure wrong, no amount of strategy, technology, or capital can save you.

Research from MIT Sloan confirms this mismatch: companies that adopt new technologies without redesigning their organizational model capture less than 30% of the expected productivity gains. In other words, **technology without structure is noise**.

And here is the crisis: in a "normal" world, org design was already behind the times. It lagged decades behind technology, customer expectations, and the way people actually worked. Enter AI, and the problem explodes.

The gap between Pre-AI organizational structures and AI First organizational requirements is a gap **that makes the Grand Canyon look like a crack in the sidewalk** Traditional leaders have absolutely no idea what to do. They were never trained to think of structure as strategic, and most organizations are nowhere near prepared to figure this out.

This is why so many companies bolt AI pilots onto old structures, only to see them fizzle. The skeleton is broken, and no amount of "innovation theater" can hide it. Unless leaders radically rethink org design, their companies will not survive the AI era.

Structure is **not a side note**. It is the skeleton of the business. It determines posture, agility, and strength. Ignore it, and your organization will lurch, stumble, and eventually collapse under its own weight.

With the Power of AI now at hand, **organizations that want to be AI first must** immediately redesign and restructure their organizations to have a change to achieve this. It must happen.

The Superpower Hidden Inside AI First Organizations: An Army of Entrepreneurs with Unlimited Resources

AI First organizations don't just have the power of AI. They have something else—a **new class of entrepreneurial leaders who thrive in this environment.** This is the real **superpower**, second only to AI itself.

For decades, CEOs and boards have dreamed of a nearly impossible combination: how to capture the creativity, urgency, and relentless outcome-focus of entrepreneurial talent, but at the scale, consistency, and durability of a large organization. Normally, those two forces are in conflict. Entrepreneurial leaders thrive in environments of chaos, freedom, and rapid iteration. Large organizations, on the other hand, survive on predictability, hierarchy, and structure. Put simply: entrepreneurship has the energy, but not the discipline. Corporations have the discipline, but not the energy.

AI First changes everything.

AI doesn't just supercharge productivity—it resolves the age-old paradox of entrepreneurship versus structure. It allows organizations to **harness entrepreneurial leadership at scale** without losing control, alignment, or cohesion. Organizations can **now** unleash an army of entrepreneurial leaders who move fast, take risks, and innovate aggressively, while still being guided and amplified by AI-driven insights, governance, and data discipline.

This is the ultimate superpower of an AI First organization: **the power of entrepreneurship at scale.** The ability to combine the creative fire of individual leaders with the alignment and power of AI infrastructure. That combination is more valuable than any single technological breakthrough—it's the structural unlock that leaders have craved for generations.

Think about it: most organizations when they achieve success have always tried to "bottle" entrepreneurship. They launch skunkworks projects, create innovation labs, or hire high-priced consultants to inject energy into a stale bureaucracy. But the problem has always been the same: **entrepreneurs hate bureaucracy, and bureaucracy crushes entrepreneurs.** Most of these efforts collapse under the weight of misalignment.

One of the most brutal truths of business is this: companies that start out as scrappy entrepreneurial rockets almost always calcify into bureaucratic machines. They grow, they scale, and somewhere along the way, they swap entrepreneurial leaders for professional managers, and innovation for process. The very thing that made them great gets suffocated by slow hierarchies, endless approvals, and **people more worried about optics than outcomes.**

Google is the perfect case study. By any measure, Google is one of the most valuable and successful companies on the planet. It is arguably one of the most successful businesses **of all time.** Yet we are watching, in real time, the early stages of its decline. For 20 years, Google's monopoly on search was untouchable — it still commands around 90% of global market share, generating $200B+ annually in ad revenue. That monopoly has papered over everything else. Most of its 200+ products have flopped, but it didn't matter — search kept paying the bills.

Now, the ground is shifting. AI threatens the very core of its empire. OpenAI came out of nowhere with fewer than 1,000 employees and put Google — a company with nearly 200,000 staff — on defense in the single most important technological race of our lifetimes. That's not just about technology. That's about organizational DNA. Google had the brains, the data, and the cash, but not the entrepreneurial structure to unleash them. Instead of risk-taking builders, it is dominated by professional managers, cautious hierarchies, and a culture where most employees hope not to get fired so they vest their stock grants rather than push to win.

And Google is not unique. IBM was once the king of computing. It owned the future of enterprise technology. But decades of professional management and org structures built for slow, careful moves turned it into a services dinosaur — limping forward while nimbler competitors passed it. Yahoo once dominated online traffic, but its obsession with process, layers of management, and lack of true entrepreneurial leadership doomed it to irrelevance. GE, once the most admired conglomerate in the world, collapsed under the weight of its own bureaucracy and an org chart designed to support lifers rather than disruptors.

The through-line is unmistakable: the combination of **a lack of entrepreneurial leaders** and **an organizational structure designed to protect hierarchy instead of outcomes** kills even the greatest companies. They stop taking risks, they stop moving fast, and they stop delivering new value. Bureaucrats accumulate power, innovators get sidelined, and entire orgs become paralyzed.

The danger in the AI First era is that this process no longer takes decades. It takes years, or even less. One AI First startup with 500 people can run circles around a legacy giant with 50,000, because AI multiplies entrepreneurial drive while exposing bureaucratic dead weight. Google still looks "great" because search is printing money. But look deeper — you see an organization that is one or two disruptive shifts away from being gutted.

The warning is clear: even the most valuable companies of all time are fragile if they are **structured for slowness and led by professional managers instead of entrepreneurs.** In the AI era, monopolies won't just fade slowly — they will collapse suddenly, because structure and leadership DNA matter more than size.

 **Cooper Callout:** The AI First world doesn't reward who you were. It exposes who you are. And if you're built for hierarchy instead of entrepreneurship & outcomes, you're already dying.

AI First Organizational Structure Breaks the Rules

AI breaks the stalemate. With AI embedded into pods, workflows, and decision-making, you can **scale entrepreneurial leadership without fear of chaos.** AI ensures visibility, accountability, and alignment across hundreds or even thousands of entrepreneurial pods. It takes the raw power of entrepreneurial leadership and plugs it into a system that can operate on a global scale.

The double benefit here is profound. First, you get the productivity explosion of AI itself—orders of magnitude faster execution, insight, and efficiency. Second, you get the unleashed human energy of entrepreneurial leaders who are no longer suffocated by traditional structures. AI multiplies both. The math is staggering: if AI can increase productivity by 3–5x on its own, and entrepreneurial leaders drive innovation and outcomes 10x faster than bureaucrats, the combination is **exponential.**

But here's the catch: this only works if **organizations are restructured to enable it**. You can't plug entrepreneurial leaders into the old structures and expect results. The old org charts, layers, PMOs, and bureaucratic bottlenecks were designed for control, not empowerment. They will kill the AI + entrepreneurial leadership superpower before it ever takes off.

This is why structure matters more than ever. If you redesign the organization into AI First pods—decentralized, lean, outcome-driven teams led by entrepreneurial leaders and guided by AI—you don't just improve efficiency. You fundamentally unlock the dream state of business: the **scalability of a corporation combined with the agility of a startup.**

This cannot be overstated: **don't mess this up by clinging to old structures.** Leaders who try to bolt AI onto outdated bureaucracies will waste the biggest opportunity of their careers. But leaders who redesign for AI First, who embrace entrepreneurial pods, who trust entrepreneurial talent empowered by AI—they will run circles around their competitors. The AI First org structure must not just support entrepreneurial leaders. It must be engineered to **weaponize them.**

> **Cooper Callout:** AI is the engine. Entrepreneurial leaders are the drivers. Without the right structure, the Ferrari never leaves the garage.

Organizational Structure Impacts Incentives and Drives Behavior

Org structures don't just describe "who reports to whom." They determine how incentives flow, how resources get allocated, and how quickly a company can pivot.

If **incentives reward maintaining headcount**, leaders resist automation. If authority requires five signatures, innovation stalls. If accountability is diluted across committees, nobody truly owns the outcome. Structure shapes culture and culture shapes survival.

In AI First organizations, structure has to reflect a different reality: that fewer people, supported by AI systems, can deliver exponentially more output. That decision cycles must compress from quarters to weeks, and from weeks to days. That entrepreneurial leaders must **not be rewarded for preserving stability, but for pushing velocity.**

A McKinsey study in 2023 found that organizations with flatter structures and empowered teams were 5x more likely to achieve breakthrough innovation during digital transformations. Deloitte reports that companies with adaptive, network-based structures were 33% faster in bringing new products to market compared to peers with rigid hierarchies.

Those numbers weren't just about technology. They were about leaders. The orgs that won were the ones that created structures where entrepreneurial leaders could move, decide, and act without friction.

Put differently: **technology without structural change is theater.** Most companies aren't losing because they don't buy AI tools. They're losing because they bury the people who can wield them under layers of corporate cement.

And this is where structure drives incentives that become reality. Structure determines what people are motivated to protect or what they are driven to destroy. In the old world, managers were incentivized to grow teams, budgets, and bureaucracies because status was tied to empire-building. In the AI First world, the incentives must flip: leaders are rewarded not for size, but for outcomes.

The smaller the team, the sharper the accountability. A pod of five entrepreneurial leaders armed with AI has nowhere to hide—every decision is visible, every outcome traceable. This creates a culture where incentives line up directly with results, not with appearances of control.

That's why AI First organizations must deliberately design incentives around lean, focused pods. The message has to be crystal clear: **fewer, more powerful people in smaller teams, fully accountable, fully unleashed.** These teams are not distracted by noise or ceremony—they are aimed like precision weapons at the outcomes that matter most.

This design doesn't just reward entrepreneurial behavior—it makes entrepreneurial behavior inevitable. When small teams own the work, are given authority, and have AI as their force multiplier, incentives and structure converge into one thing: velocity.

Flatter structures multiply this effect. When there are fewer layers, information moves faster, authority isn't trapped in middle management, and entrepreneurial leaders don't spend half their week "seeking approval." Decision-making becomes rapid, direct, and relentless.

> **Cooper Callout:** In AI First orgs, **structure isn't bureaucracy—it's a weapon.** The flatter it is, the sharper it cuts.

Flatter Organizations

AI First organizations need to be flat. Flat is good. Flat allows **speed** and iteration to become a priority.

Flattening Organizations does **not** mean chaos. It means collapsing needless bureaucracy and replacing it with direct accountability. It only works if the leaders in the organization are entrepreneurial.

Entrepreneurial leaders thrive in flatter structures because they don't need permission to move; they need **clarity of mission**.

Information doesn't need to crawl upward—it can be shared instantly. Execution doesn't need a dozen approvals—it needs one empowered leader who understands the outcome and uses AI to deliver it.

Consider a regional construction company with 80 employees. In the past, the firm had four layers of supervisors between field technicians and the CEO. Every change request in the field went up the chain, then down, sometimes taking a week to resolve. By restructuring into flatter, AI-supported crews, entrepreneurial leaders emerged—crew heads who could decide in minutes and let AI handle compliance. Projects now close 20% faster and with fewer errors, and the organization created the capacity for 15% more revenue with the same workforce!

Flattening also reduces what economists call **"the coordination tax."** Every layer of management adds a cost in time, misunderstanding, and politics. AI First orgs slash this tax by eliminating entire rungs. Instead of information flowing up and decisions flowing down, entrepreneurial leaders at the edge make the call, with AI providing instant intelligence.

And here's the cultural magic: **flattening signals trust**. When leaders at every level are trusted with authority, they rise to the occasion. When they're smothered under micro-management, they wither. Flatter organizational structures are the ideal operational construct, as it maximizes outcome-based productivity.

Flat organizational structures are not only recommended, but a strong requirement for entrepreneurial driven AI First organizations.

Examples of Flattening in Action

1. A Fortune 500 Tech Company

One of the world's largest technology firms recently began collapsing layers of management inside its product engineering division. Previously, a single feature update for a major product had to pass through at least five layers of management—team lead, manager, director, VP, and senior VP—before reaching the CTO's office. The cycle took three to four months, even for relatively small improvements.

In late 2023, they piloted an AI First flattening initiative. They reduced the management chain from five layers to two: pod leader and executive sponsor. Decision-making authority was delegated directly to AI-driven pods of 8–10 people, each with access to AI systems that handled compliance, reporting, and testing. Within one year, time-to-market for new features dropped by 60%. Revenue per employee climbed 22%, and voluntary attrition fell because employees reported they felt trusted and empowered for the first time.

The case revealed how AI could make middle layers redundant—not by removing accountability, but by automating the reporting and forecasting those middle managers once controlled. The company now plans to roll out similar flattening across global divisions, potentially eliminating thousands of mid-level roles while boosting overall organizational output. Senior executives also noticed a cultural shift: **instead of "covering your ass," teams focused on delivering outcomes.** This psychological shift reinforced agility, proving flattening wasn't just a structural change but a mindset revolution.

2. A Global Retail Chain

A multinational retailer with over 2,000 stores across North America and Europe had become notorious for slow merchandising decisions. Local store managers had to escalate requests for layout changes or product substitutions through four layers of approvals. By the time decisions came back down, the opportunity to capitalize on regional trends was gone.

In 2024, the chain adopted AI First flattening. Store managers were reorganized into AI-supported pods, each given authority to make inventory and layout decisions on the spot, guided by AI dashboards showing local demand patterns, supply chain constraints, and profitability models. Instead of a three-week cycle for approvals, managers acted in real time, changing endcaps or pricing within hours.

The results were dramatic: same-store sales increased 12% in the first year, shrinkage dropped by 9%, and customer satisfaction improved. Employees reported feeling like "entrepreneurs with corporate backing" rather than clerks waiting on orders from headquarters. The company discovered that decentralized, AI-powered authority made every store act like a startup—but with the resources of a multinational. Senior leadership noted that morale skyrocketed, as store teams could finally see the direct impact of their decisions.

3. A Mid-Sized Healthcare Provider

A regional healthcare provider with 1,200 employees and six hospitals faced critical challenges with decision-making speed. Every change—whether approving new equipment, adjusting staff schedules, or redesigning patient flow—required committee review across multiple administrative layers. Patients often waited weeks for improvements that could have been implemented in days.

In 2023, the provider flattened its structure, reorganizing around cross-functional AI-driven pods. Each pod included doctors, nurses, and administrators empowered to make patient-care decisions in real time, supported by AI tools that ensured compliance with regulatory and insurance requirements. The change reduced ER wait times by 35% and improved bed utilization by 20% in the first year.

The financial payoff was just as significant. Operating margins improved 14%, largely due to reduced administrative overhead and more efficient resource allocation. Perhaps most importantly, staff engagement scores rose sharply—nurses and physicians reported that they finally had a voice in operational decisions rather than waiting for "approval from above." Leadership highlighted that flattening didn't just speed up the organization—it rekindled a culture of accountability and pride among front-line healthcare workers. By the end of year two, the provider became a model studied by other health systems across the U.S. and Europe.

Across these examples—enterprise tech, retail, and healthcare—the story is consistent. **Flattening doesn't create chaos; it creates speed.** Middle layers vanish, not because accountability disappears, but because AI systems replace their coordination role. Decision-making flows to the edge, where outcomes happen. And whether it's a trillion-dollar corporation, a multinational retailer, or a regional healthcare provider, the effect is the same: faster cycles, higher margins, more innovation, and a culture of trust that energizes employees.

Cooper Callout: Flat isn't fragile—it's fast. And in an AI First world, speed is survival.

AI Pods

Perhaps the most important new structural construct in the AI First organizational model is the **AI pod.**

An AI Pod is a small, **outcome-focused team of entrepreneurial leaders and specialists,** tightly integrated with AI tools, designed to deliver measurable business results at speed. Unlike traditional departments or centralized functions, AI Pods own a complete outcome end-to-end—strategy, execution, and accountability—without layers of bureaucracy. They are flat, autonomous, and built to move fast, where every member's productivity is amplified by AI, making the team exponentially more powerful than its size suggests.

These pods don't just maximize AI—they maximize entrepreneurial leadership. By giving one entrepreneurial leader a pod that includes AI leverage, an AI architect, and a few experts, you essentially create a **mini-enterprise inside the company.**

Unlike traditional departments, pods are **outcome-defined, not function-defined.** Instead of "marketing" or "finance," they are "growth pods," "product launch pods," or "cost optimization pods."

Their goal is not activity—it's measurable results. AI gives them the leverage; the AI architect gives them the depth; structure gives them the accountability; and the entrepreneurial leader gives them the drive.

Spotify popularized the "squad" model in software. AI First organizations will supercharge this by integrating AI as the "extra team member," dramatically expanding each pod's capability.

Case in point: a mid-sized e-commerce retailer built three AI pods for logistics optimization. Each pod had one entrepreneurial leader, one logistics expert, one AI architect, and one AI coordinator. Within six months they cut delivery costs by 18% and reduced stockouts by 40%. Without the entrepreneurial leader driving outcomes and the AI architect weaponizing the tools, the AI systems would have sat idle.

How should these pods actually be set up? The key is **end-to-end accountability.** Each pod must have everything it needs inside the walls of the pod to deliver its assigned outcome. No endless handoffs. No waiting for another department. No begging finance, IT, or HR for support. If a pod is tasked with "new product launch," that pod has design, AI analysis, customer data, financial modeling, and compliance expertise all in one. **They own the outcome from start to finish.**

Pods should be small and lean—usually 5–10 people maximum, never more than 15. Large groups dilute accountability. Small groups move fast and make decisions without hesitation.

Each pod is measured on **outcomes, not activities.** Did the growth pod grow revenue? Did the cost optimization pod reduce expenses? Did the compliance automation pod cut cycle times and errors? Inputs and effort don't matter—only results.

AI pods also function on **short cycles.** Traditional departments measure success quarterly or annually. Pods should run on 2–4-week cycles, shipping results, testing, iterating, and compounding progress.

Their entrepreneurial leader is not a manager in the old sense. They are **general managers of outcomes,** accountable for every result the pod produces. They don't manage process—they deliver impact.

The AI architects are the pod's technical backbone. They ensure that AI is not a toy but a weapon—selecting the right tools, structuring the right data, and integrating AI into workflows so that every pod member is 5–10x more effective.

Measurement of pods should focus on three things:

1. Speed — how fast did they deliver?
2. Impact — what measurable business result did they create?
3. Learning — what did they test, iterate, or discover that makes the company smarter?

When pods succeed, the results are exponential. One cost-optimization pod can save tens of millions in a year. One product-launch pod can create an entirely new revenue stream. One customer-success pod can cut churn by 20% and boost lifetime value.

AI pods can scale infinitely. Unlike legacy departments that balloon with headcount, **pods replicate like cells.** You don't add 500 people to a department—you add 10 pods, each built to deliver discrete outcomes.

AI Pods in Action: Real-World Examples

The idea of AI Pods can sound abstract until you see them in action. These aren't theoretical exercises. They are small, tightly focused, AI-native teams that move like **special forces** inside organizations. To make this concrete, let's look at three very different examples: a Fortune 100 enterprise, a major university, and a 55-person commercial electrical and HVAC contractor.

Fortune 100 Manufacturer

For years, their product development cycles dragged on — 24 months on average from concept to launch, clogged with committees, legacy tools, and signoffs. When they stood up their first AI Pod, it wasn't a giant reorg. It was 12 people pulled from design, supply chain, marketing, and engineering, working together inside an AI-native stack. Instead of sending requirements back and forth through silos, they fed everything into AI platforms for simulation, cost modeling, and customer testing. Within six months, the pod slashed the development cycle to under six months. A single AI Pod outproduced what entire departments were delivering before.

How did they scale that?. The company didn't "roll out AI" department by department. They replicated the pod — spinning up 15 across functions like procurement, customer service, and quality assurance. In two years, the company's time-to-market was cut in half, and operating margins rose by 8 percentage points. All because small, AI First pods could move faster than the old machine.

Large, Full-Service University

Imagine the school--- with tens of thousands of students and sprawling operations — launching one of its first AI Pods: a cross-functional group of 10 people — professors, IT staff, and student affairs officers — tasked with redesigning the advising process. Traditionally, students waited weeks for an advisor, graduation audits lagged behind, and scheduling was chaos. The AI Pod plugged all that into AI-native scheduling tools, predictive analytics, and conversational AI for frontline advising. Within a single semester, wait times for advising dropped by 70%, and graduation audits that once took weeks were completed in 48 hours. The result wasn't just efficiency — it was better outcomes for students and higher satisfaction scores.

The university leadership didn't stop there. They spun up pods for financial aid processing, campus safety analytics, and even curriculum redesign. Each pod had a clear mission, operated independently, and reported **results** directly to leadership every **30 days**. The impact was immediate: the university not only cut costs but also became known as one of the most AI-forward schools in its region — a magnet for students who want to graduate job-ready.

55-Person Commercial Electrical and HVAC Contracting Firm

Before AI, their bids were slow, job costing was inconsistent, and project management was a headache. They launched one AI Pod with seven people: two estimators, two project managers, an operations lead, and two technicians. They put Simpro's AI First operating platform at the center of their workflow, using AI to generate bids, predict labor hours, automate tasks and optimize schedules. What once took two weeks for a bid now took one day.

In less than a year, this single pod transformed the business. The company expanded revenue by 35% without hiring a single additional employee. Profit margins shot up because bids were more accurate, labor overruns dropped, and customers got faster turnaround. Seeing the impact, the owner rolled out two more pods — one for service dispatch, and one for preventive maintenance. Each pod became a profit center, accountable for outcomes, not process.

The lesson here is simple: AI **pods scale rapidly and reduce risk. .** A global enterprise can deploy 20 pods and save billions. A university can launch pods to redesign student services. A 55-person contractor can use pods to double profits without growing headcount. The common denominator is structure: small, AI-native, outcome-driven, and unshackled from the old hierarchy.

> **Cooper Callout**: AI pods are not teams inside a company. They are companies inside a company—small, lethal, outcome-obsessed, and **impossible for bureaucracy to slow down.**

Fewer People, Greater Output

The power and speed of AI—and the surge in output AI First companies achieve when led by entrepreneurial leaders—force an uncomfortable truth: **AI First organizations require fewer people.** Not because talent doesn't matter, but because talent is now amplified.

AI First adoption produces **massive productivity gains—sometimes upwards of 100% within just a few months.** Teams that once needed 50 people can achieve the same or more with 25, or even 10. A product cycle that once took nine months can be compressed to 6 weeks. A back-office process that used to require dozens of analysts can be automated to near zero human touch. In other words, organizations that embrace AI quickly find themselves sitting on a mountain of new capacity.

The critical question is: *what do you do with that capacity?* This is where value is either unlocked or squandered. On the surface, the answer looks simple. If output per person doubles, then you need fewer people, so reduce headcount and harvest the gains. But history shows that this doesn't always happen. Many leaders shy away from the uncomfortable optics of layoffs, or they **lack the discipline to make hard structural changes.** Instead, they absorb the gains into "nice-to-have" projects, half-baked initiatives, or layers of reporting that don't tie back to revenue or cost.

What starts as a once-in-a-generation productivity gift **often gets dissipated into corporate fog.** A CIO might say, "We've freed up 40% of our engineering time, so let's assign them to a dozen experimental projects." None of those projects are given clear owners, deadlines, or ROI metrics. A CFO might resist cutting expenses, fearing political fallout, and instead re-labels the efficiency as "strategic reinvestment." The result? Busy teams, bloated budgets, and no measurable shareholder value. You'll hear a familiar counterargument: *"Don't reduce headcount—repurpose it. Keep everyone and just do more."* On paper, that sounds noble. In reality, it often breeds bloat, dilutes focus, and destroys accountability.

And the reason this reflex is so strong is because **leaders have been programmed for decades to equate size with success.** In the old world, the easiest way to measure a manager's importance was by counting how many people reported to them. A VP with 500 direct and indirect reports was seen as more powerful, more valuable, and more prestigious than a VP with 50—regardless of actual results. Promotions were often tied to how big your empire was, not how much business impact you delivered.

This mindset has hardened into the DNA of most large organizations. Generations of leaders have been raised to believe that "shrinking" is a failure, that getting smaller is inherently bad, and that protecting headcount is the safest way to preserve career capital. Cutting people feels like cutting status. To a career manager trained in the deep state, a leaner, more focused organization doesn't feel efficient—**it feels threatening.**

It's the organizational equivalent of muscle memory. For 30 years, if you wanted more credibility, you asked for more resources. If you wanted to signal growth, you showed that your department was adding headcount. Leaders are praised for building empires, not for dismantling unnecessary ones. No wonder they instinctively resist the idea that fewer people can mean greater output.

This **"never lay people off, always grow my org" reflex is the very definition of deep state thinking.** It is symptomatic of a system where leaders measure their self-worth by the size of their teams, not by the value they create. It's why so many transformations promise efficiency but deliver nothing measurable. Leaders default to protecting headcount because that's the scoreboard they were taught to play on.

AI First demands a 180-degree turn from this thinking. In the new world, the **scoreboard is outcomes, not org charts.** The true measure of a leader is not how many people sit in their empire—it's how much value they and their team produce relative to the resources consumed. **Value**

production, not size, is the only way to ensure the productivity gains of AI are fully realized. Without this pivot, all the efficiency in the world will just get buried under layers of PowerPoint and process.

Breaking that habit is like asking a lifelong smoker to quit cold turkey—it goes against every instinct that's been rewarded in their professional life. AI First exposes the lie: bigger teams don't mean better results anymore. In fact, AI makes it glaringly obvious that **small, entrepreneurial pods can outproduce bloated departments** by orders of magnitude.

This is why so many companies fall back into the trap of repurposing everyone instead of making the hard calls. It's not just a numbers game—it's cultural conditioning. Until leaders rewire their mental model to measure worth by outcomes rather than headcount, they will keep adding weight instead of cutting fat. And the result is always the same: **bloat disguised as progress.**

This is how the AI first organization is wired: **efficiency isn't real until it shows up on the P&L.** Organizations routinely claim "20% efficiency" after a big program, then keep all the people, add new projects, and declare victory. Meanwhile, operating expenses don't fall, revenue doesn't rise, and the company quietly slides backward. This is how the deep state wins—PMOs and consultants celebrate slides and scorecards, while shareholders get nothing.

A widely cited McKinsey finding is that roughly **70% of large transformations** fail to meet their stated objectives; BCG has similarly reported that the majority of "digital transformations" **underdeliver on hard results**. The pattern is depressingly consistent: promised savings never flow because leaders avoid the **hard calls**—true cost takeout or explicitly funded bets with revenue targets, owners, dates, and most importantly **accountability**

Consider a composite but all-too-real vignette. A global bank spends hundreds of millions on "automation at scale," forecasting a 15–20% reduction in back-office cost. Two years later, headcount is flat. The "savings" were redeployed to a constellation of initiatives with no hard

ROI gates. The PMO declares success; the CFO can't find a single percentage point of margin improvement. Efficiency theater, full stop.

Now contrast it with a lean mid-market SaaS company that reorganizes into a flat structure with AI pods. They automate Tier-1 support, onboarding, and billing ops. Before the program starts, leadership sets non-negotiables: 1) translate 60% of automation gains into **actual OpEx reduction**; 2) redeploy only the top 5–10% of freed capacity into **named growth pods** with revenue KPIs; 3) shut down or consolidate anything that doesn't move a P&L metric within 90 days. Twelve months later: support cost per ticket down 42%, days-sales-outstanding down 18%, revenue per employee up 35%, EBITDA margin up 9 points. Same technology as everyone else—**different structure, different incentives, different outcome.**

This is the pattern AI makes possible: one **product leader + AI** can synthesize customer feedback, generate wireframes, and run experiments in a day—work that used to span five roles. One **lawyer + AI** can draft, redline, and cross-check contracts with speed and accuracy that once required a para-team. One **analyst + AI** can consolidate data, model scenarios, and publish board-grade reporting in hours, not weeks. This isn't hypothetical: Goldman Sachs has estimated that AI could automate ~**25% of work tasks** globally by 2030, and Bain has reported **15–30%** headcount reductions in key back-office functions among companies deploying gen-AI at scale.

So, what does "fewer people, greater output" *really* mean in practice?

- **Make the savings real.** Pre-commit to how much automation benefit becomes OpEx reduction vs. how much is redeployed—then track it to the ledger.
- **Redeploy with accountability.** Only the highest-leverage talent moves into **small, AI First pods** with explicit revenue or cost KPIs, a single accountable owner, and 90-day proof points with ruthless accountability measures for value
- **Ban the repurposing reflex.** "We'll find something useful for everyone" is how bloat returns. If a role no longer maps to outcomes, don't invent work.

- **Keep teams tiny and powerful.** Fewer people → clearer ownership → faster cycles → visible results. Flat beats fat, every time.

And here's the paradox most people miss: fewer people does not mean less opportunity. It means the people who remain matter more than ever. They're not process-cogs; they're outcome-drivers—entrepreneurial leaders amplified by AI, operating in small, lethal pods with the authority to ship.

> **Cooper Callout:** In the AI First world, 10 entrepreneurial leaders with AI will crush 1,000 career bureaucrats with PowerPoint

Killing the Deep State: PMOs and Bureaucratic Bottlenecks

Here's where the knife goes in.

For decades, companies created specialized functions like Project Management Offices (PMOs), "centers of excellence," and process enforcement groups. These were sold as ways to "ensure quality" or "align execution." In reality, they often became a significant contributor to the **deep state of business**—slow, risk-averse, self-protecting bureaucracies that killed innovation before it could breathe.

Even in pre-AI companies, PMOs were more often value-destroyers than value-creators. Why? Because they were staffed with functional specialists, not result drivers. They knew frameworks, templates, and compliance rules—but not outcomes, customers, or real business creation. Their success was measured in **process compliance, not in results**.

PMOs *look* good on paper. Centralized expertise, standardized processes, and governance. But in practice, they **very quickly become bottlenecks.** There is little to no accountability for business outcomes. Their accountability is in the deployment of guidelines and process.

The reason is structural—**power concentrates.** And once power is centralized, it gets held tighter than Mike Tyson's fist. The instinct of a PMO is to protect control, not to accelerate value. This is why projects drag, decisions crawl, and organizations suffocate under their own red tape.

The deeper flaw is distance. Centralized PMO groups are often **two, three, or even four layers removed** from the actual business issues they're meant to add value to. They're not in the trenches with customers, operations, or products. They're professional project managers managing from afar, divorced from context, yet armed with authority. That is a recipe for bureaucracy and misalignment.

More often than not, professional PMO leaders are **professionals at professional process management.** They are experts at Gantt charts, RACI matrices, and status meetings—not at driving outcomes. Their metrics of success? Deliverables, milestones, compliance checklists. Almost never P&L. Which is why, if you ask the hard question—*"When was the last time your PMO quantified real financial outcome value?"*—the answer is silence. Or worse, a 60-slide deck with abstract ROI models that collapse under scrutiny.

This is deep-state behavior at its finest (or worst). Bureaucrats whose survival depends on opacity, on hiding in plain sight, on **avoiding accountability** for results and business outcomes. Their power comes not from what they produce, but from knowing how to stall, how to position, and how to never be seen as the reason for failure. They thrive in ambiguity because ambiguity keeps them employed.

In the AI First era, this is not just wasteful—it is lethal. **AI itself automates the very functions PMOs claim as their core purpose.** Tracking milestones? AI can do it automatically with real-time dashboards. Risk detection? AI systems can flag deviations in hours, not weeks. Governance? AI can enforce compliance programmatically, without needing a weekly committee meeting. What used to take dozens of PMO staffers can now be embedded in a pod's workflow, handled by a single entrepreneurial leader equipped with AI.

And here's the bigger truth: **AI First orgs don't need mega-programs.** The days of multi-year, galaxy-sized transformation projects **are over.** In fact, they're insane. They take so long that most of the people who were there at the start aren't even around to see the end. By the time the project closes, the market has shifted, the technology is outdated, and the business case has evaporated. This is why McKinsey found that 70% of large transformations fail to meet their stated goals. It's not the tools. It's the structure.

AI First organizational structures flip this on its head. Instead of gigantic centralized PMOs, you create **tiny, lethal pods.** Each pod owns an outcome, not a process. They ship in weeks, not years. They're staffed with entrepreneurs who understand the customer problem, not career administrators who understand frameworks. And when a pod needs project management skills, it's embedded locally—inside the pod, tied directly to the outcome—not centralized in some distant bureaucratic tower.

The role of "project manager" doesn't disappear; it gets redefined. Project management becomes a skill, not a function. It's owned by entrepreneurial leaders and, where needed, embedded as a resource in a pod. That ensures that accountability stays with the team driving the value, not with some external referee who's never carried the ball.

Contrast that with the old deep state PMO, where control was centralized, schedules were worshipped, and value was always someone else's problem. Those organizations slowed everything down in the name of "alignment." But alignment without velocity is just paralysis.

PMOs and centralized bureaucratic groups exist to reassure executives that someone is "managing the process." They practice **"control theater"**; they manage the optics, not the outcomes

Ask yourself: **when was the last time your PMO produced a breakthrough?** Not a report, not a workshop, not a governance framework—a real breakthrough that customers noticed or the P&L reflected directly? The answer is almost always "never."

This is why AI First destroys the need for PMOs. Not because project management is irrelevant, but because **bureaucratic bottlenecks are unsustainable.** Entrepreneurial pods can manage their own delivery with AI-enhanced dashboards, AI-generated reporting, and AI-driven risk alerts. They don't need a separate organization of gatekeepers. They need freedom to act and accountability to produce.

The deep state thrives on centralization. AI First thrives on decentralization. The deep state thrives on process. AI First thrives on outcomes. The deep state values headcount. AI First values value. These are not small differences. They are **diametric opposites.**

Because in the AI First era, the only governance that matters is results.

> **Cooper Callout:** PMOs don't manage projects—they manage careers. And in AI First companies, careers are made by results, not reports.

Strategy & Consulting Groups: A Diminished Role

The same disease that PMOs perpetuate infects organizations in similar ways by management and strategy consultants, both internal and external.

For decades, executives outsourced vision and insight to armies of analysts, blue-chip consulting firms, and their internal equivalents. Consultants thrived because they weren't accountable for outcomes. They delivered frameworks, decks, and "strategic recommendations," then walked away. If the ideas failed, it was the client's fault. If they succeeded, the consultants claimed credit. **Heads they win, tails you lose.**

Even in traditional businesses, this model was shaky. **Consultants often lacked business-specific creativi**ty. They were framework-focused, not outcome-focused. They didn't live in the trenches of the company, and they didn't stay long enough to ensure value. They advised, but they did not own.

In an AI First structure, this weakness becomes terminal. Entrepreneurial leaders in AI pods **don't outsource vision**—they generate it. They have data at their fingertips, simulations in real time, and AI to test scenarios instantly. The economics of insight have flipped.

A management consultant charging $5 million for a three-month engagement is now competing with an entrepreneurial leader and an AI architect who can run 100 scenarios, test them live in the market, and pivot in two weeks. The leader owns the outcome; the consultant just bills for the effort.

The numbers behind consulting failure are staggering. *Harvard Business Review* estimates that **up to 80% of consulting-led projects either fail outright or deliver only marginal value**. That means billions of dollars spent annually with little to show for it beyond PowerPoint slides and "lessons learned" memos.

One of the biggest drivers of failure is misaligned incentives. Consulting firms make their money on billable hours and long contracts. The longer the engagement, the more profitable it is for them. The result? Drawn-out projects with endless "phases" that rarely end, and frameworks so complex that only the consultants themselves can explain them. This creates dependency rather than independence

A 2022 study by Source Global Research found that **41% of clients believe consulting firms are more focused on selling additional work than on delivering measurable value**. In other words, clients themselves see the game being played, but many feel trapped because of board expectations or lack of internal confidence.

Even when "success" is declared, the results are often superficial. PwC's research indicates that **only 12% of consulting-driven digital transformation projects deliver sustained value beyond three years**. Most improvements erode quickly because the firm leaves, the client lacks ownership, and the organization reverts to old habits.

Consultants may still add value as **sparring partners or benchmarks**, but their role shrinks dramatically in AI First Organizations. They cannot substitute for entrepreneurial leadership anymore. In an AI First org, the

center of gravity has shifted permanently to those who act, not those who advise.

Example: The Fortune 100 Retailer Case

One Fortune 100 retailer famously hired a top-tier consulting firm for a $400 million, multi-year "digital transformation." The consultants produced roadmaps, org charts, and reams of "strategy documents." After four years, the company's online revenue share had grown only 1%, while operating costs ballooned. The consultants billed hundreds of millions, but the business saw little operational improvement. Eventually, a new CEO scrapped most of the work and instead built AI First pods in logistics and merchandising. Within 18 months, the company saved $250 million in supply chain costs and grew online revenue share by 9%—without consultants.

This example is not unique. In fact, it is typical. Gartner found that over 50% of organizations that rely heavily on external consulting for transformation projects end up redoing the work internally within 24 months.

In the AI First world, this model is even less sustainable. AI tools give internal leaders real-time insights once monopolized by consultants. Scenario testing that once required weeks of analyst crunching can now be run in hours. Dashboards that once came from external reports are instantly available internally. The monopoly on frameworks is broken.

The harsh reality is that **consultants often act as the deep state of business**: slow-moving, risk-averse, self-preserving, and parasitic on client dependency. In the AI First era, where speed is survival, their very structure becomes the enemy of progress.

> **Cooper Callout:** Consultants don't build companies. Leaders do. And in AI First companies, entrepreneurial leaders don't rent insight—they generate it.

Summary: Organizational Structure for the AI first Organization

Organizational structure in the AI era is not just about efficiency—it's about unleashing entrepreneurial leaders and aligning them with AI to drive exponential outcomes.

If structure rewards delay, the company dies. If structure rewards velocity, the company thrives.

And let's be blunt: as you can see, the AI First organizational structure is **different. Totally and completely different.** It requires everything to change. Reporting lines, incentives, authority, career paths, planning cycles, measurement—all of it. You cannot "tweak" your way into this. You need **extreme change management** (see chapter 5) to get there. His new structure is different. It is a new reality

Here's the bold reality:

- Flatten the Org
- Implement AI Pods
- Shrink the number of people in the organization
- Eliminate criticality and power of PMOs and internal bureaucratic blockers
- Don't outsource strategy. Reduce/eliminate internal and external management consulting to limited influence and decision making
- If your org chart looks the same as it did last year, you're already behind.

The death of PMOs, the shrinking of consulting empires, the rise of pods, the flattening of hierarchy—these aren't just trends. They are **requirements.**

The new blueprint is clear: AI is the engine. Entrepreneurial leaders are the drivers. Structure is the racetrack. Build it right—or get lapped.

Cooper Callout: AI doesn't just change what you do. It changes what you are. And if your structure doesn't change, your company won't survive long enough to find out why.

We have said this many times and we will keep saying it. **AI changes everything.** Everything! So once the org structure changes, what changes next? **The workforce itself.** Let's learn how.

Chapter 7:

Brace Yourself: The Coming End of "Jobs as Usual"

This chapter is about defining the skills, the attributes, and the motivations that make up the **workforce for the AI First Organization**. We have discussed how leadership will change. We just discussed in the previous chapter how the organizational structures need to change. Now we will talk about the people who make up those organizational structures, and how the makeup up of the workforce in the AI First Era will change.

With the Speed and Power of AI and the new dynamic organizational structures that are required, we are about moving beyond "jobs as usual" to "value as usual"—because in the future, the AI First workers will be measured not by hours logged but by **outcomes created with AI leverage**.

AI is changing everything about our businesses and organizations. Literally everything. Speed. Leadership. Structure. **Work is changing, too, in terms of the skills required by the workforce to do the work and the jobs themselves.**

For the past 200 years—especially the last 100—the formula for career success has been drilled into us with relentless consistency. Get as much specialized education as possible. Stack on advanced degrees in one narrow field. Accumulate expertise in a specific niche that makes you indispensable. Climb the ladder by knowing more about your slice of the world than anyone else around you. Demand more compensation because of your expertise.

We rewarded depth over breadth. **Specialization over versatility.** Depth made workers valuable because they controlled knowledge others didn't have. And given where the world was, it was the right thing to do.

But that world is gone.

The skills that built the workforce of the 20th century are simply not as relevant in the 21st-century post AI First era. AI has not just entered the workplace as another tool—it has **rewritten the rules** of what human contribution means and the skills and attributes requires to deliver on that contribution.

Human workers are not just competing against machines for speed or strength—they are competing against machines for intelligence, insight, and decision-making. And AI is not slowing down. Every week brings new models, new capabilities, and new breakthroughs. What was impossible last year is table stakes today.

This changes *everything*. **Entire categories of work are collapsing** while new ones emerge. The old model of "get trained once and repeat the job for decades" is dead. In its place is the AI First model, where the ability to adapt, to learn, and to wield AI directly is more important than any static credential or specialized training.

In an AI First organization, the **only irrelevant worker is the one who doesn't know how to work with AI**. It doesn't matter if you are a CEO, a line supervisor, or a field technician. If you don't know how to engage with AI, guide it, and extract value from it, you are obsolete.

By 2030, McKinsey estimates that 375 million workers—nearly 15% of the global workforce—will need to switch occupational categories entirely because of AI and automation. Many experts, myself included, feel that that number is **understated** by a factor of three and should read more like **one billion people.**

Yes, one *Billion* people. With a B.

Think about that: **upwards a billion people**, or approximately 27% of the global workforce 3.6 billion, **will be forced out of the jobs they trained for**, because the rules of the game changed. That's not a workforce shift—that's a **wholesale reinvention** of what it means to be **employable**.

And yet, here is the opportunity: AI does not diminish human contribution; it magnifies it—if we adapt. The **paradox of AI** is that the more powerful it becomes, the more it rewards workers who know how to use it, direct it, and combine it with business judgment.

Don't forget what AI *really* is. It is an ARMY of millions of specialized workers, with more productive potential than entire cities, ready to follow your lead. Ready to apply that capacity to execute *your* vision. Ready **to do *your* bidding.**

I will say it again. **To do YOUR bidding.**

AI can write code, but it cannot decide what product to build. AI can draft contracts, but it cannot negotiate the deal. AI can summarize data, but it cannot set the strategy. That is the human contribution in the AI First era: not doing the task but creating value by wielding AI as leverage.

This is why **every employee must change**. From the boardroom to the factory floor, the core requirement is no longer years of narrow specialization—it is the ability to learn, adapt, prompt, and deliver outcomes with AI. The lawyer who knows how to use AI will outperform three combined who don't. The electrician who can use AI to diagnose, plan, and optimize will outperform the one who cannot. The sales manager who knows how to train AI on customer data will outperform the one still stuck in spreadsheets.

The divide is not blue collar vs. white collar. It is not management vs. staff. **The divide is AI-literate vs. AI-irrelevant.**

This entire book is about how everything must change. It is a playbook for what organizations need to do become AI First organizations TODAY. This chapter is about defining the skills, the attributes, and the motivations that make up the **workforce for the AI First Organization.**

It is about moving beyond "jobs as usual" to "value as usual"—because in the future, workers will be measured **not by hours logged but by outcomes created** with AI leverage.

The organizations that get this right will explode in productivity, innovation, and growth. The ones that cling to the old workforce model—specialization, hierarchy, narrow expertise—will collapse. This is as certain as the industrial revolution replacing manual weavers with machines, or the digital revolution replacing paper ledgers with software.

Because one truth is now undeniable: "jobs as usual" is over. What comes next is work without precedent—and it belongs to **those who embrace AI.**

The AI First Worker Defined

For over a century, organizations measured a "good employee" by a narrow set of traits: diligence, specialization, and compliance. The model worker was someone who showed up every day, possessed a deep and capable specialization, leveraged that skill when called upon performed the same function reliably, and followed instructions. **Success was about executing tasks, not questioning them.** It was about staying within your lane, not crossing boundaries. In fact, the more specialized and compliant you were, the more secure your role seemed.

But in an AI First organization, those traits are no longer enough. Diligence matters, but if diligence is only about repeating what a machine can do better, faster, and cheaper, it's wasted energy

Specialization has value, but if that specialization makes you inflexible or unable to connect across disciplines, it becomes a liability.

Entrepreneurial Skills Remain Important

The definition of a "good employee" has been rewritten in the AI First era. The AI First worker—whether a leader or frontline contributor—must have **entrepreneurship** at their core. They are outcome-driven, not task-driven. Instead of asking, *"What does my manager want me to do?"* they instinctively ask, *"What outcome is the organization trying to achieve, and how can I leverage AI to get us there faster?"*

In a previous chapter, we discussed how leaders at all levels of an AI First organization require entrepreneurial instincts. They must be comfortable with uncertainty, motivated by results, and constantly scanning for new ways to deliver value. But this mindset can no longer be confined to the executive suite. **The rank-and-file employee must carry the same DNA**—because in an AI First company, leverage exists at every level, and even the smallest role can shape massive outcomes.

Context, of course, matters. The factory floor operator isn't expected to obsess 24/7 about optimizing company-wide efficiency. Their shift ends when their workday ends. They go home to their families, live their lives, and return the next morning. Yet even here, the entrepreneurial attribute shows up **as a skillset, not a lifestyle**. It's about **adaptability**—the comfort with change, the instinct to solve problems rather than wait for instructions, and the willingness to experiment with AI-driven tools.

The AI First employees aren't workaholics; they don't need to work more hours than their pre-AI counterparts. But they use their time **differently**. They lean into new workflows, leverage AI solutions, and ask sharper questions. They are quicker to recognize when a process is broken, and faster to try a fix. The entrepreneurial worker is not the person who clocks extra hours—**it's the person who knows how to get 3x the value out of the same hours.**

This distinction is critical. AI First workers are powerful not because they hustle harder, **but because they think differently.** They embody entrepreneurial skills like creativity, resilience, and dynamic problem-solving, even in jobs that historically rewarded repetition and compliance. And when an entire workforce develops this mindset—even on the shop floor—the organization gains a cultural engine of innovation and adaptability that compounds over time.

Workers need to be able to identify problems and translate them into AI-solvable challenges. For example, in the Pre-AI First organization, a support agent was responsible for answering customer tickets quickly and politely. In the AI First model, that same agent trains the AI on common questions, refines the system's prompts, and monitors the feedback loop to ensure customers are not only answered but delighted. The work is not about "closing cases." It's about transforming the way customer service operates, scaling outcomes with AI.

The AI First worker is also deeply comfortable with iteration. They don't fear mistakes—they expect them. They take risks, test ideas, and learn quickly. Workers who wait for perfect plans or fear stepping outside their role are not valuable to the AI -first organization.

Contrast this with the **compliance-driven worker of yesterday**. Traditional organizations rewarded people for minimizing risk, staying invisible, and avoiding failure. In AI First organizations, those behaviors are punished indirectly because they slow velocity. Standing still means falling behind.

Adaptability is another defining trait of workers that AI- First organizations require. Workers must be able to flex between functions, roles, and challenges. They aren't trapped by job descriptions. They see themselves as outcome-creators who can deploy AI to bridge knowledge gaps instantly. A marketing associate may shift into customer analytics. A field technician may pivot to predictive maintenance modeling. These shifts don't take years of retraining—they take curiosity, the ability to learn on the fly, and the confidence to trust AI as a partner.

And this leads to the **most** fundamental redefinition: The AI First worker is not a cog in the machine. They are a **co-pilot to the machine**. Their role is not to execute what AI can do but to guide, contextualize, and drive outcomes that AI amplifies.

Consider the lawyer who once billed hours to draft routine contracts. In an AI First organization, the lawyer uses AI to draft, review, and cross-check documents instantly. Their value shifts from "grinding out clauses" to providing judgment, strategy, and negotiation skills. Or consider the financial analyst who once spent weeks consolidating spreadsheets. With AI, the data is already modeled. The analyst's role is to interpret the results, identify the hidden risks, and translate them into decisions that move the business forward.

This transformation is **not about replacing skills—it's about reframing them**. Every employee must develop fluency in prompting, outcome iteration, data interpretation, and AI interaction. But those are table stakes. What separates the winners is mindset: curiosity, resilience, and a hunger for outcomes.

AI First workers understand that their power is **amplified by AI**. They don't fear being replaced by AI because they know how to harness it. They aren't defined by the size of their team or the number of tasks they complete. They are defined by the value they create, the problems they solve, and the speed at which they can adapt.

Put bluntly: in an AI First company, the most irrelevant worker is the one who doesn't know how to work with AI. The most valuable worker is the one who **sees AI as a force multiplier** and themselves as the outcome-driver.

The old definition of "good employee" is dead. The AI First worker is something entirely new—part builder, part problem-solver, part entrepreneur. They don't wait for permission. They don't cling to narrow specializations. They don't measure success in process compliance. They measure success in velocity, outcomes, and impact.

Motivation: Why It Works

Skills alone don't define the AI First worker. You can teach someone to use AI. You can show someone how to interact with an AI First machine on the factory floor. . You can train someone to interpret data. You can coach someone to use a new platform. But motivation—that runs deeper. Motivation determines whether workers lean in or hold back, whether they embrace change or resist it, whether they thrive in an AI First company or quietly sabotage its progress.

For most of the last century, worker motivation was rooted in **predictability**. People went to work to secure a paycheck, to protect their benefits, to climb a ladder that promised safety, knowing that their job wouldn't change often if at all. Organizations reinforced this by rewarding loyalty, tenure, and predictable execution. The great exchange was simple: give us consistency, we'll give you security. That model shaped generations. It built the "deep state" of business—the massive middle of organizations where resistance to change thrives.

But in the AI First era, predictability is not the primary motivator. AI obliterates routine. It rewrites processes weekly. It shifts job boundaries overnight. Workers motivated by stability will cling to the old ways just as fast as AI tears them down. The result is paralysis. Stability-driven employees in AI First companies are like anchors dragging behind a rocket ship.

The AI First worker is motivated by something entirely different: **accomplishment**. They find energy **not in holding the line, but in crossing it**. They don't want to preserve—they want to create.

Of course, every human craves stability and knows that they will have a job tomorrow. The AI First employee is no different. However, the AI First employee leans in more than the average worker toward disruption. Their reward is not in "being safe," but in "making impact."

These workers are motivated by **speed**. They feel alive when projects move in days, not quarters. They thrive in environments where iteration is fast and failure is treated as fuel, not shame. Speed doesn't scare them—it excites them, because speed means progress, and **progress is their oxygen.**

They're motivated by **ownership.** In the old model, workers were task executors. Do your part, pass it up, and wait for approval. In the AI First model, workers own outcomes. The AI executes tasks, but the human defines, guides, and is accountable for the result. That shift creates a sense of pride. The AI First worker doesn't want to "do what they're told." They want to shape, direct, and own the value they create.

They're motivated by **curiosity**. These workers poke, test, and explore. They experiment with prompts, tools, and workflows not because they're told to but because they *want* to. Curiosity is not a distraction—it's a driver. In AI First companies, curiosity creates breakthroughs.

They're motivated by **creation**. Building something new, improving something broken, scaling something beyond its limits—these are their rewards. While stability-driven workers fear disruption, AI First workers understand the need for it and enjoy being a part of it. They welcome it. They want to see things work better, faster, and smarter. And they love being the ones who make that happen.

They're motivated by **competition**—but not the old zero-sum, ladder-climbing competition of traditional orgs. Their competition is with the status quo. With inefficiency. With impossibility. They get satisfaction from proving that what others thought couldn't be done can be achieved with AI and grit.

They're motivated by **winning**. Not just personal wins, but organizational wins. The AI First worker feels real satisfaction in seeing their company advance, their customers succeed, their work drive outcomes that matter. Their scoreboard isn't hours worked—its value created.

And critically, they are motivated by **change itself**. While traditional workers see change as a threat, AI First workers see it as opportunity. Change means movement. Movement means progress. Progress means they're winning. This flips the motivational equation of the industrial era on its head.

This motivation isn't just a personality quirk—it's a cultural requirement. Without it, AI First organizations collapse into friction and resistance. With it, they become unstoppable.

Hiring for skills is not enough. You can train how to use the latest AI-enabled project management software, but you can't train hunger. You can teach AI fluency, but you can't **implant curiosity**. AI First companies must recruit and retain people who are motivated not by safety but by impact, not by stability but by creation, not by predictability but by progress.

This is why deep-state employees—the ones who are motivated by protecting their turf, keeping their headcount, preserving their role—are deadly in AI First environments. Not just the leaders, but the workers themselves.

AI First workers **aren't driven by fear of being replaced—they're driven by the thrill of becoming irreplaceable through impact.** They don't want to stay in their lane—they want to redraw the map. They don't want to slow things down—they want to break barriers and speed things up.

That is why motivation is the ultimate differentiator. It's not who can "use AI." It's who is motivated to *leverage AI to create change.* Skills fade, tools evolve, but motivation endures.

The AI First worker is motivated by building, winning, and changing the game. They are not clock-punchers. They are not ladder-climbers. They are creators, disruptors, explorers. Their fuel is not stability—it is velocity, progress, and outcomes.

And this is the **cultural line in the sand**: In AI First companies, workers motivated by stability will hold you back. Workers motivated by accomplishment will propel you forward. The future belongs to the latter.

New Skills Framework: What Every AI First Worker Must Master

If the last century was defined by diplomas, certifications, and years of accumulated expertise in narrow lanes, the AI First century will be defined by a new set of skills that cuts across every role, every function, and every industry. Titles matter less. Hierarchies matter less. What matters is whether you can thrive in a workforce where humans and AI collaborate to create exponential output.

The first competency is **AI Literacy**. This doesn't mean everyone must become a data scientist or machine learning engineer. It means understanding, at a functional level, what AI can and cannot do.

The AI-literate worker knows that AI can surface patterns in millions of data points instantly, but AI cannot (yet) replace human judgment in complex ethical tradeoffs. AI-literate workers know how to spot AI "hallucinations" and when to push back on output. **Think of it as the ability to drive the car safely without needing to know how the engine was manufactured.**

Second, **Prompting Mastery**. We will cover this in incredible detail in the next chapter, but it is very important to understand that **Prompting is literacy for AI**. This is the universal communication medium of the AI First workforce.

Third, **Critical Thinking**. AI accelerates, but acceleration without direction is chaos. The AI First worker must be able to validate output, challenge assumptions, and refine responses. If AI produces 20 options, the critical thinker identifies the one that creates actual business value. If AI drafts a legal document in seconds, the critical thinker ensures the clauses align with strategy, compliance, and risk. In other words, they don't take output at face value—they sharpen it into impact.

Fourth, **Data Fluency**. Every worker in an AI First company must have basic comfort with data. Not deep statistical analysis, but the ability to feed AI the right inputs, interpret the outputs, and use dashboards or metrics to guide decisions. A nurse who can interpret AI-driven patient data on a tablet, a factory worker who can understand production metrics in real-time, or a sales rep who can analyze lead scoring recommendations—all are demonstrating data fluency.

Fifth, **Entrepreneurial Problem-Solving**. The AI First worker treats every challenge as if they were founding a start-up. Limited resources, big problems, no clear playbook—that is the default environment. Instead of waiting for instructions or falling back on "this is how we've always done it," they lean on AI to prototype, test, and refine solutions quickly. They view AI not as a crutch but as leverage—an amplifier of creativity and resourcefulness.

Sixth, **Collaboration with AI Pods.**. AI First companies thrive on small, agile pods that combine entrepreneurial workers with AI systems to drive specific outcomes. This requires new collaboration skills: not just working with humans, but working seamlessly with AI agents, delegating tasks to them, and integrating their output into team workflows. A pod might consist of three humans and a suite of AI models—and that team may outperform a traditional department of 50.

Seventh, **Adaptability**. AI First organizations evolve at breakneck speed. What worked last quarter may be obsolete today. Workers must be able to unlearn and relearn constantly. Adaptability isn't just about picking up new tools; it's about embracing discomfort, experimenting without fear, and thriving in environments where the ground shifts daily.

The World Economic Forum projects that 60% of workers will require retraining in AI-related skills by 2027. *2027 !*—that's practically tomorrow. Organizations that fail to re-skill their workforce will collapse under the weight of irrelevance. Workers who fail to re-skill themselves will be stranded.

The blueprint is clear: AI literacy, prompting mastery, critical thinking, data fluency, entrepreneurial problem-solving, collaboration in AI pods, and adaptability. These are the non-negotiables of the AI First workforce. They are the difference between being a cog in the old system—or a value creator in the new one.

Beyond White Collar: AI for Every Worker

One of the biggest misconceptions about AI is that it's only for "knowledge workers"—the engineers, the analysts, the lawyers, the consultants. That's a dangerous myth. The truth is AI is just as powerful for frontline and blue-collar workers as it is to white-collar workers. This is often called **AI for the middle class.** AI is becoming just as essential to frontline and blue-collar workers as it is to white-collar ones. The AI First organization is not an organization where only executives and coders prompt machines and interact with AI. It is a world where **every single worker**—on a factory floor, in a hospital wing, or on a construction site—interacts with AI as naturally as they would with a wrench, a drill, or a clipboard.

Consider the technician in the field, working on a complex HVAC system. Instead of flipping through manuals or waiting hours for a senior expert, they can use AI-assisted diagnostics to run real-time tests, troubleshoot issues, and get repair recommendations instantly. A construction worker can use AI on a mobile device to scan safety procedures for a specific site condition, ensuring compliance and preventing accidents on the spot. A factory worker can simply use voice-AI to optimize shift schedules or identify machine downtime patterns that would have taken a manager days to analyze. Nurses—already stretched thin—are now using AI to surface real-time patient data, highlight risk factors, and even recommend interventions before a crisis occurs.

These aren't hypotheticals. **They're happening now**. Walmart is training its store employees with AI-driven learning tools that adapt in real time to each worker's pace and role. Caterpillar deploys AI diagnostics for heavy machinery, enabling frontline operators—not just engineers at HQ—to catch maintenance issues before they cause costly breakdowns. Delta Airlines equips mechanics with AI-enabled maintenance apps, shaving hours off aircraft turnaround times. Hospitals like the Mayo Clinic are piloting AI copilots for nurses to monitor patient vitals continuously, reducing the burden of manual charting and freeing staff for higher-value care.

The frontline workers are no longer just "doing tasks." They are decision-makers, enhanced by AI, able to catch problems early and act with more precision than ever before. This fundamentally **redefines what it means to be "skilled."** It's no longer about memorizing procedures or relying solely on seniority. It's about leveraging AI tools in the moment, interpreting recommendations, and making faster, more accurate calls.

The skills required are shifting fast. Workers need to be comfortable with mobile and voice-based AI tools, fluent in interpreting AI recommendations, and confident enough to apply critical judgment when the AI gets it wrong. Blind obedience to AI is just as dangerous as blind obedience to a flawed boss. The best workers in the AI First company will be those who can balance trust and skepticism—knowing when to follow AI's lead and when to override it.

This balance is critical because **AI isn't perfect**. It can hallucinate, misinterpret, or overfit to bad data. Imagine a nurse who takes an AI's recommendation at face value without checking vitals—lives could be at stake. Or a factory operator who trusts a scheduling model without recognizing a real-world bottleneck on the floor—production halts could cost millions. The human skill of judgment, combined with AI literacy, becomes the ultimate differentiator.

This is a massive cultural reset. For decades, many frontline jobs were about compliance, repetition, and rule-following. Workers were rewarded for showing up, doing the task as instructed, and not asking too many questions. In an AI First company, the frontline worker must become entrepreneurial too—constantly adapting, **questioning**, and driving outcomes. They must treat AI not as a boss or a replacement, but as an amplifier of their output.

Take **logistics** as an example. Truck drivers are already using AI route optimizers that shave hours off delivery schedules and save millions in fuel costs. But the best drivers aren't just following the AI blindly— they're feeding it context: weather, local traffic quirks, or even knowledge of where safe rest stops are. They're co-pilots, working with AI to deliver better outcomes than either human or machine could achieve alone.

Or consider **agriculture**. Farmers are using AI drones to monitor crop health, AI models to predict irrigation needs, and AI-driven robotics to automate harvesting. But the farmer's judgment—spotting early disease signs or recognizing soil anomalies—remains vital. The AI can surface patterns, but it's the farmer's entrepreneurial instincts that decide when to act.

AI literacy is no longer a luxury skill. It's the new baseline. Whether you're a janitor who uses AI to optimize cleaning routes in a skyscraper, a warehouse picker guided by AI efficiency algorithms, or a nurse balancing patient loads with AI scheduling tools, you will need to speak the language of AI to be effective. Those who don't will struggle, not because they're lazy or unskilled, but because the tools around them will be unintelligible.

That's why the organizations that win in the AI First era will be the ones **that democratize AI literacy.** They won't reserve AI training for executives or specialists—they'll embed it into **every role**, from frontline to C-suite. Walmart is already investing in this, building AI literacy into their global workforce development programs. Amazon trains warehouse employees to use AI-driven robotics systems rather than fear them. Forward-thinking construction firms are rolling out voice-AI assistants for safety checks and project planning.

AI First literacy isn't about coding. It's about commanding machines to amplify human output, no matter your role or collar color. In the AI First organization, a nurse, a factory worker, or a construction foreman will need to be as AI fluent as a software engineer. **The companies that understand this—and train their people accordingly—will dominate.** Those that don't will find their frontline workforce stuck in the past, unable to keep up with competitors who have supercharged every role with AI.

AI and the Middle Class

While the early tides of change and media coverage related to AI focus on impacted white collar and higher paid jobs, ultimately AI will become a **middle-class revolution.**

AI isn't just for Wall Street bankers or Silicon Valley coders. It's for welders. It's for carpenters. It's for electricians. It's for nurses. It's also for the middle class. And it is going to transform the organizations that employ the majority of middle-class workers more than any other economic group—because AI is going to determine which middle-class companies thrive and which get left behind.

Organizations in the **Trades**, the technicians, the builders, the operators, the drivers—will be 100% impacted and evolved by AI. These are not edge cases. These are the jobs that keep cities running, keep homes warm, keep our children safe, keep our hospitals functioning, keep industries alive. These are the people and organizations that keep our way of life possible and humming. And in the AI First era, the companies in these fields—whether a fifteen-person electrical shop or a national logistics and freight forwarding organization—will rise or fall based on one factor: whether their workforce is AI literate

For commercial and residential trade companies, **AI is not an accessory; it is a make-or-break tool.** The electrician who can use AI-assisted diagnostics will outpace the one who cannot. The plumbing company that trains dispatchers and technicians to use AI-powered scheduling, routing, and customer communication will crush competitors who still rely on spreadsheets and sticky notes. The HVAC firm that teaches its techs to run AI-driven predictive maintenance will deliver service that is faster, cheaper, and more reliable than anything the market has ever seen.

The AI First commercial and residential trade organization will **double** its profit margin within 6 months. For the trades, the heroes of our modern economy who keep everything running, this is game-changing. The average pre-AI commercial and residential trade organization has a profit margin of approximately 10%. Relative to the importance and value they provide to society, that feels like a crime. For the trades, AI delivers swift justice. The trades are ripe to benefit from the value that AI provides, and once a commercial or residential contractor becomes AI first, their profit margins almost immediately double. This will bring the average profitability for a contractor to a respectable 20%. This is still too low a profit margin, frankly, given the value they provide our society.

This is the middle-class economy and the organizations that make it up are being rewritten in real time. Those who cling to "the way it's always been done" will become irrelevant faster than they can imagine. The winners will be the AI-literate companies that treat prompting, diagnostics, and machine collaboration as natural as using a wrench or making a service call.

There is a new phase emerging that will be as common a phrase as "blue-collar" or "white-collar": **AI for the Middle Class.**

Closing: The Workforce Blueprint of the AI First Era

The future of work has never been clearer—or **more unforgiving**. The AI First organizational playbook is not about chasing the latest shiny tool. It is about talent. It is about rewiring the workforce so that every individual—whether in the C-suite, the factory floor, or the construction site—becomes an entrepreneurial force, amplified by AI. AI without entrepreneurial workers is wasted potential. Entrepreneurial workers without AI are underpowered. But together, they unlock the superpower of the 21st-century company.

The traits we once rewarded—compliance, specialization, ladder-climbing, and gatekeeping knowledge—are now anchors that drag organizations down. In its place rises the AI First worker: entrepreneurial, outcome-obsessed, fluent in prompting, critical in judgment, and fearless in adapting. These are not employees in the old sense. They are value creators. They treat every project like a start-up, every task like a chance to drive impact, and every AI interaction like a partnership with a thousand invisible experts.

The workforce of the AI First organization must be wired for prompting, fluent in data, relentless in problem-solving, **and unafraid to disrupt.** This is not limited to knowledge workers. The transformation of the middle class—the trades, the technicians, the frontline staff—is where AI's power will echo loudest.

This is the moment when organizations decide whether they will be slowed by the "deep state" of business—bureaucracy, incrementalism, and fear—or whether they will unleash the entrepreneurial workforce that can harness AI for velocity and creation. The AI First company is not a place where hierarchy dictates value. It is a place where outcomes do.

In AI First companies, your value is not measured by how many hours you put in, or how many people you manage. Your value is measured by how much you can create—with AI as your amplifier. The workers who master this shift will lead not only their companies, but entire industries.

The organizations that embrace this workforce blueprint will dominate their markets. Those who don't will be fossils of the pre-AI age.

This is not evolution—it is revolution. And only the organizations who staff their AI First organizational structures with entrepreneurial, AI-literate, outcome-driven workforce will survive it. This revolution has a new language. A new tool for communication. A new required skill for survival.

And the new language of this revolution is called **prompting.**

Chapter 8:

Prompting As the New Literacy In the AI First World

AI is not a tool you download. It is not just another piece of software running quietly in the background. It is a workforce—an army of hyper-specialized, highly skilled digital workers capable of producing more knowledge, analysis, and output than entire industries of the past. Consider that AI offers you tens of thousands of experts, each trained in a specific domain, available at your command 24/7.

The critical question is: How do you get that army to deliver the outcome you want? The answer—the only answer—is prompting. **Prompting the communication paradigm of the AI First era.** Without it, AI's power sits idle, like a billion workers standing around with nothing to do. With it, organizations unleash capacity at a scale humanity has never seen.

Prompting can be defined as the disciplined, iterative practice of communicating the *outcome* you want to AI so that AI can deliver your desired outcome. It is not simply asking questions. It is not giving the system a checklist or step-by-step script. It is **articulating** the result you want, **providing** the right context and constraints, and **refining** the message until the output matches your vision.

Prompting is the language of communication in the AI First age. Just as great managers don't hover over employees telling them each keystroke to press, great AI First workers don't tell AI how to do something. They focus on ***what*** needs to be achieved—and let the machine figure out ***how***.

This distinction is massive. When most people first interact with AI, they default to micromanagement. They treat AI like a junior assistant: "do this, then that, then the other thing." That is by very definition "Supplemental AI." But that defeats the purpose. **AI is not waiting for a script—it is waiting for direction.** Prompting is about setting the destination, not dictating the route. You say: "Here's the result I need, here's the audience, here are the constraints, now go." The AI army— your invisible workforce of specialists—handles the rest.

When people fail with AI, it's usually because they misunderstand this relationship. They try to force AI into being a rules-based machine when in fact it's a reasoning-based one. It's not a calculator. It's more like a room full of PhDs who can each run a thousand experiments instantly. You don't tell them exactly how to think—you communicate the goal, the boundaries, and the context, and then **you let them produce outcomes.** That is the essence of prompting.

This shift in mindset changes everything about how humans work. Prompting forces workers to think in terms of results and outcomes, not tasks. It forces clarity: what exactly do I want? What **does success look like?** What constraints or context matter? The act of prompting elevates the worker's role **from "doer" to "director."** It transforms them into outcome managers guiding a vast army of machine talent.

Consider the marketers who once spent weeks iterating on a campaign. In an AI First company, they can generate 20 campaign variations in 10 minutes, and prompt again and again based on the results until the desired outcome is achieved. Consider the paralegals who once spent days drafting boilerplate contracts. With AI, they can produce drafts at 10x speed while focusing their energy on nuance, negotiation points, and client strategy. Or the developer who used to toil over code for weeks— now they can turn a vague product vision into a working prototype overnight, because AI handles the boilerplate and the detailed logic, syntax and work. **These are not fantasies:** they are already happening in thousands of AI First organizations. All done by those who are very **successful at prompting.**

The numbers back this up. Accenture found that "prompt engineers"— workers trained in outcome-oriented prompting—deliver productivity boosts up to 40% compared to their peers who use AI without structured prompting. And that's just the beginning. When prompting becomes universal, not a micro-specialty, the impact multiplies across every corner of the business.

Prompting is not a skill for a handful of AI specialists. Prompting is the **universal literacy of the AI First workforce**. Just as the ability to read once separated knowledge workers from the illiterate masses, **prompt literacy and proficiency will separate the relevant worker from the irrelevant one**. In the AI First company, *everyone*—from the CEO to the field technician, from the nurse to the electrician, from the customer service agent to the janitor—will interact with AI daily. Prompting is not a niche technical trick. It is the universal language of productivity in the AI First era.

> **Cooper Callout:** In an AI First company, the only irrelevant worker is the one who doesn't know how to work with AI. And working with AI means learning how to communicate with it, lead it, and direct it. That is prompting. And that is why prompting is not just a skill. It is a new form of literacy—the baseline for human contribution in the AI First age.

What Makes a Great Prompter

If prompting is the universal literacy of the AI First workforce, the natural question becomes: What makes someone good at it? What separates a mediocre prompter from one who can unlock the full potential of AI's massive army of specialized workers? The answer is **not about technical coding skills**, advanced degrees, or narrow subject-matter expertise. Instead, it comes down to traits and habits of mind that look very different from the 20th-century definition of a "good worker." **To reiterate, prompting has nothing to do with technical skills. Nothing**. It is all about **communication**.

Great prompters are **excellent communicators**. They know how to clearly describe what success looks like, even if they don't have the technical or specialized know-how to get there themselves. They can frame problems in terms of objectives rather than instructions. They are comfortable saying: "Here's where we need to go, here's what matters most, here are the non-negotiables—now deliver."

At its core, prompting is the skill of *articulating to a massive army of specialists what a desired outcome is.* You are not telling them how to do their jobs. You are not micromanaging their processes. You are **defining the vision**, providing the context, clarifying the constraints, and then letting the system bring that outcome to life. That makes prompting much closer to leadership than to execution.

This is why prompting fits seamlessly with the strengths of people who have **worked successfully with a strong chief of staff, or who know how to leverage an assistant effectively.** Think about what it takes to make those relationships work. If you dump tasks without clarity, you get frustration and misfires. But if you provide a clear vision, define what matters, and leave room for them to contribute, the results are exponentially better. Prompting AI works exactly the same way—only the assistant you're working with is an army of hyper-specialized machine experts.

A good prompter, in other words, behaves like an **effective delegator**. A detail- and- outcome-obsessed delegator. Good prompters set the destination and allow the AI to chart the route. They recognize that their job is not to *do* every step, but to *guide* toward the outcome. That makes prompting the **opposite** skill set of the specialized worker who prides themselves on doing everything alone. For centuries, the path to career success was to become so narrowly indispensable that nothing could move without you. In an AI First organization, that instinct becomes a liability. The new winners are those who can work with others— especially with AI—by clearly defining goals and empowering execution.

Good prompters also share another key trait: **curiosity**. They are willing to experiment with wording, framing, and context until they get the best possible result. They don't stop after the first output; they iterate, refine, and push for excellence. In this sense, they treat AI not as a vending machine but as a conversation partner—one that requires clarity, patience, and refinement.

Skilled prompters are outcome-driven rather than task-driven. Instead of obsessing oversteps, they keep their eye on results. This allows them to **avoid the trap of micromanagement** of the how, and allows them to use AI's vast capacity for creative problem-solving to micromanage the what (output) A specialized worker might say, "Here's exactly **how** this has to be done." A great prompter says, "Here's what we need to achieve—surprise me with how you get there."

Finally, great prompters bring **humility** to the process. They don't assume they know best. They recognize that their value is not in providing all the answers but in asking the right questions and setting the right direction that will yield the optimal outcome. This humility is a **radical shift from the old model of being the expert** who has to own every detail. In the AI First era, the prompter's power lies in unlocking the intelligence of the system—not hoarding expertise for themselves.

In short, a great prompter looks less like the traditional deep specialist and more like a visionary director, sharp communicator, skilled delegator, and an outcome-obsessed leader. They can clearly articulate to AI's massive army of specialists what the desired outcome is and then guide the iterative process until it becomes reality. That is the essence of the skill—and it is what separates those who thrive in AI First organizations from those who get left behind.

The Prompt Playbook: How to Prompt Like an AI First Leader

Good prompts don't happen by accident. They are structured, intentional, and precise. They frame the AI's role, define the context, set the constraints, and spell out the deliverables. In other words, they mimic what a great manager would do if they were briefing a top-performing direct report. Without that structure, you get generic, surface-level work. **With it, you get real outcomes.**

The first ingredient is **role**. Telling AI to "write an email" produces bland, one-size-fits-all results. But if you start with a clear role, the AI can step into that mindset and deliver higher-quality output. Saying, *"You are the head of marketing for a $500M consumer brand. Create a 5-email drip campaign for our new product launch,"* is night-and-day better than simply asking for "an email campaign." The difference is that you're making the AI act like a professional operator, not a general-purpose chatbot.

The second ingredient is **context**. Context is what separates a simple example from a board-ready deliverable. If you tell AI to "forecast next year's sales," it will give you a generic table with invented numbers. But if you say, *"You are a financial analyst for a mid-size HVAC company with $120M revenue. Use our last five years of sales data to build a forecast that factors in seasonality, supply chain volatility, and new federal green energy incentives,"* you've now grounded the AI in reality. The richer the context, the more relevant and valuable the output becomes.

Next is **constraints**. and this is where many people fall short. Constraints force specificity and actionability. Without them, you'll get broad essays that sound smart but don't drive outcomes. A weak prompt says, *"Write a speech."* A strong one says, *"You are a university president addressing 1,200 incoming students. Write a seven-minute speech in an inspiring but approachable tone, reference AI as the future of learning, and provide both a full transcript and a 150-word summary version."* Suddenly, the AI is working like an assistant who knows your time, audience, and requirements matter.

Finally, you need **deliverables**. Always define what you want back. Do you want a campaign broken into five emails with subject lines? A redlined NDA draft with commentary? A three-scenario financial model with charts? The form of the output matters as much as the content. If you don't tell the AI what "done" looks like, you'll get walls of text that require more editing than they're worth.

The formula is simple but powerful: **role, context, constraints, and deliverables**. When you layer them together, you stop getting "answers" and start getting *outcomes*. You stop asking AI to do your homework and start asking it to deliver finished work products that would otherwise take teams of humans days or weeks.

That's why good prompting is not a trick—**it's a discipline**. It's how an AI First leader compresses entire workflows. A marketing campaign that used to take 14 days to plan and launch can now be done in two hours. A legal document that once took six billable hours can be drafted in 30 minutes. A financial forecast that dragged on for weeks can be built in a single afternoon.

Long Tail Prompting

One of the most underappreciated aspects of prompting is what we might call **long-tail prompting**—prompts that are not one-liners, but detailed conversations spanning 4, 10, even 50 sentences.

In traditional work, managers write long emails, detailed memos, or multi-page briefs to align teams on outcomes. That same concept applies to prompting. The best outputs often come not from the shortest instructions but from the most thoughtful **context-setting**. A long-tail prompt might include background, desired tone, examples of success, and constraints on what *not* to do.

For example, instead of saying:

- "Draft a sales script."

A long-tail prompt might say:

- "Draft a sales script for our inside sales team targeting small construction companies. The goal is to schedule demos of our project management software. The audience is typically non-technical, time-poor, and skeptical of new tools. The script should be short, conversational, and focus on three pain points: lost time on paperwork, missed project deadlines, and poor job-site communication. Include two objection-handling examples and a suggested closing line."

That is not overkill. It is the difference between a generic script that must be reworked multiple times spending countless hours preparing it to be ready, and one that wins customers after the first attempt

The reality is that in an AI First organization, **strong prompting combined with long-tail prompting becomes yet another superpower.** It transforms AI from a toy into a strategic asset.

Prompting Efficiency: The Mark of an AI First Worker

In an AI First world, prompting a measure of effectiveness. The better someone prompts, the less often they need to circle back, reword, or endlessly tweak what they're asking for. The best AI First workers know that **time is their scarcest resource**, and they treat prompting like an art form: the cleaner and sharper the input, the faster and more valuable the output, and the fewer iterations are required to generate the outcome

Think about the difference: one employee takes 100 prompts to get to the outcome they need. Another gets there in 10. That's not just a little more efficient—it's an order-of-magnitude difference. Over weeks and months, the "100-prompt worker" wastes days running in circles, while the "10-prompt worker" delivers projects, insights, and results at lightning speed. In competitive environments, that gap can decide who gets promoted, who gets replaced, and which company wins the market.

Great prompting is **iterative, but it's not sloppy.** Strong AI First workers don't fire random prompts into the void hoping something sticks. They know how to refine, build, and layer each prompt so that the AI "learns" exactly what outcome is required. Their first attempt gets them 70% of the way there. Their second gets them to 90%. By the third or fourth, they're at 100%. That's prompting excellence.

This discipline mirrors other professional crafts. A master carpenter doesn't hack away at a piece of wood with 100 random cuts; they measure twice, cut once, and get it right. A great attorney doesn't file 50 sloppy drafts of a contract; they structure their work, so each revision tightens and improves. Prompting is no different—**precision up front reverberates down the line.**

Efficiency in prompting is one of the purest metrics of AI First fluency. You can measure it: ratio of prompts to usable output. If one sales rep needs 50 prompts to generate a compelling client deck, and another needs five, the second rep isn't just faster—He is 10 times more valuable to the organization.

Efficiency doesn't mean taking shortcuts or asking less of the AI. It means being intentional. It means embedding role, context, constraints, and deliverables into the prompt from the start. The AI First worker knows how to anticipate what's missing and front-load the clarity that prevents wasted iterations.

This is why **prompting should be treated as a core competency.** Companies should track it, coach it, and reward it. Just as salespeople are measured by close rates and software developers by clean code, AI First employees should be measured by prompting efficiency. It's not enough to "use AI"—the real differentiator is how **well** you use it.

The truth is that most workers today are still amateurs. They blast AI with vague commands and then spend hours refining. That's the same as giving instructions to a team member without context or clarity—you're setting them up to fail. The pros know better. They treat AI like a partner, not a magic box. They prompt with discipline, precision, and iterative logic. That is not AI First. That is a very limited value add form of supplemental AI at best.

And here's the clincher: prompting efficiency **compounds**. The worker who learns to hit outcomes in 10 prompts instead of 100 will not only deliver faster—they'll build confidence in the AI, and the AI will generate better outputs because of the cleaner instructions. Over time, the gap between the efficient prompter and the inefficient one isn't just 10 times—it's exponential. One looks like the future. The other looks obsolete.

Direct Financial Costs of Poor Prompting

In the very near future, **financial costs will make the difference even sharper**. Every prompt consumes compute power, API calls, and data resources. As providers tighten governance and usage models, we will start to see _considerable_ AI usage fees and throttling adjustments by the AI Infrastructure providers. This has begun in small pockets, but over the coming 12-24 months, the fee structure to leverage AI will be fully consumption based, charging for items like prompt volume, token consumption and data governance. These costs will add up quickly as AI

First sweeps the globe. A worker who burns through 500 sloppy prompts opposed to 8 well-structured prompts isn't just wasting time—they're racking up **hard expenses for the company**. At scale, the difference is staggering: a team of efficient prompters can cut hundreds of thousands, even millions of dollars, off an annual AI bill compared to a team of inefficient ones.

Let's look at a few examples.

Micro Case Study 1: Marketing Team Efficiency. A mid-sized consumer goods company has two marketing teams piloting AI for campaign generation.

- **Team A** treats prompting casually. They rely on vague instructions, producing low-quality drafts that require dozens of retries. On average, each project takes **100,000 prompts per month** across the team. At $0.002 per prompt (a common API rate today), that's **$200 per project in compute cost alone**—before factoring in wasted labor hours. Over a year, the excess prompts add up to **$2.4 million in avoidable AI costs**.
- **Team B** invests in prompting training. They structure prompts with role, context, deliverables, and constraints. They iterate logically. They achieve the same quality outcomes in **10,000 prompts per month**. Their annual cost: **$240,000**.

The difference? Both teams generate similar outputs. But Team A burns through **10 times the compute budget** and takes **weeks longer** to reach final campaigns. Team B operates lean, fast, and financially efficient.

For executives, this is a stark wake-up call: in an AI First organization, sloppy prompting is not just a workflow issue—it's a **P&L issue**.

Micro Case Study 2: Finance Forecasting Team

A regional bank with 3,000 employees runs two parallel finance teams to test AI adoption.

- **Team X** uses generic prompts like "Make me a financial forecast." The AI produces vague charts that require dozens of follow-ups. Each quarterly forecast requires **50,000 prompts** and two full weeks of analyst refinement. The total AI cost: **$100,000 per quarter**—plus analyst salaries for work that AI should have done.

- **Team Y** is trained in precision prompting. They specify role, context, datasets, and deliverables in each prompt: "You are a senior banking analyst. Build a three-scenario forecast using our uploaded loan data from the past ten years, factoring in interest rate volatility and regional housing trends. Deliver charts and commentary for board review." Each forecast requires **5,000 prompts** and is finished in two days. The AI cost: **$10,000 per quarter**, with analysts spending their time on strategy rather than rework.

Over the course of a year, Team Y saves the bank **$360,000 in AI usage costs** and produces forecasts **85% faster**, allowing the executive team to make moves weeks ahead of competitors.

The outcome is clear: efficient prompting doesn't just save compute—it changes the tempo of decision-making and the financial health of the company.

Cooper Callout: In the AI First era, it's not who prompts the most—it's who prompts **the best.** And the best prompters don't just save time—they save millions and win markets.

The Power of Good Prompts: Real-World Examples

One of the most overlooked truths of the AI First world is this: the difference between a mediocre outcome and a world-class outcome often comes down to the quality of the prompt. Good prompts collapse workflows that used to take days into minutes. Bad prompts create noise, rework, and frustration.

Below are several examples from different industries showing how great prompts create exponential outcomes.

Marketing Campaign Creation in a Global Consumer Brand

Consider a consumer brand in the premium skincare market. A weak prompt to AI might simply say: *"Write me an email campaign for a new product."* The output would be predictable: a generic, uninspired draft with no segmentation, no customer journey, and no brand voice. A marketer would spend hours reworking the material, essentially doing the heavy lifting themselves.

Now compare that to a strong prompt: "You are the head of digital marketing for a premium skincare brand targeting women 30–45. Create a five-email drip campaign for our new anti-aging serum. Each email should build on the previous one, moving the customer from awareness to urgency. Include subject lines under 50 characters, A/B testing variations, and a call to action linking to a product page. Maintain a confident, science-backed but approachable tone. Provide a suggested send cadence."

This prompt produces a complete strategy: segmented messages, A/B tested variations, tone-perfect copy, and even recommendations for timing. Instead of two weeks of workshop-style brainstorming, the marketing team has a fully formed campaign in two hours. What makes this prompt effective is that it frames the AI as a role ("head of digital marketing"), defines customer context, sets a tone, provides constraints, and asks for structured output. The result is a campaign cycle compressed from 14 days to just a few hours — a staggering 98% productivity gain.

Legal Drafting in a Mid-Market Law Firm

Law firms provide another clear example. A weak prompt such as: *"Write me an NDA template"* would lead to a generic document packed with boilerplate, completely misaligned with client needs. Lawyers would then spend hours tailoring and revising, wasting billable time.

By contrast, a powerful prompt might say: "You are a corporate attorney specializing in venture capital transactions. Draft a mutual non-disclosure agreement (NDA) between a U.S. startup and an EU-based venture capital firm. Include GDPR-compliant data protection language, define 'confidential information' broadly, and limit the term to three years. Highlight areas where state law differences may require adjustment. Deliver both a clean draft and a redline with comments explaining your rationale for each clause."

With this, AI generates a tailored, jurisdiction-specific NDA complete with flagged risks and explanatory notes. What once required six hours now takes thirty minutes. The prompt succeeds because it specifies expertise, context, scope, risks, and even dual output formats. Instead of AI producing a "template," it behaves like a seasoned lawyer. The cycle time drops by 90%, showing how precision prompts eliminate waste.

Financial Forecasting in a Manufacturing SMB

Forecasting is another area where poor prompting leads to hollow results. A weak prompt like: *"Make me a sales forecast for next year"* produces a table with arbitrary numbers, disconnected from reality. Executives can't rely on it.

But a stronger, more thoughtful prompt might say: "You are a financial analyst for a mid-size HVAC manufacturing company with $120M in annual revenue. Using historical sales data (attached CSV for the past five years), build a 12-month forecast model that incorporates seasonality, raw material price volatility, and a projected 15% increase in demand due to federal green energy incentives. Deliver the output as a three-scenario model (conservative, expected, aggressive). Include charts and commentary on assumptions."

The output in this case is a robust multi-scenario financial model, complete with visuals and commentary on assumptions. Instead of weeks of analyst work, executives get actionable insights within hours. This prompt works because it provides **clear context** (industry, revenue), **specifies modeling factors** (seasonality, policy, input costs), **sets structure** (three scenarios), and asks for **particular output formats.** A forecasting cycle that used to stretch over two to three weeks now happens in a single afternoon.

Academic Administration in a University

Universities face similar challenges when implementing AI. A weak prompt like: *"Write a plan to use AI in admissions"* yields nothing more than a vague essay — no priorities, no actionable steps, no alignment with values or regulations.

A well-constructed prompt, however, might say: "You are an AI strategy officer for a mid-sized public university. Create a two-year implementation plan to integrate AI into admissions, focusing on improving application review speed, reducing bias, and personalizing communications to applicants. Include phased milestones (quarterly), required technology investments, potential risks, and metrics for success. Show how this plan aligns with diversity goals and compliance with U.S. Department of Education regulations."

Here, AI delivers a detailed roadmap with milestones, budgets, risk assessments, and compliance notes. What once would have required six months of committee work can now be condensed into three days of refinement. The strength of the prompt lies in defining the role, timeline, objectives, compliance boundaries, and alignment with institutional mission. The result is a shift from vague ideas to board-ready strategy almost overnight.

Field Operations for a Commercial Contractor

Even in blue-collar settings, prompting matters. A facilities manager might weakly prompt: "Optimize my maintenance schedule." The AI gives a generic calendar. A strong prompter says: "Generate a preventative maintenance schedule for a hospital HVAC system with 30-year-old chillers, high uptime requirements, and regulatory inspection every six months. Prioritize minimizing downtime during summer months." That output saves real money and prevents system failures.

Legal Services

A paralegal using weak prompting might ask, "Summarize this case law." The result is a generic overview with little practical value. A strong prompter reframes: "Summarize this case law for a litigation attorney preparing for cross-examination. Focus on precedents that limit liability, highlight language judges have quoted in rulings, and present in bullet form." The result is a tool the attorney can use in court—work that might otherwise take days, done in hours. Of course, the paralegal or attorney has to check all the AI's citations to ensure that they are real and not hallucinations.

Across the above cases, the difference between a "bad" and a "good" prompt is striking. **Bad prompts treat AI like a search engine**; good prompts treat it like a senior collaborator with expertise, responsibility, and context. By framing the AI's role, defining constraints, clarifying deliverables, and embedding strategic context, good prompts collapse entire workflows.

Good prompting simulates expertise, defines scope, includes constraints, and specifies output format. Instead of "asking a question," skilled prompters assign a role, provide context, and demand deliverables. Across functions, **good prompting shrinks AI First work cycles by nearly 100%.** In many cases, what was once a multi-week workflow is reduced to a same-day iteration. This is the secret weapon of AI First organizations: speed, clarity, and execution at the pace of thought.

Summary: Prompting as the Core Skill

The workforce of the AI First organization must be wired for prompting. Prompting is not a niche task for AI specialists; it is the universal language of productivity for all workers in this new AI First era. The winners will be entrepreneurial, outcome-focused workers who can make prompting as natural as walking. They will treat AI's massive army of specialists as partners, not tools, and communicate outcomes with clarity, depth, and precision. In an AI First company, the best communicators—those who can frame problems, set direction, and iterate toward results—will set the pace for everyone else. Prompting is not simply a skill; it is the defining literacy of the 21st-century workforce.

Prompting is the new language of the AI First age. It is how humans and machines collaborate, how ideas are translated into execution, and how organizations capture value at scale. Mastering it isn't optional—**it's the baseline for relevance**. Workers who cannot prompt with precision and efficiency will fall behind just as surely as illiterate workers did in the Industrial Age.

Efficiency in prompting matters as much as clarity. AI is not free; the cost of processing, compute cycles, and API calls is already climbing, and industry projections suggest that by 2027, large AI First organizations will spend 8–12% of total operating expenses directly on AI infrastructure and compute, rivaling labor as one of the largest costs on the corporate P&L. For some industries—finance, healthcare, software—the figure could be closer to 15–18%. That means sloppy prompting isn't just a workflow issue—it's a financial liability. If one team requires 100 prompts to get an outcome that another can achieve in 10, the cost difference is not marginal; at scale, it can mean millions of dollars annually in wasted compute.

The organizations that thrive will be those that cultivate prompting excellence across every role. Just as the internet made basic digital literacy non-negotiable, AI is making prompting the **universal skill** that determines who accelerates and who stagnates. Prompting is no longer just "communication with AI"—it is the operating system of productivity, cost efficiency, and competitive advantage in the AI First era.

Prompting is the language of the AI First organization.

But how do you find the people to staff your AI First organization? That's the job of HR, as we'll see in the next chapter.

Chapter 9:

HR's Crucible - The Coming Talent War

As we have said throughout this book, AI is changing everything about the organizations that make up our society. In the previous chapters, we discussed how the AI First organizations have a different means of communication: prompting. In Chapter 8, we discussed the AI First organizations changing need for workers with new sets of talents, motivations and characteristics that organizations need their workers to possess.

These changing labor realities are forcing organizations all over the globe to become participants in a new kind of global conflict. Not a "hot Conflict", fought with bullets and bombs. Not a conflict for technology or markets. It is the **Conflict for talent**—the battle for the world's best **AI First leaders and workers.** This conflict will be fought by different rules, and with the highest stakes. And for all AI First organizations, the department that is responsible for winning this conflict is **Human Resources.**

This conflict will be unlike any labor competition we've seen before. It will touch every function of every organization *__simultaneously__*—from CEOs and CFOs to Directors of Operations, to field service technicians in the trades, to factory operators, to electricians to radiologists. Organizations need to restaff and retrain the entire organization immediately and **all at once.** No role is immune. That is because **the nature of ALL work itself has changed.** In the AI First company, the worker is not just an employee who robotically follows their manager's instructions. They are a **force multiplier.** One person equipped with AI, with the right mindset and skills, can achieve what once took entire departments.

This creates an entirely new organizational risk: **worker concentration risk.** In past eras, when one worker left, the damage was limited, as one individual, even the best of the best, was **just one worker.** But in an AI First company, where each person's productivity is exponentially amplified by AI, the departure of a single key worker **could cripple a team,** delay critical outcomes, or stall innovation. The leaner the organization, the greater concentration risk becomes—and the more precious each employee becomes.

The **talent war** for these AI First individuals will make all previous recruiting battles look trivial. You think the competition for software engineers in Silicon Valley from 2020–2023 was cutthroat? That was a skirmish compared to what's coming. This time, it won't just be tech firms fighting for scarce developers. It will be every company, in every industry, competing for entrepreneurial, AI First employees **across every job category.** The HR manager at a hospital, the recruiter for a logistics company, the COO of a mid-market manufacturing firm—**all** organizations will all be hunting for the same kind of worker for **all** positions.

And here's the paradox: organizations will have fewer workers overall, but the **battle for each one will be fiercer.** How can that be? Because AI magnifies the output of every role. One AI First marketing lead can launch ten campaigns in the time it used to take to launch one. One AI First nurse can triage patients with data support that makes them twice as effective. One AI First field service technician can solve problems in half the time with AI diagnostics. The fewer workers you have, the more essential it becomes that each individual worker is the right one.

The challenge that all organizations face is that the skills required to thrive in this environment are rare. Entrepreneurial drive is not common. Comfort with constant change is not common. A craving for accountability is not common. Outstanding communication, the ability to translate vision into AI-directed outcomes, the grit to fail fast and adapt quickly—**these are not skills you find in every résumé**. And yet, these are the exact skills every organization now needs, across every level.

Research already confirms the gap. A Gartner study shows that less than **20% of HR leaders believe their organizations have a strong strategy to identify and recruit AI First talent**. In other words, the demand for AI First workers is surging, but the supply is nowhere near ready.

This puts enormous pressure on HR. They are the ones responsible for ensuring their organizations attract, retain, and motivate the new kind of talent. But here's the rub: HR itself now has to **unlearn** decades of lessons. For the last 30+ years, talent management was about finding, training, and rewarding specialized workers—people with certifications, degrees, and linear career paths. Compensation, benefits, retention strategies, and culture programs were all designed to appeal to workers motivated by stability and specialization.

That model is dead. In its place emerges a demand for entrepreneurial, outcome-driven, AI-literate workers. The messaging must change. The job descriptions must change. The compensation systems must change. The very definition of "top talent" must change. Everything HR thought it knew about talent strategy must be dismantled and rebuilt for the AI First reality.

And **HR itself must evolve as a profession**. For decades, HR drifted into being treated as a cost center. Too often, HR became the "policy cop", the enforcer of rules, the keeper of bureaucracy, a glorified compliance organization. In many organizations, HR is seen as the beating heart of the **deep state**—risk-averse, process-obsessed, preventing change and evolution, and resistant to change. HR is seen as the advocate for the employee, opposed to an organization producing the human talent required for organizations to succeed. This kind of culture cannot survive in the AI First era. Instead, HR must be entrepreneurial reinventing how to attract, assess, and develop talent.

HR has a dual **challenge**: it has to **re-talent the entire organization** while simultaneously **re-talent-ing HR itself**. This is among the most critical challenges any organization faces in its journey to AI First. It must build new capabilities around AI tools, analytics, and workforce insights, while also becoming the best recruiters of entrepreneurial talent in the world. And all of this must be done at speed, because the talent war has already begun.

As we will see in the rest of this chapter, the stakes are massive. HR will need to rethink how it hires, how it motivates, how it retains, and how it rewards. It will need to redefine culture for a world where agility, experimentation, and accountability matter more than hierarchy, specialization, and the status quo. HR needs to understand not only the change in skills required, but the change in **personality type** that make up this new workforce, and the implications those changes have on everything. And it must do this while also becoming a poster child for what AI can do: automating away repetitive administrative work, freeing HR professionals to focus on strategy, talent vision, and impact.

The message is clear: in an AI First company, **HR is not a support function. HR is the front line.** The war for AI First talent will decide which organizations thrive and which collapse. And HR will be the army in that war.

Why HR is the Epicenter of the AI First Shift

People are the most critical asset in most all of organizations.

In the AI First era **every organization must rebuild itself from the inside out.** This isn't about software licenses or tech stacks. It's about people and organizational structures. And the people responsible for making that shift happen are the ones most leaders have historically ignored: HR and Recruiting.

In the past, HR was seen as a back-office cost center --administrators of payroll, compliance, benefits, and job postings. Important, yes. Strategic? Rarely. But in an AI First world, HR sits at the epicenter of survival and growth.

Why? Because building an AI First organization requires an entirely new class of talent: entrepreneurial leaders, AI-literate workers, adaptable thinkers, and outcome-driven operators. This talent is very different from the talent objectives of the Pre-AI world. No longer is HR looking for the most specialized talent, the deepest areas of expertise They are on the hunt for the ideal AI- first worker and AI -first skills. To meet this challenge, HR must transform itself so that it can develop the skills to identify, attract, hire, curate and develop this new skill set for its entire workforce.

What makes this task even more important is the reality that the AI First organization will have **fewer people.** AI is such a hugely productive transformation that organizations require **far fewer workers** than they did previously to produce the same level of output. That means organizations are much more dependent on each and every leader and worker than ever before.

To meet these new talent and people goals of the AI first company, someone has to find them. Someone has to train them. Someone has to re-structure how talent is deployed across the business. **That "someone" is HR.**

HR has perhaps the most difficult and important task of all. Not only does it need to become AI first in its operations and how it functions, but it must **completely change what it delivers as an organization;** its product if you will. It **must** transform itself from delivering talent solutions and culture that focuses on a specialized traditional labor force, to one that is the future: the AI First workforce.

New Culture for HR

To make this type of massive and critical transformation, HR must rethink its role in the organization, how it is perceived in the organization, and how it perceives itself.

Over the last several decades, HR has been built and branded as a "people-first" function, but not in the way that actually drives results. Instead of building elite teams and shaping high-output cultures, HR has too often taken on the role of the "corporate mother hen," focused on employee satisfaction, handholding, catering to the **lowest performers,** performance plans to prevent termination, and making sure no **one feels uncomfortable**. It has become the **department of rules and policies, not results**.

Historically, HR was supposed to be a strategic partner—fueling talent pipelines, shaping culture, and ensuring the business had the right people in the right seats to deliver outcomes. But along the way, it morphed into something else: **the police of the workplace**. The PC police. The compliance officers who slowed down disruptors, punished risk-takers, and buried entrepreneurial energy under a mountain of policy manuals.

The data shows the drift. A 2023 PwC survey found that **only 28% of CEOs believe HR drives measurable business outcomes,** while nearly 70% said HR is primarily a "policy enforcer" and "employee service center." Compare that to thirty years ago, when SHRM research reported that over half of senior leaders still saw HR as "critical to business strategy." The fall has been steep.

Over the past decade, too many organizational leaders, weak in their own people management skills, outsourced accountability management of their teams to HR. Instead of confronting underperformance or rallying their teams, executives handed the job of discipline and culture-shaping to the HR function. The result? **HR became the manifestation of the deep state**: acquiring even more control while remaining slow, bureaucratic, risk-averse, and far from the business.

In this form, HR is a blocker of transformation. It resists extreme change management because it is built to protect the status quo. It punishes anything "offensive," **even if that offense is the spark of innovation**. It prizes consensus over speed, harmony over outcomes, compliance over competitive advantage.

That cannot stand in the AI First Era.

AI First HR organizations will thrive or die based on their ability to recruit, develop, retain, and unleash entrepreneurial change agents— outcome-obsessed individuals who move fast, embrace discomfort, and live to drive transformation. HR cannot enable that if it is still busy writing policy handbooks and playing referee on "hurt feelings."

The importance of this transformation is amplified by the workforce volume dynamics. To put it simply, fewer workers in organizations will deliver far greater output per worker than during the Pre-AI First era. While there are tremendous social implications from this (we will discuss this in the final chapters), the harsh reality is that since AI makes organizations so much more productive and efficient, they just don't need nearly as many people.

Every worker is exponentially more valuable to the organization than previous eras, as they are responsible for producing a much higher percentage of the productive output than any 5–15 employees in the Pre-AI First era.

This means HR is no longer a side function— **Every single employee** matters more, every promotion carries higher stakes, and every mis-hire can set back entire teams. In a leaner, faster AI First organization, HR is directly tied to the P&L. Get talent right, and the business thrives. Get it wrong, and the business stalls.

HR must stop seeing itself as a service center and start acting like a **venture capital firm for people.** That means evaluating talent based on future potential and entrepreneurial drive, not just past credentials. It means looking for workers who can create value with AI leverage, not just execute tasks.

It also means HR's own culture must flip. Instead of being risk-averse, it must reward calculated bets on unconventional candidates. Instead of protecting comfort, it must push people into growth. Instead of measuring success by compliance checklists, it must measure by the business outcomes its people deliver.

Simply put: in the AI First era, HR must be as entrepreneurial as the workers it hires.

Worker Concentration Risk

One of the most underappreciated dynamics of the AI First era is **worker concentration risk.** In the past, companies employed many people to spread work across departments, functions, and teams. Scale was built by adding headcount, and when one person left or underperformed, the damage was absorbed by the system. That world is gone.

In the AI First organization, fewer people produce dramatically more outcomes. A finance analyst armed with AI can build models, automate reports, and advise executives at a speed that once required a team of 10. A field service technician can use AI diagnostics to do the work of several peers in a fraction of the time. Across the board—from factory floor to executive suite—every AI First worker is producing at a scale that would have been unthinkable even five years ago.

That reality creates a new kind of risk: every individual worker carries exponentially more **weight. Bad employees don't just underperform;** they drag down outcomes that once might have been buffered by dozens of people. A single employee departure can stall entire workflows, cost millions, or even derail product launches. Where the Pre-AI world absorbed bad fits in volume, the AI First world amplifies their damage to an unprecedented degree.

Put bluntly: one AI First worker can easily do the work of multiple traditional employees. That's concentration. That's leverage. **And that's risk.**

Now add turnover. A 2023 Mercer study found that 36% of U.S. workers were considering leaving their jobs within the next 12 months. Korn Ferry reports that nearly 50% of executive hires fail within 18 months. At non-executive levels, studies show up to 80% of turnover is caused by poor hiring decisions or mismatched fit. In an AI First company, those stats are catastrophic. When one hire equals the productivity of ten, one bad hire equals the failure of ten. When one executive flames out, it's not just a lost leader—it's the lost output of an entire business unit.

This flips HR's mission on its head. In the old world, success meant "being fully staffed." Volume was king. As long as jobs were filled, the system could grind forward. In the AI First world, rate of success is king. The cost of failure is too high. Every hiring decision matters all the more, every retention effort carries outsized value, and every cultural misstep has multiplied consequences.

HR has almost no margin for error. Retention policies that don't resonate? They bleed out irreplaceable talent **too fast**. Compensation strategies that reward the wrong behaviors? They lose high performers to competitors **too fast**. Culture programs that coddle mediocrity? They drag down the entire company. In this reality, HR can't afford to "get most of it right." They need to get **all** of it right, faster, and with sharper judgment than ever before. HR **must** adjust to the new reality of AI **speed and power.**

So how do you mitigate worker concentration risk? By changing the playbook:

- Hire for entrepreneurial traits, not credentials. Degrees and certifications don't predict success in an AI First org—adaptability, curiosity, and outcome obsession do.
- Use predictive analytics in hiring. AI recruiting tools can assess traits, past behavior patterns, and even team compatibility to flag risk before the hire is made.
- Redefine retention. Pay and perks aren't enough. AI First workers stay where they are empowered, where they can innovate, and where outcomes are celebrated.
- Develop leaders differently. Focus on accountability, communication, and outcome ownership—not on process or empire-building.
- Build redundancy into critical roles. In leaner orgs, cross-training and overlapping skill coverage ensure one exit doesn't cripple productivity.

All of the themes in this book about becoming AI First apply to organizations of every size. Whether you're a five-person startup, a Fortune 10 giant, a public university, or a federal agency—the principles are the same. At first glance, many of these ideas may seem more relevant to large enterprises, with their complex structures and massive headcounts. But after careful analysis, it becomes clear: **AI First transformation is size-agnostic** and often the impact is felt more acutely within smaller organizations.

In fact, leaders of small organizations sometimes feel that worker concentration risk hits them harder than it does larger organizations. And while it may feel more acute when you only have a handful of employees, the truth is that concentration risk is **equal and universal**. In an AI First world, every organization—big or small—is lean by design. Each worker carries outsized impact, each departure hurts more, and each hire matters disproportionately.

The bottom line is simple: in AI First companies, **each employee is worth exponentially more**—and **each bad employee costs exponentially more**. HR has to stop playing a volume game and start playing a precision game. Worker concentration risk makes talent strategy the single biggest competitive differentiator of the next decade. Companies that recruit and retain the right AI First talent will dominate. Those that don't are likely to collapse under the weight of a single bad hire.

Changing Motivations and Incentives of AI First Workers

To significantly minimize the reality of AI First based Employee Concentration risk, HR must understand, at its foundation, that the AI First employee is **motivated by different things** than the employees of the past. If HR is to be successful in building and maintaining the AI First workforce, they have to fully understand this new worker -- Not only the new skill sets that they must have, but them as unique people.

The **personality** traits of these individuals tend to be vastly different than those of previous eras.

In thinking about the actual **people,** the human beings that have the skills and talents required to be AI First, HR needs to consider their motivations. What kind of culture do they want? What kind of compensation structure do they want? How should HR recognize, reward, incent, retain them? How can HR make the best in the world want to work with **your** organization?

The HR industry has gotten good at incentivizing the **current work force**. Organizations spend billions of dollars a year studying how to attract and retain "A" talent. Entire industries are created around teaching HR leaders how to structure performance reviews to identify and recognize "the best", create compensation structures that retain "the best", create job titles and support groups to attract and retain **"the best"**.

In the AI First world, the definition of "**the best**" has done a complete 180.

The motivations of the **AI First worker** are fundamentally different from the traditional specialized worker of the past 25 years. The traditional worker was driven by stability, structure, and clearly defined roles—security in knowing that if they followed the process and stayed in their lane, they would be rewarded with steady pay, promotions, and predictability. The AI First worker, by contrast, is entrepreneurial at their core. They don't want to repeat the same tasks day after day; they want to create, solve, and adapt in real time.

What drives them is **mission and impact**—the ability to see their work change outcomes, not just fill a seat. They are motivated by compensation models tied directly to results, where their performance and creativity dictate their upside. They want **autonomy and control** over their destiny, not layers of bureaucracy and micromanagement.

The AI First worker is drawn to organizations that reward speed, innovation, and ownership rather than conformity. They see technology as leverage, not a threat, and want to harness AI to multiply their impact. They crave environments where **outcomes are celebrated more than optics**, and where performance is the ultimate currency of value. For this new class of worker, stability is not the prize—**freedom, influence, and measurable achievement** are.

In the decades before this shift, employee motivation looked very different. Gallup research throughout the 1990s and 2000s showed that the top reasons people joined and stayed at companies were **job security, benefits, and a predictable career path**. In fact, a 2001 Conference Board study found that over 70% of workers ranked **stability and steady pay** as their primary motivation. Retention strategies in the pre–AI era leaned heavily on pensions, healthcare packages, and long-term promotion tracks. The most talented individuals often stayed with employers for decades because of **loyalty programs, prestige of tenure, pensions, and the safety of defined corporate ladders**. In 1995, the average tenure of a skilled professional at a single company was nearly **11 years**; today it has dropped to less than **4 years**.

The old model valued **compliance and consistency**. This is why so many companies focused on employee handbooks, annual performance reviews, and incremental raises. Retention was built on predictability, not inspiration.

By contrast, today's AI First employees are motivated by something more. According to LinkedIn's 2023 Global Talent Trends report, the top three reasons high performers stay at a company are **growth opportunities, meaningful work, and the ability to innovate**. McKinsey research in 2022 found that **41% of employees left jobs where they felt their impact wasn't visible**, even if pay and benefits were strong. This shows a massive generational shift: the best workers will no longer trade creativity and mission for stability.

AI First workers don't expect to spend decades at a single company; they expect to maximize their performance and impact in two-to-five-year cycles. They'll move on **if the environment stifles them**. They want **results-based rewards**, fast cycles of learning, and direct recognition of their contributions. In short, where traditional workers were motivated by **security and structure**, AI First workers are motivated by **freedom, outcomes, and the chance to shape the future**.

The AI First HR organization must fully understand this as they rapidly and immediately restaff their organizations with these workers.

AI First Workers Demand to Work with Great People

Another critical dimension of the **AI First worker's mindset** is their insistence on working alongside great people. For them, the quality of their colleagues is not a "nice to have"—it is at the very top of their hierarchy of needs. They know that their own ability to succeed, to innovate, and to win is directly tied to the caliber of the people around them. If they are surrounded by mediocrity, their performance suffers. If they are surrounded by top talent, their potential multiplies.

This is a profound shift from the past 20–30 years. Of course, workers in every era wanted to succeed, but in the pre–AI First decades, most employees placed a higher value on stability, benefits, or personal advancement over the raw quality of their teammates. They would tolerate weaker colleagues so long as the paycheck cleared and the promotion path was visible. Today's AI First worker will not. They will walk away from a company that tolerates underperformers, cultural deadweight, or "bad people" who drain momentum.

For them, talent density is survival. A 2023 MIT Sloan study found that the highest-performing teams were over **50% more likely to describe their colleagues as "exceptionally capable"** compared to average teams. Netflix famously codified this principle years ago: adequate performance gets a generous severance. The AI First generation takes this same philosophy to heart.

This raises the stakes for HR. It's no longer enough to enforce policies or manage compliance. HR must become the engine of **talent density**—relentlessly recruiting, developing, and retaining only the very best. They must have the courage to say no to mediocrity, to adjust quickly when someone isn't the right fit, and to create a culture where every player is an A-player.

If HR isn't excellent, the AI First workforce will notice—and they will leave. In this new era, HR must be good, because the workers who drive transformation demand it.

For the AI First worker, winning depends not just on themselves, but on the **strength of everyone around them**. And HR's role is to make sure those people are world-class.

HR as an Operating Function Must Become AI First

In addition to all the change that HR needs to make to its culture and how it serves the business, they have to do all that **while simultaneously transforming themselves as an operating organization to AI First.** This is not optional. HR cannot preach AI First while still running like a paper-pushing bureaucracy from the 1990s.

HR, more than almost any other function, is ripe for massive efficiency and automation through AI. Why? Because so much of what HR does today is administrative, repetitive, and compliance driven. Resume screening, policy documentation, payroll processing, benefits enrollment, regulatory reporting, compliance training—the list goes on. These tasks are necessary, but they are also highly structured, rules-based, and deeply process-heavy. In other words, they are the exact kind of work that AI is built to obliterate.

A 2023 McKinsey report estimated that **up to 56% of HR functions could be automated with AI today**—making HR one of the top five corporate functions most impacted by artificial intelligence. Gartner has gone further, predicting that HR may see efficiency gains of **40–70% in the next five years** if organizations fully embrace AI tools for workforce management. Put simply: outside of the factory floor, HR may be the single largest part of an organization where AI can unleash transformational productivity.

Take talent acquisition as one example. Today, recruiters spend endless hours reviewing resumes, scheduling interviews, writing job descriptions, and tracking candidates across multiple systems. AI can do all this faster, cheaper, and more accurately. Smart systems can automatically scan thousands of resumes in minutes, surface candidates that match outcome-driven skills (not just keywords), generate tailored interview questions, and even automate initial candidate outreach. What once took a recruiting team of five can now be done by two entrepreneurial recruiters amplified by AI.

Employee onboarding is another ripe area. Traditional onboarding requires HR to shuffle paperwork, ensure compliance, and distribute handbooks that few employees read. An AI First HR org can flip that into a personalized, interactive experience—AI chatbots that answer questions 24/7, adaptive learning modules that guide new hires through culture, compliance, and skills training, and automated workflows that provision all tools and accounts in minutes. Instead of two weeks of orientation drudgery, onboarding can be compressed into two days of value-driven ramp-up.

Performance management is also transformed. Instead of relying on quarterly or annual reviews (which are often biased and inconsistent), AI can monitor outcomes, feedback loops, and productivity metrics in real time. Entrepreneurial workers don't want to wait six months to know how they're doing—they want continuous feedback. AI can provide it at scale, surfacing coaching opportunities, flagging risks, and even suggesting development resources based on an employee's evolving performance profile.

Compensation and benefits, historically one of the most complex HR responsibilities, can also be streamlined with AI. Dynamic compensation models powered by AI can benchmark salaries against real-time market data, identify compensation mismatches, and suggest retention-oriented adjustments instantly. Benefits queries—one of the largest sources of HR workload—can be handled by AI-powered agents that answer employee questions on coverage, policies, or claims instantly, without human bottlenecks.

Compliance and risk management—long the domain of HR "policy police"—is practically tailor-made for AI. Tools can scan for regulatory changes, auto-update policy manuals, track employee certifications, and audit for compliance gaps, all without requiring an army of administrators. What once required dozens of compliance specialists can now be handled by one or two HR leaders with AI systems running in the background.

The story is consistent across every HR workflow: recruiting, onboarding, training, payroll, benefits, compliance, performance management. Each process is heavy with repetitive tasks and rules. AI turns all of that into automation, freeing HR professionals to focus on what actually matters: identifying, developing, and unleashing entrepreneurial workers.

By transforming HR into an AI First function, companies not only save costs and increase speed—they also make **HR a role model for the rest of the organization.** If HR can shed its deep-state tendencies, adopt AI at scale, and demonstrate exponential efficiency gains, it sends a message to every other function: this is how it's done.

The productivity math is staggering. Studies say AI's impact on HR should drive at least a **50% efficiency gain.** —Not only will HR shrink and become incredibly more efficient, but costs can also be reallocated outside of HR into the business. At the same time, HR's performance will improve. Recruiting timelines collapse. Employee issues get resolved instantly. Culture-building and workforce planning get the attention they deserve. Instead of being seen as the compliance cop, HR becomes the entrepreneurial engine that staffs, supports, and scales the AI First company, all at a fraction of the cost and resources it consumes today.

The paradox of AI First HR is this: the more work AI takes off its plate, the more strategic HR becomes. Instead of drowning in administration, HR leaders can focus entirely on building the workforce of the future. And in the AI First era, **that is the single most important thing an organization can do.**

HR Workflows Transformed by AI

As mentioned earlier, HR is an area of every organization ripe for the speed and power of AI to add tangible transformative business value immediately.

Recruiting and candidate sourcing have always been some of the most time-consuming parts of HR. Traditionally, teams could spend weeks screening resumes and reaching out to talent. Now, AI tools like HireVue, SeekOut, Paradox Olivia, and LinkedIn AI Recruiter automate the heavy lifting. They can scan thousands of resumes in minutes, handle initial outreach, and surface the best-fit candidates up to 40–60% faster, giving HR professionals more time to focus on relationship building and closing. In fact, Deloitte estimates that AI-driven sourcing can reduce hiring costs by up to 35%, while cutting average time-to-hire from 42 days to just under 20. That's not incremental—that's transformational.

Once candidates are in the pipeline, the next challenge is **assessment and interviews**. Here too, AI has transformed the workflow. Platforms such as HireVue, Pymetrics, and Retorio analyze video interviews, evaluate behavioral cues, and score skills assessments with structured consistency. The result is reduced bias, faster decision-making, and a clearer picture of which applicants are most aligned to both role and culture. More importantly, studies show AI-enabled interviewing can lower turnover by 20–25% because new hires are better matched to organizational values and expectations. Of course, the final hiring decisions will be made in conjunction with human HR staffers.

Onboarding and training, historically cumbersome and generic, have become smarter and more adaptive with AI-driven learning systems. Docebo, Workday Learning, and Sana Labs personalize employee orientation, compliance training, and knowledge transfer. These platforms tailor the content to each individual's needs, cutting training time by 30–50% while improving retention of critical information. Companies report that employees trained with adaptive platforms ramp up to full productivity in 30% less time, meaning faster ROI on talent investment.

Employee engagement and retention, once measured with clunky annual surveys, now benefit from real-time insights. AI tools like Peakon, Qualtrics XM, and CultureAmp constantly monitor sentiment, pulse-check employee satisfaction, and even predict attrition risks. This allows HR teams to act before top talent walks out the door, turning engagement into a proactive, data-driven function rather than a reactive scramble. When companies deploy AI-driven engagement monitoring, voluntary attrition drops by as much as 15%—a massive financial impact in industries where replacing a single employee can cost 50–200% of their salary.

Even core administrative tasks like **payroll and benefits** have been reinvented. ADP Next Gen, Gusto, and Rippling automate payroll calculations, flag errors instantly, and offer 24/7 AI-powered chat support to answer employee HR questions. What used to require long cycles and significant manual effort is now nearly seamless. Some firms have reported reducing payroll error rates from 8% to under 1% with these systems, saving both time and credibility with employees.

Performance management is another area where AI brings precision and accountability. Tools like Betterworks, Lattice, and 15Five track goals, streamline feedback cycles, and use predictive analytics to surface both high and low performers. They can even recommend promotions or highlight misalignments, ensuring that HR decisions are directly tied to business outcomes rather than subjective judgment. In high-growth organizations, these systems often boost productivity by 10–15% simply by aligning incentives with measurable outcomes.

Finally, **compliance and policy enforcement**—always a high-stakes responsibility—has become significantly more manageable with AI. Platforms like DocuSign AI, Trusaic, and Vault Platform automate record-keeping, review contracts for regulatory risks, and run audit checks in real time. What once demanded armies of compliance officers can now be handled with precision by leaner teams. A PwC report found that AI-enabled compliance reduces audit preparation time by up to 80%, freeing legal and HR staff to focus on strategic initiatives rather than administrative drudgery.

Taken together, these workflows show how AI has become the backbone of modern HR. From recruiting to compliance, every layer of the employee lifecycle is accelerated, de-biased, and made more efficient. HR's role is no longer about drowning in process—it's about leveraging AI to elevate people, culture, and outcomes. The shift is so profound that many CHROs are rebranding themselves as "Chief Talent & AI Officers," acknowledging that talent strategy is now inseparable from AI fluency. For employees, this means working in organizations where HR is not a gatekeeper of forms and policies but a driver of empowerment, efficiency, and growth.

Case Study: SMB HR Before and After AI

Consider a regional services company with 500 employees. Before AI, their HR team of eight was underwater—spending nearly 70% of their time processing resumes, managing payroll errors, and running slow, reactive engagement surveys. Recruiting took an average of 45 days per role, payroll error rates hovered around 7%, and voluntary turnover sat at 18% annually. Employees routinely complained that HR was slow to respond and more focused on paperwork than people.

Then they went AI First. They deployed LinkedIn AI Recruiter and Paradox Olivia for sourcing, Gusto and Rippling for payroll and benefits, and CultureAmp for real-time engagement monitoring. Within six months, the HR team shrank from eight to five—but performance skyrocketed.

Time-to-hire dropped to 20 days. Payroll error rates fell below 1%. Attrition dropped from 18% to 11%, saving the company hundreds of thousands of dollars in replacement costs. Most importantly, employees noticed: internal surveys showed a 25% jump in satisfaction with HR, not because HR suddenly got "nicer," but because the systems worked seamlessly and freed the team to focus on people rather than process.

And the savings weren't just theoretical. Two of the eight HR staff were transitioned out entirely, creating direct hard-dollar savings on salaries and benefits—over $220,000 annually. That came on top of all the productivity gains, lower attrition, and faster recruiting.

The key takeaway is that HR costs fell by 22% year-over-year while organizational productivity rose by double digits. What once required a bloated HR bureaucracy is now a lean, AI-powered function delivering faster, cheaper, and better results.

Cooper Callout: AI doesn't just make HR more efficient—it makes HR more human by removing the drudgery and letting the team focus on people and culture, all while delivering hard cost savings that drop straight to the bottom line.

Summary: HR as the AI First Catalyst

HR is the tip of the spear, the catalyst, to ensure successful AI First transformation. Technology doesn't change companies—people do. And in the AI First era, where **everything changes**—organizational structures, leadership requirements, worker skills, and even the very definition of what "work" means—**HR must drive the reboot.**

HR is not just recruiting, retaining and training. It's the engine of talent strategy, development, scoring, onboarding, compensation, and culture. In the AI First era, HR must pivot from hiring specialized, narrowly defined workers (the default playbook for the last 50+ years) to building an **entrepreneurial, AI-literate workforce**. Workers who are outcome-driven, adaptable, accountable, and comfortable with constant change. HR must recruit, onboard, and motivate not specialists, but **force multipliers**—employees who, when paired with AI, can produce 10–100 times the output of their predecessors.

This creates an entirely new operating environment. The old mindset of **volume and scale**—just keep the organization fully staffed—no longer applies. AI First companies are leaner, smaller, and faster, which introduces **worker concentration risk.** In this world, every hire matters vastly more. Every bad hire hurts 100 times as much. Every lost employee isn't just a gap—it's an enormous hit to productivity. HR must now become experts at precision hiring, at building environments that retain entrepreneurial workers, and at motivating them with the right incentives, culture, and opportunities.

The mission of HR in an AI First company is clear:

- Recruit and retain **entrepreneurial leaders and workers** who thrive with AI.
- Redesign compensation, culture, and incentives to reward outcomes, not headcount or tenure.
- Manage worker concentration risk by making every hire count and every retention effort succeed.
- Evolve themselves into a strategic, AI-powered function that enables the organization to move faster, not slower.

The AI First transformation is not a technology project—it is a people project. And HR sits at the center. If HR rises to this challenge, it becomes the catalyst that allows the company to thrive in the AI First era. If it fails, the organization cannot keep pace, no matter how much technology it deploys.

Cooper Callout: In the AI First era, HR is not a support function. HR is the battlefield commander of the talent war. Get it right, and your organization will soar. Get it wrong, and no amount of AI will save you.

Chapter 10:

A Field Manual For
AI First Success

So how do I do this?

Up to this point, this book has hammered home why AI First is the single most important transformation of your lifetime.— why your structure, leaders, talent, culture, approach to HR and workforce all have to change. That's the "why" and the "what." But let's be honest—that only gets you so far. The real question keeping you up at night is, ***"How the heck do I actually make this happen inside my organization?"***

This is where the rubber meets the road. This is not theory, not inspiration, not another buzzword-filled "future of work" speech. This is the tactical playbook. The moves you need to make tomorrow morning when you walk into the office. The steps to take when you sit down with your executive team. The way you push through the resistance of middle management and the inertia of legacy culture.

Think of this section as the "field manual" of AI First. It's blunt. It's urgent. It's direct. No corporate fluff, no excuses. Just the steps you must take to go from talk to traction.

Set the Groundwork: AI First Is Not Optional it is the New Operating System

The biggest mistake companies are making today is still **treating AI as an experiment**, a side initiative, or an optional technology upgrade. It is none of those things. It is the most important transformation your business and organization will ever face. Becoming AI First is not just about tools, it is about survival. Think about the speed of disruption we've seen in the last twenty years—Amazon hollowing out retail, Uber killing the taxi industry, Netflix burying Blockbuster. Those took decades. AI First will enable 10X that disruption across **all** industries over a 36- month period. That's how fast this moves.

Organizations that delay will find themselves outgunned and outmaneuvered. Even companies that are "healthy" today—profitable, well-positioned, solid client bases—will find themselves destroyed if they don't become AI First immediately. Why? Because while they are sitting atop their perch, enjoying their success, their competitors are cutting costs in half, doubling productivity, and reinvesting those savings into better products and lower prices. The gap compounds exponentially, and there's no catching up.

This book is not about adding AI into one function: It's about transforming the entire operating system of your company. Workflows. Leadership. Incentives. Culture. Everything. To become AI First requires ruthless urgency, because the clock is already ticking.

The danger for many leaders is they think they have "time." **They don't.** In industry after industry—from banking to healthcare to construction—first movers in AI are already widening the gap. McKinsey estimates that AI First companies will have cost bases 30–50% lower than their peers by 2030. That's not a long runway. That's around the corner.

With AI First, the early adopters don't just get ahead—they take it all. Once a competitor establishes lower costs, faster cycles, and better customer experiences, the flywheel spins too fast to catch. Within a year or two, the laggards aren't just behind—they're obsolete. Harvard

Business Review recently noted that AI adoption leaders are *5x more likely* to gain market share than peers who delay.

And here's the kicker: customers don't care how hard the transformation is for you. They only care about speed, cost, personalization, and results. If your competitors are delivering that through AI, your excuses won't matter.

Now let's take a look at that "field manual" to ensure that your organization is on its way to AI First, as opposed to the graveyard.

Step One: Leadership Commitment and Communication

The first and most important tactical step to achieve AI First is simple and obvious. **a public, unmistakable commitment to AI First.** Optimally, this comes from the CEO, the board, or the owners of the organization. And they must state that AI First is **the priority** – not a side project or "center of excellence." That means reallocating capital, shifting people, and making every other initiative secondary to this one.

This commitment cannot be delegated; it must be visible to everyone in the organization, from the janitors to the senior vice presidents. The CEO should personally declare it to the organization and make it clear that their career, their reputation, and the company's survival hinge on AI First transformation. This is what creates the permission structure for everyone else to act.

What does this shift look like in practice? Budgets flow to AI initiatives without hesitation. Projects that don't propel the AI First vision end immediately. Leaders are rewarded not for maintaining the status quo, but for reinventing their functions through AI. Boards track AI First adoption and impact as closely—and as seriously—as they track revenue and profit. As important as the messaging and constant recommunication top down are, another essential best practice is imperative: leading from the front.

Leadership from the Front

For as long as humans have organized into groups, the most powerful form of leadership has always been leading from the front. In ancient times, generals didn't sit in tents miles behind the battlefield—they rode at the head of their armies. Alexander the Great, Caesar, Napoleon—these leaders understood that when soldiers *see* their leader charging into the fight, it ignites something primal. Morale surges. Fear drops. Commitments harden People weren't just ordered to fight—they were inspired to because their leader was doing it alongside them.

Why was this so powerful? Because **actions cut through doubt**. When leaders risked their own lives shoulder-to-shoulder with their troops, it erased hesitation. The message was unmistakable: *This is worth it. Follow me.* Soldiers didn't just obey because of rank; they followed because they trusted what they saw. Leading from the front has always been the ultimate proof of commitment.

Fast forward to business leadership **today**. In most cases, **it's almost impossible for executives to "lead from the front,"** because corporate tasks have become so diversified. A CEO's daily work looks nothing like what frontline workers do. The CFO's spreadsheet doesn't resemble what customer support handles. The COO's dashboards don't resemble the shop floor. And because of that disconnect, leadership by example often breaks down. Leaders say the right words, but the workforce doesn't feel it—they don't see the leader in the trenches with them.

AI changes that. For the first time in modern organizational history, leaders *can* work with the same tools, workflows, and platforms as their people—and they can do it visibly throughout the organization. AI gives leaders the chance to lead from the front again. A CEO can literally show the entire company that he is building board decks with AI, analyzing data with AI, and drafting memos with AI. The CFO can show he's closing the books in half the time using AI reconciliation. The head of sales can run real AI copilots to prep meetings and proposals. These aren't symbolic gestures—they're real workflows, the same kind the organization itself is learning to transform. C-suite executives might not share the details of their work with the rank-and-file, but they can demonstrate that they are using the same *processes* to reach their objectives.

When employees see their leaders *doing* AI, not just *talking* about AI, **the effect is the same as watching a general ride into battle**. It dissolves resistance, accelerates adoption, and removes excuses. The message is clear: *If I can do this at the top, you can do it in your role.* In truth, leadership by example has always been the gold standard; AI finally makes it not only possible, but mission-critical.

Before AI, leaders could model culture—they could demonstrate values like integrity, transparency, and urgency. They could set the tone through speeches, policies, and the way they carried themselves. But they couldn't realistically model *the work itself.* A CEO couldn't show an assembly line worker how to weld. A CFO couldn't show a designer how to build a prototype. A COO couldn't write code with engineers. The nature of work was too specialized and too far removed from the C-suite.

AI obliterates that divide because now, everyone can use the tools that transform work are the same tools everyone can use—from the CEO down to the newest intern. Leading by example doesn't mean lofty values alone; it means tactical, visible, hands-on use of AI in the exact workflows the rest of the company is navigating. That's why it's so powerful. When leaders use AI to summarize contracts, generate customer emails, or analyze market data, they are modeling the same behavior that every employee must adopt. The cultural and tactical layers converge into one.

This dual power—**leading from the front *and* leading by example**— creates a new kind of leadership credibility. Employees don't just hear that AI is important; they watch their leaders live it. And when leaders live it, resistance crumbles. The fear of irrelevance gets reframed into excitement for what's possible. AI doesn't look like a threat when your boss is openly using it to make their own work faster and better—it looks like an enabler.

This is why leadership in the AI First era is so different. Words aren't enough. Slide decks aren't enough. Vision statements aren't enough. **Leaders must demonstrate through their own workflows that AI is the new operating system of the organization**. That's the real definition of leading by example in the 21st century: not only embodying the values, but embodying the *work*.

In the AI First era, all leaders—whether of a 10-person startup, a 500-person SMB, or a Fortune 500 giant—can prove their commitment in real time. They can pick up the same AI tools their teams are using and show exactly what transformation looks like. Just as ancient generals once rode into battle at the head of their armies, today's leaders must log into AI and ride into the workflows at the head of their companies.

If AI First is not clear from the very top, middle managers will bury the initiative. They'll slow-walk it. They'll treat it like every other corporate fad. That's the deep state at work, and it will kill you. Only visible, unambiguous leadership commitment breaks through that inertia.

And leaders must understand : this is existential. If they fail, they lose the company. If they succeed, they double its value in 18 months. That's the magnitude of what's at stake.

The pressure is real: Gartner predicts that by 2026, 75% of organizations that haven't made AI adoption a board-level mandate will fall behind competitors to the point of irrelevance. A CEO who hesitates risks not only shareholder confidence but also the credibility of the brand itself.

Leaders who fail to commit will lose talent. The best AI First employees—the entrepreneurial, outcome-obsessed ones—will **not stay at a company that treats AI as a hobby.** They'll flee to competitors who take it seriously. Commitment at the top isn't just about signaling to Wall Street. It's about retaining the very people who will deliver the transformation. And if leadership gets it wrong, those A-players will become the competitive weapon in someone else's organization.

Leadership Case Study: Florida International University: Leading from the front

Universities everywhere are at an inflection point. Across the United States, many institutions are struggling financially. Enrollment is declining, especially in regional and mid-tier schools. A 2023 National Student Clearinghouse report showed undergraduate enrollment had dropped by more than 7% since 2019, representing millions of lost tuition dollars. At the same time, families and students are questioning whether the traditional university model is worth the cost: tuition has skyrocketed more than 200% since the late 1980s, while student debt in the U.S. now exceeds $1.7 trillion. According to a 2022 Gallup poll, only 36% of Americans said they had a "great deal" or "quite a lot" of confidence in higher education—down from over 55% just a decade ago.

This pressure is being amplified by AI. Employers increasingly demand AI-ready graduates, alternative credentialing platforms like Coursera or Google Career Certificates. These streamlined programs are eating away at traditional degree demand, and universities that move too slowly risk being left in the dust.. In short: higher education is facing a once-in-a-century challenge, and AI is making the urgency even sharper.

Nowhere is this reality clearer than at Florida International University (FIU). FIU is the one of the largest universities in Florida, serving more than 55,000 students. It is a full-service research university with a law school, a medical school, a highly regarded business school, engineering, liberal arts, and dozens of other programs. More importantly, it is the **primary university for the middle class of South Florida**. FIU has been consistently ranked as one of the **best financial values in higher education**. In 2023, *U.S. News & World Report* ranked FIU #1 in the nation for Social Mobility, highlighting how effectively it helps first-generation and middle-class students rise economically. FIU is also repeatedly listed as one of the top public universities in Florida, and among the top 5% of universities in the nation for research activity.

Recently, FIU appointed a new president, **Jeanette Núñez**, and she has wasted no time grabbing the bull by the horns. Her stated objective is crystal clear: provide the **best preparation in the world for students** to enter the workforce and live successful lives, while also ensuring the university remains **one of the best values in higher education**. Those two goals—best education and best value—are now the laser focus of FIU's leadership.

Not long into her tenure, President Núñez made the bold decision to make FIU one of the first (if not *the* first) AI First universities in the country. She recognized immediately that AI is the future of higher education. **Her visionary insight was that if** FIU is going to remain among the best in the nation, and ascend to become **the best** university in the nation, it must go AI First.

Her vision is sweeping: every student, in every discipline—business, law, medicine, engineering, literature, the sciences—will learn not only their core subject matter but also how AI reshapes and amplifies that subject. At the same time, she has recognized the power of AI to transform the *operations* of the university itself. HR, finance, marketing, IT, legal, facilities—all of the administrative functions that keep a university running—are ripe for AI-driven efficiency. By streamlining these, FIU can free up millions of dollars to reinvest in its students, **keeping costs down while simultaneously raising the quality of education.**

This matters because most universities today are facing severe budget pressures. A 2022 Deloitte study found that 60% of U.S. universities were already running operating deficits, and many were cutting programs or laying off staff to survive. President Núñez understands that every dollar FIU can take out of administrative overhead and reinvest directly into students is the **highest ROI possible**—real value for the students who entrust FIU with their education. She knows that by leveraging AI internally, FIU can continue to expand opportunities without passing costs along to families.

I was fortunate enough to attend a leadership meeting at FIU where she set this vision in motion. With her entire executive team present, President Núñez dedicated half a day to explaining exactly what AI First means, why it is critical for FIU, and how the university would begin the transformation. The **clarity of communication, the alignment with FIU's strategic goals, and the unwavering executive commitment** were outstanding.

As a part of the session, she had the group work with AI to redesign and construct a logo for the university **in real time, with** everyone together in the room. She used multiple prompts, and in real time showed how she, the new president of one of the largest universities in the nation, was willing to roll up her sleeves and use AI in real time and iterate to create a new logo. The group was **super engaged** . They were chiming in on how to work the prompting better. At the completion, several objectives were achieved.

Everyone was exposed to AI. There were no skeptics about the power and speed of AI during and after this 15-minute exercise—and it was fun. Jeanette did a great job leading the group to the most important takeaway: what would have cost the university $25–75K in fees to an outside design agency, and taken two months to complete, was replaced with 20 minutes of effort and zero cost. That single experience opened everyone's eyes to the potential efficiencies within their own departments, forcing them to consider what they would do with those savings.

Most importantly, everyone walked away with a clear understanding of the power, speed, and importance of becoming AI First. It was no longer a buzzword or a conceptual example—Jeanette made it tangible.

That was a perfect **model of leadership for an AI First transformation.** She didn't delegate. She didn't position AI as optional. She framed it as existential—an essential move to achieve FIU's mission of value and excellence. By immediately exposing her team to AI concepts, demanding urgency from every department, and positioning AI First as the non-negotiable path forward, she set FIU up for success before the first project even began. This is exactly how organizational transformations succeed: **visible, repeated, unambiguous commitment from the very top.**

Of course, universities face additional challenges in becoming AI First. Higher education, by its very nature, is full of tradition, **slow** governance, and a "deep state" of entrenched processes and norms. Universities are some of the slowest institutions in society to change—curricula are debated for years, tenure systems resist disruption, and committees can stall initiatives indefinitely. President Núñez understands this. That's why her early moves were so critical: she built the case clearly, she communicated the "why" relentlessly, and she got buy-in from her University leadership team at the start. By setting the tone with strength and urgency, she made it clear that AI First at FIU is not optional—it's mandatory.

Keep an eye on FIU. Prediction: by the end of this decade, FIU will not just be a top-10 university—it will be **#1 in the nation for return on value.** Its commitment to being an AI First university is core to that trajectory. And that commitment is being driven by a bold, clear, and communicative leader at the very top.

Step Two: Benchmark the Baseline

You cannot manage what you don't measure. Before you can transform into an AI First company, you need a clear picture of where you stand today. That means benchmarking every department, every team, and every individual.

This benchmarking isn't about vanity metrics like "do people have access to AI tools?" outcomes. How much of their work is already being done with AI? Are they doing their entire workflow and work product with an AI first mode in AI technologies, or simply dabbling with ChatGPT?

The difference between dabbling and driving outcomes is life and death.

Organizations should create a standardized "AI utilization score" that tracks adoption. Imagine dashboards that show which functions are accelerating AI First usage, and which are stagnant. The baseline isn't theoretical. It's measurable

But benchmarking cannot stop at activity. It must extend to skills baselining. **How well are they actually using AI?** How effectively are they prompting? How financially efficient are they? Who knows how to validate AI output? Who still treats AI like a toy?

Most importantly, every company must know exactly what level of a given workflow, or work process, or departments work product is created and exists within an AI First technology and workflow **completely.**

The solution is simple: give every department, and individual employee an **AI First score**---A practical quantification that measures the percentage of their outcomes/work output that was created with AI, as well as how effectively the department and individuals within the organization are using AI. This creates a heatmap of the organization— showing exactly where it is AI first, where it is not, and within each department, who are the individuals leading the way and who is are not.

That heatmap becomes the roadmap for training or replacement. Some teams may need immediate AI bootcamps. Others may be ready to lead as internal champions. Without this baseline, leaders are flying blind. They assume adoption is happening, when in reality only a handful of curious employees are carrying the load.

Organizations need this level of detail to make real decisions. If a sales team is 30% behind peers in AI utilization, you know exactly where to train. If HR is lagging, you know where automation must be injected. Benchmarking makes it impossible to hide.

Why <u>Completeness</u> of Workflow Measurement Matters

The depth of benchmarking is what separates **Supplemental AI** from **true AI First**. As mentioned earlier in the book, many organizations feel satisfied by dabbling in AI. They claim victory as they get productivity improvements However, Supplemental AI is nothing compared to AI First. "Dabbling" in AI is the easy way out, and what is critical for leaders is to make sure that does not happen.

AI First means the *entire workflow* is run inside AI systems. From beginning to end, work is executed, iterated, and finalized within AI-powered environments—making the efficiency gains exponential, not incremental. Measuring completeness ensures you know whether teams are simply experimenting or actually transforming.

If people are given the *option* of bypassing AI, many will revert to what they already know. **Humans hate change.** Left to their own devices, employees will cling to familiar tools and habits. If they can still complete 80% of their work the "old way," most will. Which means your company will stay stuck in supplemental AI mode.

That's why **benchmarking completeness of workflow** matters. It forces visibility into whether AI is central to execution, or merely a side tool. If your developers only run 10% of their work through Cursor, as an example, you don't have AI First engineering—you have AI-supplemented engineering. If your marketing team drafts 90% of campaigns manually and only uses AI for summaries, you don't have AI First marketing—you have dabblers.

The productivity gap is staggering. Studies suggest that partial AI adoption (supplemental AI) creates 10–20% efficiency gains. Full AI First workflows create 70-120%+% gains. That's a **five times difference in output**—and it compounds across every department.

Think about it: a 100-person company dabbling with AI is basically 120 people's worth of output. The same company running AI First workflows across the board is 200 people's worth of output—with the same headcount. After one year, the gap has hardened into permanence.

The only way to ensure you're in the latter camp is to me**asure it relentlessly. Audit workflows for completeness.** Ask: what percentage of this team's tasks are fully executed in AI systems? What percentage are still done manually? Create thresholds—80%, 90%, 100%—and make those the standard.

This discipline also inoculates you against "AI theater"—where leaders think they're AI First because they see activity, but in reality the workflows are still mostly old-school. Without measurement, you're leading blind. With it, you can demand transformation, hold teams accountable, and prevent backsliding.

Cooper Call Out: Supplemental AI is a crutch. AI First is a revolution. The difference is whether you measure—and enforce—workflow completeness.

Case Study: Benchmarking AI First in Software Development

To take the abstract and make it real, let's look at how to benchmark AI First implementation in one of the most important and high-potential areas of any organization: software development.

Software development has always struggled with efficiency. According to McKinsey and Standish Group studies, more than **70% of software projects run over budget or past deadlines**, and only about **30% of projects meet all their original objectives**.

Even in the most modern companies, the industry is notorious for unpredictability and waste. That's why AI's impact here is so transformative. Early research shows that **AI First software development teams can achieve productivity gains between 100% and 200%**, essentially doubling or tripling output without increasing headcount.

GitHub's 2023 study on Copilot, for example, found developers completed tasks **55% faster** and reported higher satisfaction. Imagine those gains compounded across an entire organization where every workflow is AI First.

Yet software engineering is one of the most self-determining and least standardized functions in a business. Individual developers often pick their own tools, workflows, and styles. Surveys from Stack Overflow's Developer Report show that **over 60% of developers use their own customized tool chains**, and fewer than half of organizations enforce standardized development processes across teams. Engineers are seen as "creatives," the coders who need to be left alone to "just do their thing." That freedom has led to innovation—but also to **massive inefficiencies, inconsistent results, and bloated costs**.

And the costs are staggering. Software engineers command some of the highest compensation in any industry. According to Levels. fyi and Glassdoor, average U.S. software engineer salaries range from $120,000 to $200,000+, with elite talent commanding multiples of that. For comparison, a single top-tier software engineer can cost more than two or three employees in other business functions. And yet, the productivity distribution is wildly uneven. Some studies show that the **top 10% of developers produce 10 times more output** than the average peer. This unevenness, combined with high costs, **makes software engineering one of the ripest areas for AI to clean up.**

Why is it so perfect for AI? Because software engineering is knowledge work made of repetitive patterns, logic, and text—exactly what modern AI is best at. Writing boilerplate code, debugging, testing, documenting, and even designing architectures are all tasks that AI can perform at scale. When an entire organization—not just individuals tinkering—moves to AI First workflows, the results are profound. Accenture projects that organizations who adopt AI First software engineering practices will be **125–150% more productive** within three years compared to peers who lag.

This doesn't just affect software companies. Today, nearly **80% of all businesses consider software development or digital products core to their operations** (Statista, 2023). Banks are software companies. Healthcare providers run on software. Manufacturers, retailers, and logistics firms depend on custom applications and IT systems to compete. That means inefficiencies in software development ripple across almost every industry. AI First adoption here isn't just an opportunity; it's an imperative.

Next Generation AI First Management tools

A new category of AI First software companies is forming to help organizations understand where they are on their AI First Journey. One of the most innovative is **5th Element AI**, built specifically to help software organizations measure and accelerate their journey to AI First. Its approach is simple but powerful: measure, benchmark, and optimize.

5th Element AI (and others like it) begin with an **AI First score**—what percentage of a given application or codebase was written with AI. Imagine being able to say that 70% of your code was AI-generated, versus 20% for a competitor. Or the most recent sprint was 88%, vs. 71% one month ago.

Over time, **5th Element AI** tracks this score, benchmarks it against hundreds of other software companies, and allows its customers to measure their progress vs. industry standards.

But it doesn't stop at the percentage of the applications was written in AI. It actually provides information as to **how effectively** the organization, and individual developers in the organization, are **using AI**. Not only if they are 100% developing in it, but *how well* they are using it. It provides dozens of ratios, metrics and scores that indicate whether the developer and team are good AI First developers. It compares them to then tens of thousands of engineers that it is monitoring.

Information such as how many prompts does each engineer submit, what is their ratio of prompts-to-accepted code, are they improving week-over- week? Are they using AI to cover end-to-end workflows? What % of suggestions are accepted, and what is the modification ratio of what AI Suggested?

Once the benchmarking is in place, the system doesn't just measure—it **coaches**. It uses AI to provide suggestions based on patterns of thousands of other engineers as how the organization as well as the individual developers can be better.

If developers at a peer company are 3 times more productive at testing, 5th Element AI highlights those practices and prompts your team to adopt them. This creates a continuous improvement loop, ensuring productivity gains don't just spike once but keep compounding.

The important lesson is that organizations **monitor, measure, and manage** the completeness of their AI workflows. If you don't measure it, it doesn't happen. If you allow "dabbling," inefficiency creeps back in. If you track, benchmark, and hold people accountable, AI First becomes the operating rhythm of the entire engineering org.

The model extends far beyond engineering. Just as 5th Element AI measures software development AI First journey and status, there are AI

First platforms for **marketing, customer support, HR, finance, sales, manufacturing**....literally every functional area of an organization. The specifics differ, but the principle is identical: measurement drives adoption, adoption drives outcomes, and outcomes create dominance.

The key is not which technology you use, but whether you **commit to monitoring, benchmarking, and measuring AI adoption relentlessly.** Because AI First is not a one-time project. It's a continuous process. And the companies that master it—starting with critical functions like software development—will leave competitors scrambling to keep up.

The future is clear: in a world where AI can double or triple engineering output, companies that don't measure and manage their AI First adoption will be competing with one hand tied behind their back. Those who do will not only code faster—they will innovate faster, ship faster, and dominate faster.

> **Cooper Callout:** AI First isn't about what tools you buy. It's about what your people can do. And you don't know until you measure it.

Step Three: Software Vendor Assessment and Selection

One of the most overlooked aspects of going AI First is the **selection of the software vendors** an organization relies on to run its internal operations. Too often, leaders focus only on their own internal AI adoption—training teams, rethinking workflows, or piloting new pods—while ignoring the fact that most of their workflows already run on third-party software platforms. From HR systems to sales enablement tools, from customer support platforms to marketing automation suites, these vendors are not just utilities; they are the operating backbone of modern organizations.

Studies show that over 75% of core business workflows involve one or more third-party software applications, making vendor AI posture one of the single biggest determinants of whether your company can truly become AI First. **If the software you use is not AI First, then by definition, your organization will never be fully AI First.** You'll be chained to legacy platforms that slow you down, while competitors leap ahead with tools that compound productivity gains month after month.

It doesn't matter how entrepreneurial your leaders are, how strong your culture is, or how aggressive your strategy is—if your core software is dumb, your company is dumb. You could have the best people in the world, but if they're stuck working inside systems that can't think, automate, or anticipate, you've effectively tied rocks to their ankles. Every month you stay on legacy tools, you are handing competitors free market share. In industries where margins are thin, that can mean the difference between growth and bankruptcy. What looks like a "safe choice" in software procurement today could be the single decision that kills your business tomorrow.

That means software vendor selection must move from being an IT procurement exercise to a strategic AI First decision. Every RFP, every evaluation, every renewal must begin with one central question: *how AI First is this vendor?* Not just in their marketing, but in their actual features, roadmap, and philosophy.

The Critical First Step: Audit Your Existing Applications

Every organization should immediately conduct a full audit of the AI First capabilities within their current application stack. Most companies are already paying for dozens of tools across HR, finance, customer support, marketing, operations, compliance, etc. The question is: how many of them are truly AI First?

This audit isn't about surface-level claims. Many vendors have already slapped "AI" on their websites, but when you look under the hood, it's little more than predictive text or a chatbot add-on. you need to know:

- Does this system embed AI into core workflows, or is it just a bolt-on?
- Can it automate repetitive processes and reduce headcount, or is it just "advice" sitting on the side?

- Does it have real generative capabilities, or only legacy rule-based automation?

Organizations should build a vendor AI scorecard that rates every platform on multiple factors: current AI features, pace of AI investment, customer outcomes, **and roadmap credibility.** Each application should be scored red, yellow, or green. Red = not AI First and unlikely to catch up. Yellow = some AI features, but limited or unproven. Green = genuinely AI-native, with a roadmap that compounds.

The result of this audit often shocks leadership: companies discover that 60–70% of their workflows are running on software that will never make them AI First. These are anchor weights dragging the business down, and they must be replaced.

The audit also creates urgency. Once leaders see in black and white how much of their organization is chained to legacy platforms, the conversation changes from "we should look into this someday" to "we must start replacing tools immediately." The sooner this audit is done, the sooner you know which vendors will propel you forward—and which will bury you.

What to Look for in Vendor AI Capabilities

When evaluating whether a software vendor is truly AI First, leaders should look for AI capabilities that directly enhance outcomes across core functions. But before diving into function-specific examples, there are a set of generic AI features that every serious vendor should already have embedded into their applications. These are no longer "nice to have"—they're table stakes:

- AI Search & Natural Language Queries – every application should allow users to interact with data in plain English, surfacing insights instantly without needing complex filters or reports.
- Generative Summarization – the ability to condense long documents, tickets, or threads into concise summaries, saving hours of manual review.

- Automated Recommendations – context-aware suggestions for next steps, whether it's a workflow action, a setting change, or a decision point.
- Anomaly Detection – continuous monitoring for unusual patterns in data, whether in financial entries, customer behavior, or system performance.
- Workflow Automation – embedded AI that learns repeated user actions and suggests or executes them automatically.
- Predictive Analytics – every system should have baseline capabilities to forecast likely outcomes based on historical data, from sales pipelines to churn risk.
- Conversational Interfaces / Chat Assistants – AI copilots that sit inside the platform, helping users complete tasks faster by guiding them step by step.

If a vendor's platform doesn't offer at least some of these fundamental AI capabilities, or a realistic plan in their roadmap, it's a red flag. It shows that they're behind the curve and that you'll be left waiting for features your competitors already have.

- HR Software → AI-driven recruiting screens, predictive retention analytics, automated performance tracking, bias detection, real-time onboarding assistants.
- Sales Tools → AI-enabled lead scoring, conversational intelligence, auto-CRM updates, predictive deal forecasting, dynamic pricing recommendations.
- Customer Support Platforms → AI chatbots that resolve tier-1 tickets, intelligent triage, multilingual auto-translation, sentiment analysis, real-time escalation prediction.
- Finance Systems → AI-powered invoice automation, anomaly detection for fraud, forecasting engines, cash-flow optimization, real-time reconciliations.
- Marketing Platforms → Generative content creation, AI campaign optimization, real-time A/B testing, predictive churn analysis, adaptive customer journeys.

- Legal/Compliance Tools → Contract review automation, clause risk-flagging, regulatory compliance monitoring, case law summarization, e-discovery automation.
- Operations/Field Service Tools → AI scheduling engines, predictive maintenance, route optimization, workload balancing, digital twins for equipment management.

The list goes on, but the principle is simple: if a vendor cannot show a **meaningful portfolio of AI-native features** that save time, drive outcomes, or increase accuracy, then they are not an AI First vendor—and they will not serve you in an AI First era.

How to Evaluate Long-Term AI Posture

It's not enough to assess current features—you must also evaluate whether the vendor has a credible, compounding roadmap for AI investment.

When it comes to strategic vendor selection, **insist on an executive-level session to review their roadmap explicitly through the lens of AI First.** Don't just accept a generic product demo—sit down with the vendor's leadership and demand clarity on how AI is being embedded into both their products and their own operations. The caliber of people they put in front of you will reveal everything. If they send a mid-level product manager to explain their 'AI strategy,' that tells you exactly how seriously they take it. Run for the hills.

You should expect senior executives who not only understand AI but can connect it directly to your business outcomes. Ask tough questions:

- What percentage of R&D spend is allocated to AI capabilities?
- How many engineers/data scientists are working on AI initiatives?
- Does the vendor have partnerships with leading AI infrastructure providers (OpenAI, Anthropic, AWS, Google Cloud, Microsoft Azure)?
- Are AI capabilities embedded natively into workflows, or are they tacked on as "add-ons"?

- Do they publish updates and product roadmaps showing consistent AI improvements?
- How are they incorporating user feedback loops to ensure that AI adoption is practical and outcome-driven?
- Is the vendor themselves AI First, particularly in their software development organization?
- Can they demonstrate how AI is reshaping their own workflows, not just their sales pitch?

This level of scrutiny will quickly separate the real AI First partners from the pretenders. Vendors who lead with conviction, fluency, and vision will help you accelerate your own progress. Vendors who deflect, waffle, or delegate AI discussions to junior staff will drag you down. Choosing the right partner here may be the single most important strategic decision you make for the future of your organization.

Here are the kinds of questions you should be asking in those sessions:

- Can you show how AI is embedded natively into your product—not just as a bolt-on feature?
- Are you AI First in your own internal operations (finance, HR, customer support, marketing)?
- What measurable outcomes has your AI delivered to customers so far (time saved, costs reduced, revenue increased)?
- How frequently do you ship new AI features, and can you share your AI roadmap for the next 12–24 months?
- Who on your executive team is directly accountable for AI strategy and outcomes?

If a vendor can't answer these questions clearly and confidently, they are not AI First—and they won't get you to AI First either.

A vendor's ability to evolve with AI is as critical as their current product. AI is moving so fast that if your vendor is not obsessed with AI, their platform will be obsolete in 12–24 months—and your organization will be dragged down with them.

Special Focus: Small and Medium Businesses

For small and medium businesses (SMBs), vendor selection is even more existential. While enterprises often stitch together dozens of tools, SMBs tend to run 80–85% of their workflows on a **single vendor** platform. That means the AI posture of that one platform effectively defines whether the entire business is AI First or not.

If an SMB chooses a vendor that is slow, outdated, or resistant to AI innovation, the company will be capped in productivity and competitiveness, no matter how entrepreneurial its people are. On the flip side, if an SMB chooses an AI First platform, it gains superpowers instantly—delivering enterprise level efficiency with a lean team and punching far above its weight in the market.

That's why SMB leaders must scrutinize vendor AI features even harder than large enterprises do, the cost of getting it wrong is higher, because the dependency is higher. The right choice creates explosive growth. The wrong choice creates an impenetrable ceiling.

The Importance of Vertical Software Applications

Many SMB industries depend heavily on vertical software applications—software packages purpose-built for the unique workflows, regulations, and business models of their sector. These aren't just "nice add-ons"—in many cases, they *are* the system of record, the single pane of glass through which an entire business is run.

Think about construction, dentistry, logistics, restaurants, retail, field service companies, managed IT service providers, property management companies and many others. Each of these industries has highly specialized software designed for its specific workflows—everything from compliance and scheduling to billing and customer engagement. These systems often act as integrated platforms, meaning that if the software vendor is not AI First, the entire industry segment risks being locked into outdated processes.

These vertical system of record applications often manage 80–95% of the SMBs daily operations. If that vendor falls behind on AI, the business itself is effectively handcuffed to inefficiency. On the other hand, if the vertical platform is AI First, the productivity gains are staggering. AI can automate back-office tasks, optimize operations, personalize customer interactions, and surface insights that were previously invisible.

For these organizations, the vendor's AI roadmap becomes **your company's AI roadmap.** If they innovate quickly, you ride the wave. If they stagnate, you drown. That's why leaders in industries with deep reliance on vertical SaaS must treat vendor AI posture as existential.

In effect, vertical applications don't just enable AI First adoption—they determine whether it's possible at all. The AI First organization is only as strong as its most critical vertical platform.

Examples of What AI First Software Vendors look like

Here are several examples of software vendors that have been built to be AI First, not only in their internal operations but more importantly for you, cutting edge AI First within their platforms, serving as models of what to look for in software vendor selection:

Upshop – An AI First SaaS platform managing the entire grocery store operation, including fresh operations, optimizing inventory, and managing omnichannel orders, in real time.

Most people don't think of grocery as a high-tech business. Nor do they see it as particularly "sexy." For decades, it has been defined by one thing: razor thin margins. Traditional grocery items—packaged goods like canned tuna, bags of sugar, and boxed pasta—carry margins of just **1–7%.** The grocery industry is a pure **volume game.** Move more goods, shave costs, repeat.

But there is a massive transformation happening right now: in the grocery industry, fresh and prepared foods are rewriting the economics of grocery Fresh departments—prepared meals, meat, bakery, etc.—often operate with margins between **20–45%.** That's not just a small bump—it's a seismic leap in profitability. This is why grocers everywhere are expanding hot bars, rotisserie chicken stations, fresh sandwiches, and ready-to-go meals. The entire industry is shifting focus from 7-year shelf-stable canned goods to items that can spoil in 7 hours.

That difference changes everything. Stocking 1,000 cans of tuna that will sit safely on a shelf for years is a completely different business from managing how many chickens you'll sell today, how many PB&J sandwiches you need prepped every hour, or how much salad must be made before the lunch rush. A can of tuna doesn't spoil, a PB&J is unsellable after one day. A sugar bag lasts years, but a rotisserie chicken goes bad by closing time. Supply chains, operations, and profitability models are being turned upside down.

And this complexity is the perfect use case for AI. Managing fresh food is fundamentally a data problem. How many chickens will sell today? How much time does it take to cook them, at what cost, and in what batch sizes? How many sandwiches will be eaten at 11:30 a.m. vs. 1:00 p.m.? How many trays of pasta should a store make on a rainy Tuesday compared to a hot Saturday? These are no longer "gut feel" calls. They are precision forecasts—and only AI can handle the volume of variables, from weather to holidays to local sporting events, which drive demand.

Margins are so tight in traditional grocery that even a 1% improvement in fresh efficiency can double a retailer's profitability. Imagine a grocery chain with 100 stores, each generating $30 million in revenue, with 42% of sales coming from fresh. That's $1.26 billion in fresh revenue. A 1% efficiency gain in managing fresh translates into $12.6 million in savings annually. That is the difference between survival and collapse in this industry.

AI First platforms like **Upshop** are built for this exact reality. They don't just track inventory—they optimize it in real time. They know how many chickens should be roasting at 5 p.m. They know when to start and stop sandwich prep to avoid waste. They automatically adjust production schedules to demand curves, minimizing labor costs and maximizing revenue. They ensure that every perishable item is positioned, priced, and sold before the clock runs out.

But forecasting is only part of the story. Upshop can also verify execution through captured images, ensuring shelves are set correctly, displays are built to plan, and even that bathrooms have truly been cleaned. Instead of relying on checklists or employee self-reporting, visual AI turns compliance into certainty.

It also transforms distribution decisions. In the old world, goods were shipped on a first-come, first-served basis—whoever placed the order first got the product. That meant one store could tie up all the holiday turkeys while another was left bare. In an AI world, allocation is driven by data: demand signals, seasonality, store performance, and timing ensure that goods go where they'll create the most value.

And thanks to Upshop, AI is no longer a black box. Store managers and executives don't just see a forecast—they can ask why it changed. The system explains in plain language: "Ice cream demand is up 12% next week due to higher temperatures and a holiday weekend." What once was a mystery is now a clear, conversational answer that drives action.

Unlike the old grocery game of buying pallets of goods and hoping they sell over months or years, Upshop powered modern grocery is a fresh-first, data-first, AI First business. The new grocer isn't competing on volume—**it's competing on precision**. And the stakes are massive: U.S. food waste still runs at nearly 38% of supply, representing $473 billion in lost value annually. AI isn't just a margin saver here—it's an industry-wide reset.

That's why Upshop has emerged as the leading AI-powered grocery platform. It understands that fresh is the future, but only if it's managed with AI precision. **Without AI, grocers bleed margin**. With AI, grocers transform a 1–2% profit business into a 4–6% profit business—a leap that can change the face of retail forever.

Planet DDS - Dental practice management with predictive scheduling, AI-driven treatment planning, and real-time patient analytics.

Dentistry is a $165+ billion industry that most people don't think about until they're in the chair. But behind every cleaning or root canal is a surprisingly complex business operation: front-desk staff verifying insurance, assistants capturing X-rays, doctors building and presenting treatment plans, and administrators taking payments. For dental groups running dozens or hundreds of practices, this complexity multiplies.

Rising wages, high staff turnover, declining reimbursements, and payer complexity all squeeze margins. In fact, a recent industry survey conducted by Dental Innovation Alliance in 2025 reveals that 81% of dental executives cite staffing as their top concern, followed by rising costs (34%), patient flow challenges (31%), insurance complexity (31%), declining reimbursements (27%), and revenue cycle inefficiencies (23%). These aren't just operational headaches; they're margin killers in an industry where EBITDA pressure has become the new normal.

Traditional dental software hasn't solved the problem. **Most dental practices cobble together a patchwork of disconnected systems**: one for scheduling, another for imaging, a third for billing, and yet another for patient communications. Staff jumps between tools, manually transcribing data, chasing down missing information, losing efficiency at every step. The result is wasted time, frustrated teams, and higher costs.

In recent years, AI has quickly become the buzzword in dental technology. A wave of new entrants is selling point AI solutions. These tools that might analyze an X-ray, send reminders, or predict claim outcomes. But these tools sit on top of fragmented systems, often adding complexity rather than reducing it. **Planet DDS** is taking a different approach. As the leader in cloud-based dental software and creator of DentalOS™, the industry's first AI First enterprise dental platform, Planet DDS is not only embedding AI into the platform itself, but **AI is the platform itself**, and runs through every workflow of the platform.

Imagine a patient arriving at the office: AI checks and confirms insurance benefits in real time before treatment begins. During the exam, AI applied to imaging helps clinicians interpret X-rays more consistently, supporting better diagnoses and more accurate treatment planning. At checkout, the amount a patient owes is clear and accurate – no statement of benefits in the mail post-treatment. And when claims go out the door, AI agents attach the right documentation, scrub for errors, and even handle resubmissions, so collections that once took offices months are now resolved in a matter of days.

Today, more than 13,000 practices use DentalOS AI as their system of record to manage operations, orthodontics, imaging, and billing. Planet DDS organizes its AI vision around four interconnected pillars that work in concert to eliminate process debt.

The results show up where it matters most: fewer days in accounts receivable, lower write-offs, reduced burden on staff, and stronger EBITDA. By embedding AI into the core platform rather than mere point solutions, Planet DDS has turned the daily grind of dental operations into what it calls the **"real EBITDA unlock"**— a durable operating model that translates directly into cash flow and increased enterprise value.

For dental businesses, the message is simple: your software vendor's AI roadmap becomes your AI roadmap. With Planet DDS, that roadmap leads to a future where dental organizations don't just survive margin pressure—they scale with confidence in an AI First world.

> **Cooper Callout:** In the AI First era, the software you choose is the company you become. Select AI First vendors, or you'll never be an AI First organization yourself!

Step Four: Flatten the Organization

AI First organizations must move fast. Bureaucracy is the enemy of speed. That means flattening the organization—removing middle layers, eliminating bottlenecks, and empowering small AI pods to deliver outcomes directly. We discussed this throughout the book, and it must be done right away.

The old model—layers of approvals, committees, PMOs—kills velocity. In an AI First company, decisions need to flow to the edge, where the work happens. AI makes small teams vastly more powerful. That means fewer people can do more, faster.

Flattening doesn't mean chaos. **It means empowerment.** It means small teams with clear missions and the tools to execute autonomously. It means stripping out layers of process so entrepreneurial leaders can move at the speed AI enables.

When organizations flatten, accountability rises. Every decision is closer to the customer, the market, and the outcome. In this model, you can't hide behind process or "waiting on approvals." You either deliver results—or you don't. That cultural clarity is rocket fuel for speed.

This structure is even more critical for SMBs, where a handful of middle managers can strangle growth. By removing unnecessary layers, small businesses can **unlock velocity** that rivals much larger competitors. With AI, scale no longer comes from headcount—it comes from leverage.

Flattening also transforms leadership. Instead of being evaluators or gatekeepers, leaders become outcome enablers. Their job shifts from "approving" to "clearing the path," making sure teams have data, tools, and authority to act. And most importantly, **leaders have to actually do work!**

This manner of work makes the organization far more adaptable. Flat, AI-empowered pods can be reconfigured quickly, assigned to new priorities, spun up for experiments, or scaled down when projects finish. Traditional org charts lock companies into rigidity. AI First org charts unlock fluidity.

Tactically, this means making structural decisions that force speed.

- Limit the number of direct reports any leader can have to no more than 8–10, so decision-making stays close to the ground.
- **Push budget authority down to pods** so they can act without waiting for approvals. Replace standing committees with outcome reviews every 1–3 weeks.
- Rewrite job descriptions to emphasize ownership of results rather than process participation.

- Most importantly, **track decisions and results at the pod level,** not the departmental level, so it's clear who is delivering outcomes and who is slowing things down.

Spotify squads. Toyota lean cells. These are early glimpses of what AI First pods will look like. But with AI, their power is multiplied. One 10-person pod can deliver the work of 100 people in a traditional department. And unlike traditional departments, pods don't ossify—they replicate, adapt, and evolve like living cells.

The lesson is simple: bureaucracy is dead weight. In the AI First era, structure itself is strategy. Flat beats tall. Fast beats big. Now let's take a look at a few examples of organizational flattening.

Example: Flattening in Action

Take a mid-size financial services company that employed 3,000 people across marketing, operations, compliance, and customer support. Historically, every new product feature had to go through five levels of approvals—VP reviews, steering committees, budget sign-offs—before work could even begin. It often took **9–12 months** just to launch a simple feature.

When they shifted to AI First, the first move was flattening. Middle layers of approval were cut, and instead, cross-functional AI pods of 10–12 people were created. Each pod had direct budget authority, access to AI platforms, and a clear mission: **deliver outcomes in weeks, not months.**

One pod was tasked with redesigning customer onboarding. Instead of waiting for design, compliance, and IT to sequentially weigh in, the pod used AI-driven design tools, automated compliance checks, and generative onboarding flows to build a new experience in **6 weeks.** Previously, this project had been estimated at 9 months.

Another pod focused on fraud detection. With AI anomaly detection embedded directly into their tools, they reduced false positives by **40% in 3 months**, something the legacy compliance department had been chasing for years with twice the staff.

The results across the company were staggering. Product cycle times dropped from an average of **10 months to under 10 weeks.** Customer satisfaction scores jumped 30%. And most importantly, the organization began to run leaner—shedding 20% of redundant middle-management roles without losing productivity. In fact, they gained it.

Leaders noticed another unexpected benefit: **employees were more engaged.** Without layers of approval, talented people could see their work move into production immediately. AI accelerated their output, and the flat structure accelerated their influence. Turnover among top performers dropped, while accountability for underperformance became clearer.

This transformation highlighted the point: flattening isn't just a structural tweak—it's the foundation of an AI First culture. Without middle managers slowing things down, the company could finally move at the speed of AI. And within two years, their market share had doubled—outpacing competitors still stuck in tall hierarchies and slow committees.

Step Five: Move Non-Linearly

Traditional transformation playbooks are built around phases: strategy, design, rollout, training. That playbook will bury you. By the time you finish designing, your competitor will already be eating your lunch.

In the AI First era, **execution must be non-linear.** That means retraining, restructuring, and rebuilding workflows simultaneously. It means building momentum across multiple vectors at once, not waiting for one project to finish before starting another.

Think of it like a blitzkrieg. **You must hit on multiple fronts at the same time.** AI bootcamps. Workflow redesign. New AI pods. Flattening hierarchy. Leadership modeling. It all has to happen together.

The first 30 to 90 days of AI First adoption are critical. This is where you set the tone. If there is visible momentum—real wins, real case studies, real savings—the organization rallies. If there isn't, the deep state will strangle it. Employees will shrug and assume it's another "corporate experiment."

And this is why **speed matters more than elegance**. AI transformation is a momentum game—every early win compounds, reshaping culture and crushing resistance. If you wait for perfect alignment before launching, you're already too late. Every week that passes is a week your competitor can build advantage, learn faster, and widen the gap. Non-linear isn't optional—it's the only way to stay alive in the AI First race.

Non-linear also means being **comfortable with imperfection**. You don't need to get every workflow right on the first try. Iteration is the model. Test. Measure. Improve. Repeat. AI lets you move faster because the cost of testing is lower. Use that to your advantage.

And remember: **this isn't chaos. It's controlled speed**. You need central visibility into all the moving parts, but you **don't need central control.**

Non-linear execution is also the only way to outpace customer expectations. Markets shift weekly now, not yearly, and if you're still waiting for "perfect planning decks," your customers will have already moved on to competitors delivering real AI-enhanced outcomes. Early AI First movers show that companies running multiple initiatives in parallel capture ROI 3–5 times faster than those following old linear models.

This approach also acts as a filter for talent. Employees who thrive on ambiguity and velocity will rise. Those who need rigid roadmaps will struggle. That's exactly what you want: **a self-selection mechanism** that aligns your workforce with AI First DNA.

Case in point: some Fortune 500 firms report that their biggest early AI wins came not from carefully crafted "flagship projects," but from scrappy, fast-moving pilots that solved small problems and built confidence. These quick wins became rallying cries, proving to the skeptics that AI wasn't just hype—it was changing outcomes in real time.

Non-linearity means launching while you're still building. You start training teams before all workflows are mapped. You deploy AI pods before reporting structures are finalized. You test customer-facing AI features while internal teams are still learning how to prompt. That simultaneity is the only way to move at the speed this transformation demands.

Example: A Tale of Two Retailers

Imagine two national retailers, both with 50,000 employees and billions in revenue. Retailer A decides to "get organized" before moving on AI. They spend six months building a strategy deck, **hiring consultants**, running everything through a non-value-add PMO, and mapping every workflow **in theory.** During that same six months, Retailer B launches AI bootcamps for frontline managers, pilots AI in customer support to auto-triage complaints, starts testing AI inventory forecasting in five regions, and deploys AI copilots for their finance analysts—all at the same time.

By month three, Retailer B's AI-driven support function cuts response times by 60% and saves $15 million in labor. By month four, their inventory pilots reduce stock-outs by 25%, improving sales and customer satisfaction. By month five, finance closes the books in three days instead of ten. None of these were "perfect" projects. They were rough, fast, iterative—but real. Employees saw them working, customers felt the improvements, and investors noticed the savings. Momentum snowballed.

Meanwhile, Retailer A finally emerges with a polished "AI strategy" **after half a year**—but morale is flat, skeptics are louder, and their competitor is already boasting case studies at investor day. Retailer A is now behind, and the talent that wants to work in AI First companies begins to defect to Retailer B. Investors punish Retailer A for "talk without traction," while Retailer B's stock price jumps on proof of execution.

The **results by year's end are staggering**. Retailer B posts a 12% growth rate, fueled by faster operations, better customer experiences, and visible AI-driven efficiency. Retailer A limps in at 4% growth, **spending** millions on consultants but showing no measurable wins. Customers switch to Retailer B, because service is faster, inventory is more reliable, and prices are sharper thanks to AI-enabled cost savings.

This is why non-linear execution dominates. Retailer B didn't just move faster—they reset the industry standard. Within twelve months, they positioned themselves as the AI First leader in retail, while Retailer A was stuck defending a status quo that customers no longer valued. The contrast is not incremental—it's existential. By moving on multiple fronts at once, Retailer B didn't just "implement AI"—they seized the market.

Step Six: Drive accountability down to the individual level

AI transformation is more than a departmental initiative—it's a human one. Each employee must be individually accountable for becoming AI First. That means tracking, measuring, and reporting on their AI adoption.

Who is using AI every day? Who is getting better at prompting? Who is finding ways to increase output? Who is creating measurable outcomes? And who isn't?

Those who are falling behind must be supported —intensive training, coaching, and AI bootcamps. But the window is short:. 60 to 120 days. **MAX**. If someone cannot demonstrate AI First behavior by then, **they must be replaced.** That isn't cruelty. That's survival.

Training must be structured and relentless. Employees should go through bootcamps where they learn to prompt, iterate, and apply AI to their workflows. **Think less "seminar" and more "military drill."** Short cycles. Hands-on practice. Immediate feedback. Repeat until mastery.

And accountability must be visible. Dashboards should track adoption and results at the individual level. Leaders must know exactly who is carrying their weight—and who is not.

The difference between an AI First company and a laggard is not abstract—it's in the daily habits of every worker. If 90% of your employees are still working like it's 2019, your competitor will crush you with 10% who work like it's 2026.

This isn't just true for global enterprises. Small and mid-sized businesses (SMBs) live and die on individual performance. For SMBs, accountability has to be even sharper because there are fewer people to hide behind.

Accountability also sends a cultural signal. When employees see that **AI adoption is measured and tied to outcomes,** they know this isn't a "fad project"—it's the company's future. Conversely, when leadership ignores accountability, AI gets treated like an optional tool instead of the new standard.

Even for frontline workers—sales reps, service technicians, call center staff—accountability matters. The question isn't "are they working hard?" but **"are they using AI to work smarter, faster, and better?"** That reframes performance reviews, compensation, and recognition programs.

Example: A 40-Person Electrical Contracting Firm

Take the case of a commercial electrical contractor in Florida with about 40 employees. Historically, their growth had been capped because they simply couldn't bid on enough jobs or manage enough projects without adding headcount. Every estimator was swamped, project managers were juggling spreadsheets manually, and field technicians relied on endless paperwork to track hours, inventory, and safety compliance.

When the firm's owner declared they were moving to AI First, accountability became the centerpiece. They chose **Simpro**, an AI-empowered field service management platform, as the backbone of their transformation. Each estimator was required to run 100% of their bid preparation inside Simpro, where takeoffs, scope notes, and proposal drafts were generated in minutes instead of hours. Project managers were trained to use Simpro's AI scheduling tools that flagged bottlenecks and automated compliance paperwork. Field techs were given AI copilots inside Simpro's mobile workflows that logged hours, tracked materials, and even generated punch lists with voice commands.

The company set a 120-day accountability window: every role would be tracked on an AI adoption dashboard, showing what percentage of their workflow was AI-driven through Simpro. Estimators who still did bids manually were flagged. Project managers who refused to use the AI scheduler were put into retraining. By the end of the 120 days, 95% of the workforce was fully AI First in their day-to-day execution.

The results were staggering. In less than six months, the firm was able to bid on 40% more jobs with the same headcount, win rates rose because their proposals were faster and more professional, and job margins improved by nearly 20% due to better scheduling and fewer errors in the field.

Accountability to AI adoption didn't just modernize their workflows—it literally expanded the size of the company without hiring a single new person. And because all of that extra capacity was captured with no added headcount, the financial impact was dramatic: the business added roughly **$5 million in annual revenue** without a single new hire, which translated into nearly **$1.5 million in additional profit**. That's a 50% jump in bottom-line earnings on the same payroll—a once-unthinkable outcome for a company of this size.

Perhaps the most striking shift was cultural. Employees realized this wasn't "management's shiny new toy." When they saw their own performance reviews and bonuses tied to AI adoption in Simpro, the message was clear: this is the way we work now. The contractor who was once capped at regional growth is now competing head-to-head with firms twice its size—because every single employee is accountable for being AI First.

> **Cooper Call Out:** In SMBs, accountability to AI adoption isn't about metrics—it's about survival. One laggard drags the whole ship, but one AI First employee can pull the company into a new league.

Step Seven: HR as the Tip of the Spear

Accountability doesn't happen on its own. HR must be the spearhead of this shift, and that requires a radical cultural reset inside HR itself. As we discussed in the HR chapter, too many HR departments have spent decades acting as the "mother hens" of the company—focused on keeping peace, managing policies, and protecting underperformers rather than fueling outcomes. That culture is poison in the AI First era.

HR must transform into the anti–deep state immediately. Instead of slowing things down, they must accelerate them. Instead of writing policy manuals, they must measure adoption. Instead of protecting mediocrity, they must identify entrepreneurial, AI-proficient talent and push it forward.

Culturally, this is about flipping the script. HR is no longer the corporate cop—it becomes the AI accelerator. It doesn't matter how good HR is at policies or satisfaction surveys. What matters now is: are they driving accountability for AI adoption at every level? Are they ensuring that every individual is measured, tracked, and supported to become AI First?

If HR gets this right, accountability becomes systemic and self-reinforcing. If HR clings to the old model, the entire AI First initiative will collapse under the weight of the deep state. That's why the cultural change in HR must happen immediately, visibly, and uncompromisingly.

HR must do more than *talk* about change—it must operationalize AI First inside its own house first. That means turning HR itself into an AI First operating unit before it can credibly drive the same shift across the rest of the organization.

The first tactical step: certify every HR employee on AI. Not "awareness training." Not a one-day seminar. Full hands-on, practical certification in prompting, workflow redesign, and AI-enabled recruiting. Every HR generalist, recruiter, and business partner should be able to show they've completed a baseline "AI First HR certification." If HR can't use AI well, they cannot hire or evaluate people who can.

Second: engage with specialized AI jump-start consultancies. There are firms emerging that focus specifically on getting organizations AI First in weeks, not years. HR should be the buyer, not the blocker. They should bring these consultants in to accelerate AI bootcamps, run pilots, and establish scorecards. Smart HR leaders will outsource expertise at the start, then internalize it as capability.

Third: map the entire organization and build an AI scorecard. HR must work with department heads to evaluate:

- How much work is currently being done with AI?
- Where are the biggest productivity bottlenecks?
- Which roles have the highest "AI uplift potential"?
- Who is already excelling at AI usage, and who is resisting?

Every department gets a baseline score. And every quarter, those scores get updated. Just as finance tracks revenue and costs, HR must track AI adoption and competency.

Fourth: revamp the hiring skills matrix. For 50+ years, HR has been conditioned to filter résumés for degrees, credentials, and technical specialization. That matrix is obsolete. Instead, HR must now weight entrepreneurial traits, adaptability, collaboration with AI, and outcome-driven thinking. Interview questions must change from "Tell me about your certifications" to "Show me how you would use AI to solve this problem."

Fifth: embed AI in recruiting workflows. AI can already screen thousands of applications in minutes, surface hidden talent pools, and even simulate candidate responses to job scenarios. HR should not only adopt these tools but design them to filter for *AI First worker attributes.*

Sixth: restructure performance management. Old systems measured effort, tenure, and process compliance. The AI First system measures outcomes, AI adoption, and continuous improvement. HR must install performance scorecards that reflect this reality—and tie bonuses and promotions directly to AI First behavior.

Seventh: create internal AI bootcamps for the workforce. HR must partner with business units to design programs where employees practice prompting, workflow redesign, and AI-enabled problem-solving. These should be mandatory, hands-on, and frequent. Think hackathons, not lectures.

Eighth: partner with finance and the C-suite to realign incentives. HR must ensure compensation plans and bonus structures are redesigned so leaders are rewarded for transformation, not for headcount growth or maintaining the old way of working. If leaders are paid for size, they will resist AI. If they're paid for outcomes, they'll embrace it.

Ninth: address retention through AI literacy. Worker concentration risk means each employee is exponentially more valuable. HR must ensure the best talent not only stays but keeps getting better. That means personalized development plans, AI-driven learning platforms, and clear career trajectories in the AI First world.

Tenth: build partnerships with vendors who are AI First. HR must evaluate its own stack of HR tech—ATS, payroll, performance management, L&D—and ensure every system is infused with strong AI. If the tools HR itself runs on are not AI First, the department will become the bottleneck for the entire company.

Finally, HR must stop being reactive and become the AI transformation engine. That means:

- Owning the scorecarding of every department's AI adoption.
- Driving cultural alignment around AI First principles.
- Replacing deep state blockers quickly.
- Becoming the board's primary reporting function for AI adoption progress.

This isn't incremental. It's existential. HR must reinvent itself as both an AI First operator and the architect of an AI First workforce. Done right, it will be the most powerful function in the company. Done wrong, it will be the anchor that sinks the ship.

Summary

This chapter is the field manual, not a pep talk. It takes you from "AI is important" to "here's exactly how to flip your company into AI First before your competitor turns you into a case study." The core message: this is not a tool rollout; it's a new operating system. You either install it across leadership, structure, workflows, and culture—or you get installed as someone else's cautionary tale. **Speed decides the winner.**

First principle: AI First is not optional. It's binary—**AI First or AI Finished.** The cost curve, cycle times, and customer experience gap are compounding every week. Early adopters don't just get ahead; they take it all. If you're waiting for perfect plans, you're already donating market share.

Step one is leadership commitment that's loud, visible, and personal. The CEO doesn't "sponsor" AI; the **CEO becomes the Chief AI Operator.** Budgets shift, incentives flip, and every other initiative gets subordinated to this one. No ambiguity, no split focus, no middle-manager sandbagging.

Lead from the front—literally.

Next, baseline ruthlessly. **You cannot manage what you won't measure.** Create an AI utilization score by department, team, and individual. Track not just "access to tools," but outcomes: hours saved, throughput gained, error rates reduced. Make the dashboards unavoidable.

Then fix your software and tools operating stack to AI First vendors. Vendor selection and curation needs to be done now. Over 75% of your workflows ride on third-party software; if those platforms aren't AI-native, you can't be either. Audit everything. Score red/yellow/green. Replace anchors with AI First platforms. The software you choose is the company you become.

Flatten the org. Bureaucracy kills velocity. Build small, cross-functional AI pods with budget authority and outcome SLAs. Leaders stop gatekeeping and start path-clearing. Flat beats tall. Fast beats big. One 10-person AI pod should replace a 100-person legacy department's output—then replicate, not ossify.

Move non-linearly. No more "phase 1, phase 2." Launch training, pod pilots, workflow redesign, and leadership modeling simultaneously. Ship rough, learn fast, iterate weekly. Momentum is the moat. Quick wins crush skepticism, attract talent, and unlock budget. Sequential is suicide; parallel is survival.

Drive accountability to the person. Every employee gets an AI score and a 90–150-day window to level up. Bootcamps, coaching, drills. If it sticks—promote. If it doesn't—replace. That's not heartless – it's surgery to save the patient. In lean AI First orgs, worker concentration risk is real one naysayer can sink the ship.

Ensure that HR can become the tip of the spear, not the hall monitor. Certify every HR pro on AI. Rewrite the hiring matrix for entrepreneurial, outcome-driven talent. Implement AI scorecards, tie comp to AI adoption and results, and stand-up relentless training. HR must be AI First internally before it can credibly demand it from everyone else.

This is **extreme change management in action**. Over-communicate the why. Model the how. Remove blockers fast. Celebrate evidence, not theater. Make "done inside AI" the default, not the exception. Repeat it daily until the muscle memory sticks.

Here is the cadence, distilled: **Commit. Demonstrate. Baseline. Replace. Flatten. Parallelize. Measure. Promote. Remove. Repeat.** That loop is your engine. Run it hard for 90–150 days and the flywheel takes over. And remember, AI First **never stops**. There is no end game. It is a process of continuous innovation.

Here's the payoff: lower costs, faster cycles, sharper pricing, better experiences, and a talent magnet effect—compounding quarter after quarter. Here's the risk: hesitation that turns your healthy business into someone else's acquisition.

Final word: This chapter doesn't hand you a plan—it hands you ignition. Light it now. Adapt it for what will work within your organization. Your people. Your culture. In the AI First era, the team that moves first writes the rules, sets the prices, and owns the market. Everyone else writes the postmortem.

Chapter 11:

The Shock Wave – The Coming Short-Term Disruption

AI is not just another business tool—it's the tectonic plate shifting beneath civilization. We've seen disruption before. We've seen empires rise and fall because of coinage, navigation, electricity, and the internet. But AI is different in one fundamental way: its unique mix of **Speed** and **Power.** The AI First disruption will shake our entire society to its core. Not only business, but every aspect of society. This rapid change will cause panic, disruption, change and fear on a scale never seen before. The potential for considerable suffering and damage is very high. Navigating this transformation is critical not only for the survival of the organizations that you work in, but the entire society that we all live in.

The transformation to an AI First society will occur in three distinct phases. In this chapter, we will start with the first phase, which will last approximately 3 years. This first phase will be the **most challenging for society**; in which shock waves reverberate around the world.

For the first time in history, **every** function of human organization—business, education, government, agriculture, conflict, everything—is being transformed at the same time. No prior revolution touched _every sector_ this quickly. **AI does impact them all,** and does so **1000 times faster** than anything humanity has experienced prior. Farmers, lawyers, engineers, architects, teachers, factory workers, and CEOs all feel the tremor at once. The implication is simple: this is not a revolution that the world can manage quietly. It is a **civilizational reset.**

This means that there are two simultaneous realities: **massive disruption and massive opportunity**. Productivity gains of 75%, 100%, even 200% **per year** are destabilizing job markets, educational infrastructure, geopolitical power alignment, profit structures, and entire industries. At the same time, those gains fuel new business models, new levels of abundance for the winners, and entirely new standards of living.

This is what business leaders, governments, and workers need to internalize: **There is no time to adjust slowly.** What feels stable today can be obsolete within 90 days. The AI wave does not arrive politely: It crashes like a tsunami.

The central question is not whether AI will change everything. That is already settled. The question is which organizations, societies, and individuals can keep pace without collapsing under the weight of their own inertia. The new AI First world will be composed of the those who set the pace and succeeded in their AI First journey.

Let's look at how the organizations that make up our society will change in the short, medium, and long terms, and how these changes will impact our society.

Short-Term Future (0-3 years): The Shock Phase In the immediate short term, the AI First transformation will feel like massive **whiplash.** Shock and fear will set in. Many people and organizational leaders simply won't understand the signs and what is happening. It is a period when those who are AI First in their understanding and mindset will have absolute **competitive advantage** over those who do not.

Companies and organizations that embrace AI aggressively see their profitability skyrocket as their labor costs drop substantially relative to their revenue production. We see near instant panic over job security setting in among white-collar workers of all functions. Product cycles shrink from quarters and years to **weeks.** Innovation in most industries accelerates significantly. Stock markets reward AI First companies instantly, as their profitability hits levels never before seen.

White-collar unemployment rises sharply and in shockingly disproportionate ways never seen before. These reductions happen at **all** companies, in large volumes, impacting primarily the highly skilled white-collar population that just 2 years ago felt they had the most job security. This happens all while companies are posting **record profits**.

Reports suggest that by 2026, **20–33% of roles in clerical, support, IT, legal, and back-office functions may be eliminated**. This level of dislocation has no precedent in modern economies. Unlike prior transformations, when new industries slowly absorbed displaced workers, AI moves too fast. By the time retraining programs are designed, another wave of jobs has already evaporated.

In the first 12-24 months, experts expect that 20%+ of HR jobs, 15% of finance roles, 20–25% of customer service jobs, and 21% of legal support work **will vanish**.

The experience inside organizations will feel almost surreal. Departments once buzzing with activity suddenly go quiet as AI systems rapidly transition and handle the bulk of tasks. Employees who were once central to the daily rhythm of business find themselves waiting for work, then eliminated altogether. **Meeting-heavy cultures collapse** because AI drafts agendas, takes notes, and produces action items instantly. Entire swaths of corporate bureaucracy vanish almost overnight. The **Deep State players panic** and try to slow down progress unsuccessfully in the AI First companies.

Culturally, this short-term disruption reshuffles social identity. People who built their lives around professional prestige now face a sudden loss of status. The lawyer whose contracts are reviewed faster by AI, the consultant whose PowerPoint deck is replicated in minutes, the financial analyst who is supplanted by an AI dashboard—all struggle with the shock of becoming irrelevant.

Families start to talk differently about work. Parents who once proudly said their child was "going into consulting" now question the longevity of that path. Dinner table conversations shift: "Is your son learning AI?" replaces "Which firm did he join?" The cultural symbols of success are already changing.

Young professionals—those in their first decade of work—panic more intensely than any other group. They are just starting families, weighed down by student debt that suddenly carries a brutally limited ROI in an AI First world. What was once a "safe bet" on higher education now feels like a trap, leaving them both financially burdened and professionally displaced. Many have just poured their limited savings into a first-time home purchase, only to find themselves locked into a massive liability with shrinking career prospects. Their anxiety about stability, identity, and belonging in society snowballs at breathtaking speed, creating a generational panic without precedent.

For many, this isn't just about money—it's about the **collapse of a promise**. They entered adulthood believing that education, home ownership, and hard work would guarantee upward mobility. Instead, they face the shock of industries evaporating just as they were stepping into them.

New parents in particular feel crushed under the weight of pressures they already struggle with—sleepless nights, fragile relationships, and financial responsibility—only now compounded by systemic uncertainty about their careers and future. The result is not just financial strain but deep emotional stress that destabilizes marriages, family dynamics, and community networks.

What was once considered the natural cycle of life—college, career, home, family—now **feels like quicksand**. The very milestones that should bring pride and stability instead bring heightened vulnerability and fear. This generation finds itself disillusioned and restless, suffering not only from economic insecurity but also from a profound crisis of identity and status.

Micro Case Study: The Collapse of Stability for First-Time Buyers

Consider Jason, a 29-year-old software developer, and his wife, Maria, a nurse. Just twelve months ago, they proudly bought their first home in a suburban neighborhood, pouring every dollar of savings into the down payment. They also welcomed their first child, believing they were stepping into a stable, upward trajectory. But within months, Jason's role was eliminated when his company shifted aggressively to AI First engineering, and Maria's hospital introduced AI diagnostic tools that cut back her hours. Their mortgage looms large, their student debt remains unforgiven, and daycare costs exceed $2,000 a month. The very symbols of "making it"—the house, the degree, the career—now feel like chains. Their story is replicated across thousands of households, showing how the disruption hits not the reckless, but those who did everything society told them was right.

Yet thru all this, **AI First companies' profits soar to almost unimaginable levels.** Picture a company that once earned $100 million on $500 million of revenue. With AI cutting labor costs in half and doubling output, the same revenue now produces $200 million in profit. Doubling profit in just one year. Analysts call it **"the AI dividend."** Investors call it inevitable. Workers call it terrifying.

In this period, **Super Companies** begin to emerge. A handful of AI-Infrastructure giants' growth rates are astronomical, with no end in sight. Markets reward this growth with previously unimaginable valuations. Several will approach or even exceed **$15-20 trillion** – a level never imagined previously for a company. These AI Infrastructure winners will impact global commerce in ways that commercial organizations have never seen, these megaliths' power and influence exceeding many of the nations on earth.

In these first years, the divide between AI First companies and laggards widens into a canyon. **SMBs that leap immediately embrace an AI–First strategy suddenly find themselves competing** toe-to-toe with large enterprises. A 40-person electrical contractor that adopts AI First software and workflows can bid on 40% more jobs and deliver them with higher margins, while a competitor with twice the staff loses ground, and perhaps folds. Those slow to adopt AI First cannot afford to keep their highly trained employees. These staff members need job security, so they leave for the AI First competitor who continues to grow and take market share.

For large corporations, the results are even more staggering. Whole departments of internal consultants, analysts, and coordinators—**tens of thousands of jobs**—are revealed as redundant almost overnight. The deep state of corporate bureaucracy— project management operations (PMOs), "centers of excellence," management consultants, and bloated middle managers—**faces extinction because** they are too far from delivering rapid value in AI Pods. Those who survive do so only by visibly adding entrepreneurial value and adjusting to the new normal. The rest find themselves unemployable because other firms don't want to **import dead weight**.

Companies that once prided themselves on "bench strength" suddenly recognize they were paying armies of people to push paper that AI now handles in seconds.

Governments face pressure almost **immediately** and respond clumsily. Laid-off professionals flood job markets. Calls for **retraining programs spike**. Political candidates weaponize the fear, claiming that AI is destroying the middle class. Some nations accelerate tax credits for retraining. Others experiment with wage subsidies. But the mismatch is brutal: a 45-year-old compliance officer cannot become a plumber overnight, and even if he does, the **prestige hit** devastates the social order, particularly in the white-collar middle and upper middle class.

Calls for Universal Base Income (UBI) mount. Politicians float policies like corporate AI levies or "**AI profit redistribution**" taxes, but corporations argue that slowing adoption means losing global competitiveness.

Despite these societal disruptions, no nation dares slow AI adoption. The global race is too fierce. Slow-walk AI, and you hand the crown to other nations or organizations that are sprinting forward. Regulators may threaten restrictions, but leaders know: Regulating AI

First adoption is a death sentence. Nations that try will watch industries migrate abroad as the standard of living for their citizens starts to suffer from inflation.

Global Conflict Changes

AI begins to reshape how global conflicts are prevented and (unfortunately) fought. AI enhances logistics, battlefield simulations, drone coordination, and cyber-defense. Nations test AI-assisted targeting systems, and smaller militaries start adopting AI tools to multiply force.

Cyberattacks rise in frequency and speed as AI probes for vulnerabilities and exploits them faster than humans can patch them. Police departments begin experimenting with AI crime prediction and real-time video analysis, sparking both efficiency and controversy, as civil-liberties watchdogs worry about surveillance overreach.

AI introduces a chilling new paradigm in global conflict: the rise of "mini-wars" fought not with massive troop deployments, but through drones, cyber offensives, and autonomous, non-human weapons systems. Instead of tanks and missiles, nations increasingly target each other's infrastructure—power grids, data centers, satellite constellations, and AI processing hubs.

What makes this shift so dangerous is perception. Historically, the horror of war has been measured by human casualties. A bombing raid that destroyed factories was tragic, but acceptable in the brutal calculus of geopolitics if civilian loss of life was limited. In the AI era, however, attacks that produce few or no human casualties will be seen as more "tolerable" by governments and the public—**yet their consequences may be vastly more destructive.** Conflict will become more tolerated, frequent, and justified by nation states.

Consider the difference: In 2021, dropping a bomb on a rival's power plant or launching a cyberattack might disrupt operations for weeks. Painful, costly, but repairable. In 2026, that same action could cripple 25% of a nation's AI capacity—**paralyzing its economic output,** freezing supply chains, and grinding digital infrastructure to a halt. This is not just disruption: it is systemic incapacitation.

The terrifying reality is that such strikes are comparatively easy to execute. Knocking out a server farm, severing a fiber backbone, or crippling GPU clusters with cyber-exploit requires far fewer resources than fielding an army. That is the essence of asymmetry: small actors, even quasi-state groups or rogue regimes, suddenly gain the ability to inflict disproportionate damage on global powers.

This dynamic will upend geopolitics. Nations that once relied on sheer size, industrial capacity, or nuclear deterrence will find themselves vulnerable to adversaries who can undermine them with keystrokes or drone swarms. **Global power balances may shift overnight.**

The response will be predictable: **defense spending will skyrocket.** Just as nations scrambled to build cyber commands and cyber-defense budgets 15 years ago, they will now pour unprecedented resources into AI defense. But this time, the escalation will be faster and larger. Protecting AI infrastructure and capability will become the number one priority in defense strategy.

Resource-rich nations—those with energy reserves, semiconductor fabrication capabilities, or advanced aerospace expertise—will double down, pouring billions into defending the "arteries" of AI-powered economies. Expect to see **new military branches dedicated to AI defense,** alliances forged around digital infrastructure protection, and even the emergence of "AI defense treaties" modeled on NATO's collective security principle.

The race will not stop there. Space will be militarized even further, as satellite networks critical to AI communications become high-value targets. Nations will deploy orbital defenses, harden undersea cables, and treat GPU supply chains with the same strategic importance once reserved for oil.

The AI First battlefield will be defined by who can keep their AI infrastructure online while crippling their adversary's capabilities. And in this new reality, the cost of failure is measured not only in lost lives, but in lost economic capacity and global relevance.

Cooper Call out: In the AI era, wars may produce fewer casualties—but their destruction will cut deeper, striking at the nervous system of nations.

Biggest Risk: Social Unrest at Global Scale

This short-term phase is the most **socially volatile and dangerous** moment of the AI First era for society. The gap between soaring corporate profits and rising unemployment creates the perfect tinderbox for **near universal social unrest**. As history repeatedly shows—from the bread riots of the French Revolution to the youth unemployment that fueled the Arab Spring—economic dislocation, both commercially and emotionally, ignites instability at frightening speed. And in this case, the dislocated are not only large in number but also highly educated, wealthy, and convinced that they were entitled to a better life. That combination makes the unrest sharper, more organized, and far more dangerous to political and social stability.

The psychology of the displaced white-collar worker matters. To a Harvard MBA, a mid-career lawyer, or a data analyst, losing a job to AI feels fundamentally **different**. These individuals invested years of education and hundreds of thousands of dollars into careers they believed were safe. They feel not just economic loss, but a moral injustice—that the system betrayed them.

History shows that when the **most educated classes** face downward mobility, they often lead revolts. They have the organizational skills, political networks, capital, and confidence to challenge authority in ways that underemployed or impoverished groups cannot. From the French Revolution, where educated lawyers, merchants, and mid-level professionals helped ignite revolt against the monarchy, to the American

Revolution led by wealthy and upper middle class leaders of society, to the Arab Spring, where large numbers of unemployed university graduates mobilized protests that toppled governments, the pattern is clear. These groups feel more than economic pain; they also harbor a **deep sense of betrayal.** They were promised stability, prosperity, and influence --- and suddenly they find themselves stripped of the fruits of those promises.

The first groups to be hollowed out by AI disruption are **not** the low-wage service workers, but the educated professional classes—the software engineers, analysts, consultants, lawyers, and managers who believed their degrees and career tracks made them safe. And special

When their skills are automated away, it's not only their income that vanishes, but also their sense of identity and self-worth. They don't just lose a paycheck—**they lose prestige,** relevance, and their place in society's hierarchy.

This class is also the most influential. Most of society's assets—stocks, retirement funds, real estate—are in their hands. Their political connections are second to none, built through donor networks, alma mater ties, and professional associations. They represent and manage local communities, churches, and non-profits. They lead PTAs, sit on boards, and drive civic activity. When unemployment strikes, the psychological impact is devastating: people long accustomed to power and influence find it **ripped away in an instant.** What took decades, and often generations to build is gone in a matter of weeks or months. The realization that there is little hope of returning to their previous status makes the blow even more devastating.

We've seen this movie before. In Russia in 1917, the professional classes—the so-called "intelligentsia"—were central to the early revolutionary movements, driven not only by hunger but by their exclusion from decision-making. In Weimar Germany during the 1920s and 30s, downwardly mobile professionals and educated elites who felt betrayed by economic collapse became some of the most aggressive backers of radical movements.

Now apply that lesson to the AI First upheaval. Imagine a 35-year-old software developer with a master's degree who suddenly finds his job replaced by AI. Their $180,000 salary is gone. He's competing with high school graduates for $25/hour service jobs he is not trained for and doesn't want. He is saddled with student debt and, in many cases, a mortgage and young children. The financial blow is devastating—but the psychological blow is worse. **People like this feel humiliated**, their status evaporates, and they perceive that **the system they bought into has failed them.**

These are precisely the people who will have both the motivation and the capability to organize, lobby, and revolt. They know how to use the tools of power. They know the donors, the journalists, and the politicians. They sit at the center of society's networks, not at its margins. And now, stripped of their professional identities, they have nothing to lose but their diminished status. When they feel disenfranchised, the system is shaken at its core.

Cooper Callout: Revolutions don't begin when the poor have nothing left—they begin when the comfortable realize they have been lied to, and they have the means, influence, and fury to fight back.

Within the first 12 months of widespread AI adoption, the signs of this social unrest will begin to emerge. At first, there will be **ridicule and denial**: laid-off consultants and lawyers mocked on social media for complaining while tradespeople and gig workers "still grind it out." But this laughter will turn quickly. Once professionals across multiple sectors—finance, HR, law, marketing—realize there is no comparable alternative employment, frustration will give way to anger.

These displaced workers cannot simply "downshift" into lower skilled jobs. Not only are those roles paid far less—often 50–70% less—but many AI-disrupted workers are now competing directly with high school graduates and foreign nationals (immigrants), for what limited roles remain. And because they **lack the practical skills for these positions,** they often lose out to candidates with more relevant hands-on experience.

The humiliation compounds the rage. A mid-level HR professional with a master's degree applying for an entry-level retail job, or even an entry level HR job, and being turned away is not just financially troubling for the individual—it sparks a **profound identity crisis**. When multiplied across **tens of millions of people**, that crisis can easily metastasize into social instability. What begins as quiet frustration in online forums quickly becomes organized protests, rallies, and ultimately political movements. Governments will be caught flat-footed, forced to respond with piecemeal retraining programs, wage subsidies, or even emergency welfare expansions. Yet these solutions will not match the **speed or scale of the dislocation.**

Imagine protests outside shuttered consulting firm offices in New York, London, or Frankfurt, with thousands of unemployed professionals demanding government intervention. Or strikes not from factory workers, but from recently unemployed financial analysts and paralegals blocking city streets to demand AI regulation. These scenarios, unthinkable just a few years ago, are likely to become reality shortly after large-scale corporate AI layoffs.

Consumer Confidence Plunges

In the middle of this first phase, another critical indicator starts flashing red: **consumer confidence** among the educated middle and upper-middle classes plunges to **historic lows.** This is profoundly challenging for society as these are the households that traditionally drive consumer discretionary spending—vacations, new cars, home improvements, and dining out.

Naturally, as white-collar layoffs accelerate and uncertainty spreads, this consumer segment pulls back sharply and **significantly retail** sales reports show declines in categories long considered recession-proof, like luxury goods, travel, and private education. By some measures, household spending among the top 30% of earners could contract by 25% within 18 months.

The paradox is striking. Corporate profits accelerate to record highs because operating costs collapse—AI replaces labor, shrinks waste, and drives margin expansion. Earnings per share climb, but revenue growth begins to feel pressure as consumer demand weakens. Investors celebrate profitability but quietly note that the top line is under pressure. Analysts warn of a "K-shaped economy" where companies thrive financially even as their best customers retrench. **The tension is unsustainable**: if consumer confidence among educated professionals continues to erode, it risks dragging down broader demand, creating ripple effects even for AI First winners.

The irony is that initially, many **unaffected** workers will dismiss the problem. A software engineer might dismiss his risk compared to an unemployed consultant,. But as AI accelerates, the wave engulfs them too. By the end of the first several years, the realization spreads: **Nowhere is safe**. Entire industries are being hollowed out, and no amount of credentialing, pedigree, or past success guarantees relevance in the AI First labor market.

This is why the short-term disruption is so dangerous. It doesn't just strip people of income; **it strips them of identity, pride and hope for the future**. It attacks the very people society thought were immune to decline—those with degrees, prestigious jobs, and social standing. That sense of betrayal makes them far more likely to organize, revolt, and demand systemic change. The world has seen food riots and youth uprisings. What happens when it is the former ruling class, the MBAs and lawyers and consultants, who are the ones rioting? That is the social powder keg of the AI First era.

Government Response Around the World

Governments are not ready for this scenario. They have not game-theorized the social disruption unleashed by AI, and the economic models they rely on to guide policy responses are breaking down. Traditional labor models assumed that unemployment spikes are not this rapid nor deep, and they hit low-income workers first, leaving elites and the professional classes relatively insulated. The situation modeled protects tax revenues and buys governments time to find solutions through various social and unemployment schemes.

But the AI First transition is the opposite. Unemployment surges among the highest-income, **highest tax-paying,** best-educated citizens—the software engineers, accountants, consultants, designers, and analysts whose jobs can be digitized instantly. These are not only the most connected workers in society, but also the friends, neighbors, and donors of the political class. The pressure on politicians becomes unbearable, as their donor base demands solutions that simply do not exist in the short term.

The mismatch is brutal. For decades, the policy response to technological disruption was to slow it down—regulate, stall, or cushion the transition until retraining and reallocation could take place. This time, **slowing down is not an option**. To fall behind in the AI First race is to lose permanently, both economically and geopolitically. Governments know this, which makes the political situation uniquely combustible: they cannot stop the disruption, even as the disruption ignites unrest among their most powerful constituencies.

As white-collar workers scramble for alternatives, they quickly discover there are none. The jobs they once held **are gone forever**, erased by AI productivity gains. What remains are lower skilled positions in other industries. A product manager once earning $150,000 a year may now face employment opportunities as a junior product manager at $75,000 a year (if he is lucky) or even more extreme $15-25 an hour as a barista, house cleaner, or warehouse worker. Even if retraining programs exist, they do little to bridge the yawning income gap. To stabilize society, these new jobs would have to provide at least 40–60% of previous earnings— otherwise the loss of income, dignity, and security will be too great to bear.

Government Fiscal Squeeze

The AI First disruption begins with the middle- and upper-middle class—the very groups who make up the **backbone of income tax receipts**. According to IRS data, the top 25% of earners account for nearly 90% of all federal income tax collected, while the top 10% alone contribute about 70%. These are the lawyers, analysts, engineers, consultants, and managers whose jobs are first in line for AI-driven automation. When millions of them are displaced in a matter of months—not decades—the **shockwave will ripple directly into federal, state, and local budgets.**

Income tax revenues will fall sharply just as calls for government intervention, retraining programs, and social safety nets explode. This creates a unique and destabilizing paradox: governments are being asked to do more with less, at a scale and speed unseen in modern history. Unlike past downturns, which unfolded gradually, the **AI First shift compresses fiscal disruption into quarters.** That means taxation frameworks and budget allocations will have to be realigned almost immediately, forcing governments to rethink operations in ways they have never had to before.

Consider the local level. Property tax receipts will fall as unemployed professionals default on mortgages, and sales tax revenues will shrink as consumer confidence collapses among high earners. Cities with large concentrations of white-collar workers—think New York, San Francisco, Washington D.C., and Boston—will feel the pain first and hardest. State governments that rely heavily on personal income taxes, like California and New York (where the top 1% already provide nearly 40% of all state tax revenue), **will suddenly be staring at deficits that make the 2008 crisis look tame.**

Federal deficits will balloon in parallel with states and cities. Even if corporate profits soar due to AI productivity gains, the tax structures in place are **not designed to capture enough of that surge quickly.** As governments push to increase corporate tax rates, corporations will threaten to shift their operations abroad—just as in earlier globalization eras. The fiscal reckoning will be swift and unavoidable.

Meanwhile, the political pressure will be suffocating. The displaced are not powerless—as stated earlier, they are the donor class, the educated class, the ones with media access and political connections. They will demand relief, subsidies, income guarantees, and retraining investments. But unlike low-income groups in past downturns, these displaced workers represent the majority of the nation's tax base, so their pain translates directly into government paralysis.

History gives us a preview of how governments respond when their fiscal models collapse. In World War I, the U.S. federal government introduced the modern income tax system in 1913 and then rapidly expanded it to fund wartime expenditures, raising rates **from 7% to more than 70% for top earners in less than a decade.** In World War II, governments across the world invented payroll withholding and mass taxation virtually overnight to fund the war effort. Entire fiscal systems were rebuilt in two or three years because the alternative was collapse. The AI First era will create the same kind of urgency, except this time the "enemy" is technological disruption, not a foreign military.

Within the first 36 months of the AI First era, we will likely see emergency fiscal measures: temporary tax holidays for corporations to keep them at home, deficit-funded relief programs to calm displaced professionals, and ad hoc transfers to states in crisis. **But these are stopgaps, not solutions.** Realignment will require structural changes—corporate tax increases, or entirely new mechanisms like AI productivity levies. Governments will have to capture value from where it now resides—in super-profitable AI First corporations—because individual income taxes will no longer provide the stability they once did.

The scale and speed of this tax disruption cannot be overstated. Just as World War I and II forced fiscal revolutions that permanently reshaped how governments funded themselves, the AI First disruption will force an equally radical reset—one driven not by bombs, but by algorithms. Governments that fail to adapt quickly will see social instability intensify, because when the tax base collapses just as demands for spending surge, the crisis is not only economic— it threatens the foundation of governance itself.

New and Radical Ideas

Early on, radical ideas will surface. Ideas that some will love, some will hate, but all ideas will be on the table, as governments focus on **preserving social stability at all costs.**

Some governments will flirt with universal basic income, others with massive increases in corporate taxes or emergency retraining subsidies. Proposals that would have been unthinkable just years earlier will gain traction, driven not by ideology but by necessity. But none of these proposals will change the hard truth: **the old jobs are gone.**

This reset will drive the next major transformation; the re-emergence and revaluation of low and medium skilled workers through a **new concept of unionization of workers**. Not the cross-industry unions of the past, but **new AI-era unions** embedded within companies and organizations themselves, leveraging collective bargaining and political influence to reshape the balance of labor and capital to a **true** collaborative incentive, aligning structure for the sole objective of social stability. This is not the classic "Management vs. Labor" or "us vs. them" union, but rather a "we". This revolution will demand new legal frameworks, new social perceptions, and entirely new social contracts.

A New Kind of Union for the AI First Era

As we move through the first phase of AI First disruption, governments, corporations, and citizens will all face the same unavoidable question: **how do we stabilize society** when millions of high-paying white-collar jobs evaporate almost overnight? How do we provide high or high enough paying jobs, with meaningful social value to the *__tens of millions__* of displaced white-collar workers?

Until this point in history, the dominant assumption in any major business transformation has been that displaced **workers would simply "reskill"** or "move into new industries." History is filled with examples of this. While painful, society eventually adjusted and the reskilling and "re-industrying" worked. However, as we will see, with AI it is different.

In the Industrial Revolution, the first century of factory work was brutal. —workers were exploited to extremes, forced into unsafe conditions, with starvation wages and no protections. Labor unions arose not because workers **wanted** them, but because workers' **survival demanded** them.

Over time, those unions became extraordinarily powerful. In many industries, they secured essential rights: the weekend, overtime pay, pensions, workplace safety standards. But then, in many countries, the **pendulum swung too far** in the other direction. Union demands became so expensive that companies with domestic unionized workforces could no longer compete globally. American and European manufacturers shifted production to low-cost countries, fueling decades of globalization and hollowing out middle-class industrial jobs.

Now, for the first time in history, we face a scenario where **both sides— companies and workers—need unions equally**. Workers need them to protect wages and dignity in a world where AI has erased much of the white-collar ladder. But companies need them too. Without unions ensuring wage floors and bargaining power for labor, there is no stable consumer base left to purchase the products and services these hyper-efficient AI First organizations will generate.

This period will mark the rebirth of unions as not as defenders of workers, but as pillars of macroeconomic stability. **True incentive alignment between the organization and its labor is the reality in the AI First World.** Unions and companies **together** with government support will agree to push for radically higher wages in sectors historically considered "low skill." Agricultural workers making $50 an hour, hotel service workers earning $62 an hour, and lifeguards being paid $55 an hour will no longer be outliers—they will be the backbone of the new middle class. These are not symbolic raises; they are survival raises---very good strong middle and upper middle-class wages. This is all possible because as AI automates accounting, legal, drafting, software engineering, and dozens of other high-paying professions, the economy must rebalance by elevating the pay of manual and service roles.

The effect will be transformative. **Jobs that today carry little prestige will become desirable careers.** The social map of "good" versus "bad" jobs will be rewritten. For decades, white-collar work was viewed as the pinnacle of economic achievement. In the AI First economy, dignity and financial stability may flow instead from unionized, service-driven roles that cannot be automated away. This is not to say that the AI First white collar worker is not the most desired career path. Rather due to the massive displacement that will be taking place, reality on the ground will force new self-perceptions.

This transition will also alter politics. Both major parties in the United States—and governments across the world—will support unions, not just grudgingly but proactively, as will the organizations that employ them. Why? Because they will recognize unions as a stabilizing force, ensuring that displaced white-collar workers do not fall into poverty, radicalize, and destabilize society itself. **Higher wages will keep consumer spending alive** at a time when corporate profits are soaring, but payrolls are shrinking.

Cooper Callout: AI makes companies richer than ever, yet it forces those same companies to rely on new AI First unions to ensure there are still customers left to buy their products.

AI First unions will also look different than their predecessors. This will be the first time in history where unions are perceived as **vital mechanisms for economic balance**—ensuring that society can handle the redistribution shock caused by AI. This shift will lay the foundation for the second and third phases of the AI First economy: one where service roles become the new middle class, where consumers retain purchasing power, and where political stability is maintained by raising the floor of wages for millions of workers.

Education in the AI First Era: Learning How to Learn

Education will be one of the most profoundly disrupted industries in the AI First era. For centuries, the model was largely fixed: four-year universities for the elite, later democratized to the masses, with careers built on static degrees. **That model is collapsing.** The defining skill of the future will not be memorization of facts or even mastery of narrow disciplines—it will be the ability to **learn how to learn**, adaptively, continuously, and in partnership with AI.

Traditional four-year universities will face massive structural pressure. Enrollment in U.S. colleges has already dropped by 15% since 2010, and analysts projected that even Pre AI impact that more than 500 colleges could close by 2030 due to declining ROI and demographic shifts. With AI automating knowledge retrieval and technical execution, the idea of spending $200,000+ **and four years** to prepare for a career will be seen as antiquated. Students and families will increasingly demand shorter, cheaper, more targeted learning pathways with measurable job outcomes.

In place of traditional models, **trade schools and company-sponsored skill academies** will emerge as dominant forces. Some within universities, and some standalone. **Corporations of all sizes (including SMBs),** recognizing the need for workers trained specifically in AI First skill sets, will sponsor their own credential programs. Imagine a major contractor running a three-month HVAC and electrical automation academy, or a global bank offering six-week AI-driven finance bootcamps. These programs will not just fill immediate hiring pipelines—they will reshape the entire notion of postsecondary education.

Liberal arts education will survive, but in a transformed way. Philosophy, history, literature, and ethics will still matter—perhaps more than ever in an AI First world—but much of this instruction will move online, part-time, and bundled into broader career-preparation tracks. Instead of 18-year-olds leaving home for four years of residential learning, many will weave in and out of liberal arts coursework across their careers, combining intellectual grounding with agile skill bursts.

The **costs of higher education** will face relentless downward pressure. Universities that survive will be those that reinvent themselves: **modular programs**, AI First research hubs, and partnerships with employers to guarantee work placement. Those that fail to adapt will shutter. Already, in 2023–24, we have seen small private colleges like Cabrini University and Alliance University announce **closures due to unsustainable finances.** By 2030, hundreds—possibly thousands—more will follow, unable to justify their tuition against job market realities.

Faculty roles will also shift. Professors in high-demand, job-linked fields—AI engineering, healthcare, energy systems—will command strong salaries. But non-vocational faculty in traditional liberal arts disciplines will see compensation fall as delivery moves online and demand shrinks. The prestige of research universities will persist, but only if they become **AI First research institutions**, embedding AI into everything from lab experiments to grant writing to global collaborations. Universities that fail to harness AI in research will quickly become irrelevant.

The student experience itself will be unrecognizable. Education will no longer be structured into rigid four-year degrees and 15-week semesters. Instead, degree timelines will shrink dramatically. We will see a surge in **two-year community colleges**, **six-week to six-month micro-academies**, and **stacked credential programs** designed for speed and direct applicability. These shorter, focused pathways will carry just as much value as the traditional four-year model.

Today, there's still a certain mystique around a four-year degree—a cultural signal of prestige, commitment, and completeness. But in the AI First era, that mystique disappears. **Four years is simply too long**. The world can change two, three or four times in that span. By the time a student graduates under the old model, half of what they learned in year one could already be obsolete. Employers, parents, and students alike will no longer see that as an investment—they'll see it as wasted time.

Instead, education will be **interwoven with work** in agile, ongoing bursts. Professionals will return to school—not in semesters, but in **13-month sprints** of concentrated, high-value learning, integrated directly with their careers. A future software developer might start with a single semester of coding basics, then pivot immediately to AI-assisted programming platforms. From there, they'll return for one-month increments to master new frameworks as technology evolves. A healthcare worker may spend three months learning AI diagnostics, then return a year later for an advanced robotics course. A logistics manager could take a two-month sprint on AI supply chain modeling, apply it in their job the next day, and return six months later for a new sprint on autonomous vehicle routing.

The old model of six semesters of study for a field that changes every 12 months is not only obsolete—it's counterproductive. The **AI First worker will live in a constant cycle of work, learn, apply, repeat**, with each learning module directly tied to immediate outcomes. In this new reality, the prestige isn't about finishing a four-year track. The prestige comes from staying current, adaptive, and ahead—measured not in years enrolled, but in outcomes delivered.

High schools will also adapt. By the end of the first phase of disruption, **most high school graduates will be work-ready**. Instead of funneling the majority into full-time universities, many will step directly into the workforce, supplementing their careers with short, agile education cycles—one to three months of training at a time, repeated throughout life. Education will become **continuous, modular, and deeply intertwined with work itself.**

This is a massive conceptual leap: the "school-work-retirement" lifecycle is gone. Instead, the AI First citizen will live in a world where **education and work blur permanently.** You'll work, learn, upskill, and pivot— over and over. A marketing manager might take a two-week AI prompt engineering course at 32, a healthcare worker might learn robotic systems at 41, and a logistics operator might do a trade-up bootcamp at 50. **Agile education becomes the fuel of career resilience.**

Summary: AI Speed Makes Change Happen

AI is all about Speed and Power. **Speed defines first phase of the AI First era.** Not gradual, not incremental, but **blinding**, disorienting acceleration. The disruptions are so massive and so sudden that they feel like near chaos. Entire industries, labor markets, and social structures shift in months. The introduction of AI First organizations doesn't ripple across society slowly the way the steam engine or the personal computer did. It detonates, sending shockwaves through every institution that underpins modern life.

Given this speed and power of AI, the first three years of organizational and societal change in the AI First Era equals 60+years societal change in any previous eras. The change that once took generations to impact institutions, organizations and how people felt about themselves, now happens in less time than a presidential election cycle. That math is tough to swallow. The competitive drive for human survival ensures this speed. No company, no government, no military can afford to pause and debate for long. Once AI delivers a 100%+ annualized productivity advantage, adoption is no longer optional. It becomes the defining factor that separates organizations with a future from those destined to disappear. Refusing to move fast means falling behind permanently. And so, every organization—from banks to hospitals, from universities to construction firms—must adapt at breakneck pace. Their profit models, labor needs, and entire operating structures change instantly.

This speed forces society's hand as well. Education systems cannot take decades to adjust curricula. They must pivot in real time to teach AI First literacy and skills, with high schools preparing students for work directly and universities collapsing four-year programs into months-long intensives. Labor strategies cannot wait for "natural attrition" to balance the workforce. They must redeploy displaced white-collar workers immediately, while service and trade wages rise to stabilize purchasing power. Social fabrics and safety nets have to be reinvented almost overnight to keep society from tearing apart. Unions, once thought to be relics of the industrial age, surge back with a very different identity, structure, and charter way, providing wage social stability and dignity in jobs that AI cannot automate.

Corporate structures flatten in the same burst of speed. Layers of bureaucracy collapse, AI pods replace entire divisions, and entrepreneurial leaders rise as professional managers fade. **Investors** punish firms that move slowly and reward those who demonstrate measurable AI First productivity gains. **Governments** scramble to react, often without useful playbooks, while trying to manage civil unrest triggered by sudden job losses in professions once considered secure. Moreover, **defense and geopolitics** shift as AI capacity becomes a national security asset, vulnerable to cyberattacks or sabotage in ways no one predicted just a few years earlier.

And yet, the speed is not just a risk—it is also the mechanism that forces change to happen. If transitions dragged out for decades, resistance would build, and entrenched interests would slow progress. In Phase One, the sheer pace overwhelms resistance. By the time debates rage about whether AI is "good" or "bad," organizations have already restructured, universities have already retooled, unions have already reemerged, and companies have already doubled their margins. The adjustments, however painful, take root quickly because they must.

By the end of Phase One (~36 months), much of the **scaffolding for the new world of AI First is already in place—or at least being built at full tilt.** The shock is real, the turbulence is violent, but the adjustments are underway because there is no alternative.

And through it all, markets cheer. Investors flood into AI First firms, while valuations of laggards plummet. Wall Street analysts openly talk about "two economies": one where profits surge, and another where collapse feels imminent. The short term is **chaotic,** but it is a new type of chaos The short term is a crazy time for organizations and individuals alike—an exhilarating boom for some, a devastating bust for others.

It is only in the Medium Term that people begin to **normalize these changes. They will** accustom themselves to the new reality. But make no mistake: the foundation is laid in Phase One. The world adjusts at a pace unmatched in history, because in the AI First race, slowing down is the same as losing.

Chapter 12:

Final Thoughts -- The AI First Future Equals Adaptation and Abundance

Between phase one of AI First adoption and full adjustment to a society where AI First is the norm for organizations, the world will pass through two more phases: Restructuring, then finally Cultivating the Abundance. By the end of phase three, the world as we know it and the organizations within it, will be a relic.

Abundance or annihilation in this new, AI First world: the choice is ours. If we embrace AI and harness it for good, we will see a rapid real-life manifestation of the old adage "a rising tide lifts all ships." But if we fail to migrate society to AI First in a thoughtful way, of the AI revolution and reskill our workers, we might face a different kind of revolution --- one that no one wants to see.

Let's consider Phase 2, the mid-term future of four to six years, and get a sense of what the post-shock period of restructuring might look like.

The Medium-Term Future: Restructuring

The initial short-term period broke many institutions and norms that governed the organizations of our society. However, it also created the foundations and scaffolding for the AI First future. The medium term is when those new foundations are tried, tested, and shaped, and **adjusted**

This is the **restructuring phase.** Economies, companies, and nations reinvent themselves to survive in an environment where AI is no longer optional—it is the air everyone breathes.

During the medium term, the AI First world **stops being shocked. Acceptance sets in,** bringing with it stability and predictability. The panic of mass layoffs, corporate reorganizations, and early super-profits begin to **harden into a new reality.** Organizations have absorbed the shock, but the ripple effects of Phase 1 have reshaped everything— business structures, labor markets, social contracts, and geopolitics. The suffering and challenges of the new normal still exist, but society is into full solution mode, as opposed to the panic and chaos of phase one.

The Continued Rise of the Super Companies

Four years from now, AI Infrastructure Super Companies will dominate global AI commerce. These aren't mere trillion-dollar firms anymore— they are multi-trillion-dollar behemoths, worth upwards of **$20-40 trillion.** Their valuations climb because they can deliver profit margins once thought impossible. These powerful organizations begin to exhibit **major** nation-state-like influence and power around the world.

Across industries, we will see the AI First companies achieving value at levels not thought possible in prior eras. Energy, finance, manufacturing, banking---every industry now requires 30-70% fewer labor costs. Their profit margins **explode.**

Investors are uncompromising. They reward companies that demonstrate mastery of AI First with huge valuation premiums. Firms that cannot demonstrate measurable AI-driven productivity gains face swift and severe consequences. Shareholders no longer only ask, "Are you making money?" but **"Are you AI First enough to double margins?"**

This shift to an AI First mindset is not abstract—it is visible in every function of every organization in every industry. In energy, AI-driven predictive maintenance reduces downtime by 60%, allowing power plants to run continuously while cutting labor-intensive inspections.

Finance firms let go of thousands of back-office staff as AI handles fraud detection, compliance checks, and reporting in real time. In manufacturing, factories become nearly autonomous, with AI orchestrating supply chains, scheduling machine usage, and forecasting demand down to the hour.

Businesses are also fundamentally redesigned around **AI-driven pods** rather than legacy departments. A single AI pod in retail can oversee merchandising decisions for 1,000 stores, dynamically adjusting pricing, promotions, and inventory based on real-time consumer behavior. Marketing departments that once employed hundreds now run lean, with AI producing and testing campaigns at a fraction of the cost and in one-tenth of the time previously required.

Meanwhile, the explosion of AI First software products and tools forces traditional software vendors to either reinvent themselves or disappear. Products without AI capabilities rapidly lose relevance, as customers expect every tool to not just store data but analyze it, predict outcomes, and recommend actions. The bar has shifted: "software" without embedded AI feels empty.

The cultural change inside companies is equally dramatic. Executives no longer talk about cost control or incremental efficiency gains—they talk about compounding AI leverage and rapid outcomes. Strategic planning shifts from five-year roadmaps to rolling 90-day cycles, because competitors can leapfrog entire industries in a single quarter. AI is not a supporting function; **AI is the business model.**

Collapse Of White-Collar Jobs

The labor shock of the short term hardens into **permanent restructuring**. The trends that began in Phase 1 become permanent. White-collar job losses become staggering.

- **Customer Support**: 60–80% of roles are eliminated. AI copilots resolve tickets, handle voice calls, and escalate only rare-edge cases. Humans step in only for complex B2B cases, difficult customer conversations, or regulatory-sensitive interactions.

- **Finance & Accounting**: 40–60% of roles are cut. AI runs reconciliation, forecasting, and even scenario modeling. Finance teams shrink from 200 to 40. The few that are left focus on oversight and strategic interpretation.

- **Legal Support**: 30–50% of paralegal and contract-review jobs are gone. AI conducts discovery, redlines contracts, and drafts filings. High-end trial lawyers and strategists remain, but much of the industry is gutted. Human "hallucination" monitors will doublecheck the AI's citations to ensure that they are valid.

- **HR & Recruiting**: 40–70% reduction. AI manages screening, onboarding, compliance, and even performance management dashboards. HR transforms from "process managers" to "AI utilization enforcers." Of course, humans will set employment strategies, vetting promising prospects in person before offering a job.

- **Consulting & Project Management**: 60–90% gone. PMOs collapse as AI First pods take over. The consultants that survive are entrepreneurial specialists who solve edge-case problems, not broad process designers. Instead of overpaid management consultants, AI First entrepreneurial leaders will set strategy and direction. Endless PowerPoint presentations will be things of the past.

- **Marketing & Advertising**: 35-50% fewer roles. Creative ideation survives, but campaign design, testing, and execution are automated end-to-end. Agencies collapse unless they become AI-native. A small number of copywriters will be retained to finesse the output of AI and check it for hallucinations.

- **Engineering & Software Development**: 30–40% fewer absolute roles, but the productivity of those who remain doubles or triples. One AI First engineer does the work of 5–10 traditional coders.

In the medium term, the hardest truth emerges: **upwards of 100 million** highly educated professional knowledge workers around the world have become economically irrelevant almost overnight.

Let that sink in.

Hundreds of millions of highly educated, highly skilled, highly intelligent, highly trained, highly prepared financially successful individuals are **no longer economically relevant** in their chosen fields.

It has happened: People who spent hundreds of thousands of dollars on advanced degrees find themselves competing with AI systems that can do their job better, faster, and cheaper. The imbalance between educational investment and market value becomes unbearable.

Micro Case Study: Law Firm Reinvention¶

A top 50 law firm reduces its headcount of junior associates by 60% within three years. Instead of charging clients for the billing hours of armies of associates, they market themselves as an "AI-powered firm." They move most of their work to fixed-price engagements. Clients pay half the fees for faster, more accurate results. Former associates, saddled with $200K in student debt, scramble to retrain as mediators, compliance advisors, or even switch to trades or other lower skilled **and lower compensated professions.**

SMBs: The New Powerhouses

While Super Companies dominate global capital markets, SMBs (small and mid-sized businesses) become hyper-leveraged competitors in local and regional markets.

Think of it: a 40-person local advertising agency can suddenly compete with global giants because AI First workflows let them produce 60% more campaigns with the same staff. AI handles media planning, audience targeting, creative iteration, and performance optimization in real time, allowing the boutique shop to deliver results once reserved for New York or London Based global agencies with thousands of employees.

Similarly, a boutique manufacturer running AI-native design and supply-chain optimization can deliver at scales once reserved for Fortune 500 firms. In short: **AI collapses the scale advantage of large companies** while retaining the competitive scale of its enormous capabilities. SMBs don't need massive staff to compete. They need AI-native platforms.

As a result, capital shifts. Venture funding flows not just to startups but to SMBs that prove they can run AI First. Private equity firms roll up trades and mid-market firms across vertical industries, applying AI First playbooks to turn $50M firms into $500M powerhouses.

Societal and Cultural Shifts

By the end of this phase, cultural norms have realigned. The **collapse of white-collar prestige is irrefutable.** Families no longer view a finance or HR career as aspirational. Instead, pride grows around trades, entrepreneurship, and practical skills. A plumber running an AI-optimized contracting business earns more than a mid-tier lawyer. A machinist in advanced manufacturing commands a salary equivalent to a pre-AI corporate VP.

People no longer deny AI or call for its demise. **Acceptance has arrived.** AI continues to grow, because of its inevitability as well as the advantages it provides in everyday life. New Unions with new structures and alignments—not for white-collar jobs, but for the many white-collar displaced workers changing careers. Unions emerge in sectors that suddenly form the backbone of society because they cannot be automated completely. Wages rise exponentially for the AI-literate or those whose labor cannot be replaced by AI. In some cases, wages for these groups will grow 5-10X within 5 years, as AI First skills drive organizations success.

Evolution of Government and Policy Responses

During the first phase, 100% of governmental focus was on maintaining social stability ---preventing the global meltdown of organized society. Governments in the medium term are caught in a high-wire act. They cannot slow AI adoption without crippling their competitiveness, yet they cannot ignore social unrest from displaced workers. Policy debates become fierce:

- **Corporate Taxation:** With corporate profitability soaring, tax rates on Super Companies increase. Relatively quickly nations debate whether to institute minimum effective global corporate tax rates to redistribute the new "AI dividend," which has propelled profitability to unprecedented heights across industries. Pressure intensifies to tax the "super companies" that dominate the AI infrastructure.

- **Universal Base Income & Wage Subsidies:** Universal Basic Income (UBI) is piloted in multiple countries with various results and incentive perversion. Wage subsidies for retraining programs expand, though they lag behind the speed of disruption.

- **Immigration Policy:** Nations compete fiercely for AI First talent, offering fast-track visas and tax incentives. At the same time, they restrict inflows of non-AI-skilled workers to protect fragile domestic labor markets, as many low-skilled jobs that were previously filled by immigrants are now higher paid unionized jobs being filled by displaced white-collar citizens.

- **Education Reform:** Governments pump billions into trade schools, apprenticeships, and AI First training programs. By 2028, enrollment in vocational programs rises 60%. Universities that fail to pivot collapse.

Social unrest flares in multiple regions. Protests from displaced white-collar workers, sometimes turning violent, pressure governments to act. However, regulators face the unavoidable truth: **AI cannot be stopped.** If they impose restrictions, other nations surge ahead and capture their markets. No democratic leader wants to be remembered as the one who killed national competitiveness by throttling AI.

Energy Policy to Meet AI's Thirst for Power

The AI revolution will rewrite global energy strategy as profoundly as it rewrites business. The sheer compute costs required for large-scale AI adoption **demand massive amounts of electricity,** turning energy independence into a top-tier matter of national security. Nations will no longer view electricity primarily as an infrastructure resource—it becomes the backbone of competitiveness, sovereignty, and survival in the AI First world.

For countries without oil, natural gas, or coal, **nuclear energy** will surge to the forefront. Expect a new wave of nuclear investment across Europe, Asia and beyond as governments scramble to secure stable baseload power. Nations rich in carbon-based energy resources—particularly natural gas and oil—will reap extraordinary economic windfalls, as their exports now underpin not just transportation and heating but the digital engines of the AI economy.

Renewables like solar and wind will remain part of the mix, but their intermittency, high cost, and current scalability gaps mean they cannot ramp up fast enough to match the explosive growth in demand. Moreover, their relative cost is still too high to compete with other resources The reality is undeniable: **AI's hunger for power is immediate and exponential,** and only nuclear and fossil fuels can bridge that gap in the short and medium term. The geopolitics of energy will be redefined—those who can supply AI-grade power will lead, and those who cannot fall behind.

Projections:

- By 2030, AI data centers alone are expected to consume as much as 8–10% of total U.S. electricity demand, up from ~2% in 2023.
- Globally, AI workloads could require equivalent power output of 40–50 large nuclear reactors by 2035 just to sustain compute growth.
- Nations like France, South Korea, and the UAE are already accelerating nuclear builds; the International Atomic Energy Agency projects that nuclear capacity could double worldwide by 2050, with AI-driven demand being a primary factor.
- In fossil fuels, natural gas exporters like the U.S., Qatar, and Australia are positioned to see double-digit export growth, as gas-fired plants provide the fastest scalable solution to meet AI-driven energy spikes.
- Transmission and grid investment is expected to surge. McKinsey warns that by 2040 the world must pour $21 trillion into upgrading power grids to withstand the new load patterns of an AI First economy.

Military, War, and Crime in the Medium Term

By the mid- to- late- 2020s, AI is fully embedded in national defense strategies. Militaries deploy AI to manage battlefield logistics, autonomous drones, and cyber-defense at scales never seen before. **AI-augmented simulations** allow generals to test thousands of battle strategies in hours. Nations that fail to keep pace militarily in the AI arena find themselves dangerously exposed.

Policing also transforms. AI-powered surveillance and predictive analytics become widespread. Crime prevention improves, but privacy concerns spark mass protests. Facial recognition, bodycam analysis, and real-time anomaly detection redefine law enforcement. Criminals adopt AI too—fraud schemes, identity theft, and AI-driven scams skyrocket, forcing constant escalation in the eternal **cat-and-mouse game between law enforcement and criminal networks.**

Summary of the Medium Term

The medium-term future of the AI First world marks the restructuring phase—roughly years 4 thru 6—when the initial shock of mass layoffs, corporate upheavals, and panic transitions into stabilization and acceptance. AI Infrastructure Super Companies emerge as multi-trillion-dollar giants. Legacy firms struggle, while new AI First entrants leap into dominance, just as Facebook and Uber did in the digital revolution.

Every sector is reshaped – energy firms, manufacturing, retail, and software. Investors punish companies that are not "AI First enough," even if the firms remain profitable. Inside organizations, cultural norms shift from long-term planning to 90-day cycles of compounding AI leverage.

The labor market undergoes irreversible restructuring. White-collar roles collapse: Highly educated professionals—**tens of millions** with advanced degrees—find themselves economically superfluous almost overnight, sparking social unrest and identity crises.

Culturally, society revalues trade and practical/manual work. Plumbers, machinists, and contractors earn as much as mid-tier lawyers, while unions resurface in agriculture, services, logistics and other industries to secure higher wages and stabilize society. Governments respond with corporate tax hikes, wage subsidies, UBI pilots, and massive vocational training programs, though these often lag disruption.

This is also the period where governments themselves begin to fundamentally restructure. Ministries and agencies shrink layers of bureaucracy, replacing them with AI-driven service delivery—tax processing, licensing, benefits, and even parts of policy analysis become automated. Educational systems undergo dramatic realignment as four-year universities crumble, giving way to two-year programs, micro-academies, and company-sponsored trade schools. These new models cycle students through intense 2–6 month bursts of learning. What started as experimental pilots in Phase 1 are now the dominant model of workforce preparation.

Healthcare systems, too, standardize AI triage, diagnostics, and administrative automation, slashing costs and reducing wait times. Financial regulators adopt real-time AI oversight to prevent fraud, and law enforcement agencies normalize AI surveillance, with debates about privacy becoming a permanent feature of democratic politics. In short, the seeds planted during the chaos of Phase 1 become the entrenched structures of Phase 2—hardwired into government, education, healthcare, and business at every level.

Energy emerges as a national security issue, with AI's massive compute demands driving nuclear expansion, fossil fuel windfalls, and $20+ trillion in grid investments. Countries unable to secure affordable, reliable power face economic collapse. Militaries also embed AI deeply, using it for logistics, battlefield simulation, and autonomous drones, while cyberwarfare and AI-driven crime escalate sharply. Law enforcement and surveillance adopt AI too, creating major privacy battles.

By the end of this phase, society has entered a new normal. The chaos of the short-term gives way to hardened realities: AI dominance is entrenched, economic structures are permanently reshaped, governments have adapted, and both corporations and nations operate in ways that would have been unimaginable just a few years before.

Long-Term Future: The Age of Abundance or Annihilation

If the short-term (0–3 years) is chaos, and the medium-term (4–6 years) is restructuring, the long-term (7+) is where we can finally see the true fruits—and risks—of the AI First society. By this point, the shockwaves have been accepted, and much has been absorbed. Entire industries have collapsed, rebuilt, and stabilized around AI First models. And the result is a world that looks radically different from anything we've seen before.

A New Normal: Phase 3 Benefits of the AI First World

When the dust of the first two phases finally settles, something remarkable happens. Out of the chaos of mass displacement, social unrest, corporate restructuring, and political upheaval emerges a society that is fundamentally **more efficient, more productive, more**

balanced, more entrepreneurial, and more prosperous than anything humanity has ever experienced. This is the new long-term normal.

Over the initial 7-year period of the AI First era, human productivity doesn't just climb—it **skyrockets**. Conservative projections suggest a 500–1000% increase in output and productivity over this period.

To put that in perspective, it's the equivalent of the **productivity gains humanity achieved over the last 1,000 years, compressed into less than 90 months.** That is not hyperbole—it is the direct outcome of AI amplifying every human action, every organizational process, and every industry.

The potential benefits cascade everywhere. Food production becomes nearly limitless, as AI-driven agriculture maximizes yields, reduces waste, and distributes resources with near-perfect efficiency. Hunger, which has plagued humanity for millennia, has become a solvable **logistics problem** rather than an intractable tragedy. Energy, once a choke point of industrial society, shifts toward abundance. Smart grids, optimized fossil fuel extraction and consumption, nuclear expansion, and AI-optimized renewables ensure that power is cleaner, cheaper, and more reliable than ever before. AI doesn't just power society—it redefines what "energy security" means, turning it into a foundation of prosperity. And unlike previous eras of abundance that were unevenly distributed, this wave touches every corner of the globe faster, as AI erases many of the structural inefficiencies that once locked out entire regions.

Medical advances accelerate in ways that border on science fiction. AI-assisted research reduces drug development timelines from 10-15 years to 12-18 months. Personalized medicine, tuned by real-time analysis of individuals' genetic code and health data, eliminates entire categories of disease before symptoms emerge. **Life expectancy rises sharply**—20, 30, even 40 years in some projections. The era of AI First healthcare doesn't just cure—it prevents, preserves, and enhances. In many cases, people are living healthier at 90 than they once did at 60. Hospitals become hubs of wellness, monitoring preventative systems powered by AI, and shifting the focus of health from treatment to optimization.

Education also undergoes a renaissance. Learners flow between short tactical bursts of skills training and lifelong enrichment in the classics. The result is a society that is both more technically competent and more deeply human. At the same time, trade schools and company-sponsored academies thrive, ensuring that new generations have a practical pipeline into high-value roles. Universities that survive transform into hybrid institutions, blending advanced research with short-cycle skill training and broad humanistic education. This is not education for status—it is education for adaptability and meaning.

The economy becomes not just bigger, but more efficient. The realignment of labor markets ensures that disenfranchisement - **though it never disappears completely**—is held to stable, tolerable historical norm levels. Unions and corporations align together in a **symbiotic relationship** to ensure higher wages for manual and service labor.

Corporate labor alignment for AI-literate workers skyrockets incomes. The rising tide, for once, truly does lift all boats. Workers in roles once dismissed as "low prestige"—from hotel staff to tradespeople to agricultural workers—now command wages of $50, $60, even $90 an hour, supported by AI-driven efficiencies that allow companies to absorb the increased costs while still expanding margins. This rebalancing of wages creates an inversion of social prestige: jobs once seen as marginal become the backbone of stable societies.

AI First Super Productivity Allows Less Work for the First Time

The AI First era productivity explosion yields so much surplus productivity per worker that society does not need humans to work harder to achieve exponential gains. For the first time in our history on the planet, efficiency and abundance no longer require exhaustion. The asymmetry of output is so massive—ten or even one hundred times the productivity per unit of effort—that the same worker can produce more in a few hours than an entire team once could in weeks. That surplus allows **humanity to finally step off the treadmill of perpetual travail.**

Yet the most profound change isn't material—it's temporal. This stage brings another first for humanity --- work is no longer the dominant rhythm of life. AI's compounding productivity gains free up something we've never had at scale: time with freedom of choice. People still work, and work hard, but work no longer dominates identity or defines existence. Leisure, family, friendships, exploration, and creativity take a central place in daily life. Parents spend more time with their children; caregivers have more freedom; communities rediscover forms of connection that had long been eroded by the relentless pace of industrial and digital life.

This is unprecedented. Every prior productivity revolution—coinage, industrialization, digitization—**ultimately demanded that humans work more,** scale faster, and compete harder. Yes, output per worker increased, but so did the hours, the intensity, and the demands on the human body and mind. The farmer who once tilled more acres with better plows had to work longer hours to meet the new market's demands. The factory worker of the Industrial Revolution endured longer shifts despite machinery multiplying output. The knowledge workers of the digital revolution found themselves tethered to email, Zoom, and smartphones—working harder, not less, even as their productivity soared.

What AI creates is **not laziness, but liberation.** People will still strive, but for the first time, striving can be a **choice**, not a condition of survival. Humans will pour energy into pursuits that deepen their lives rather than just sustain them. Believe it or not, **AI will enable more human connection, not less**—more time to sit with family, talk with neighbors, create art, build, teach, play, and explore.

This opens the door to a new kind of renaissance. People begin to rediscover activities that were once abandoned to the pressures of industrial schedules. Arts, music, crafts, and literature flourish as millions of people return to working with their hands—not because they must, but because they can. AI co-pilots enhance these efforts, making creation more accessible while leaving the joy of the process intact. Hobbies that were once luxuries become central to life. Health becomes a greater focus too, as individuals invest time in exercise, nutrition, and preventative care. Communities grow stronger when individuals can actually participate in them.

The transition is not frictionless, but once achieved, it redefines what a "normal" human life looks like. Work remains part of life, but because of the astronomical productivity of every worker, work is for the first time no longer the center of life. The rhythm of society shifts toward balance, where productivity and abundance do not come at the cost of exhaustion and alienation, but instead fuel freedom and reconnection.

The result is more freedom. Some will continue to work at a frantic pace, measuring themselves by accomplishments and greatness. Others may choose a more balanced life of family, community and leisure. For the first time in history, society doesn't need work to rule people's lives.

Humanity can now produce the resources to survive—and even thrive—without a work-obsessed existence. The sense of fragility that defined Phase 1 has been replaced by a new sense of possibility, and with it, a society that feels more human than it has in centuries.

Long-Term Permanent Transformation of Labor

By the third phase of AI transformation, the labor market looks very different. It has permanently transitioned into three groups:

1. **AI First Knowledge Workers (10–15%)**: A small elite of highly skilled, highly compensated, entrepreneurial, AI-fluent professionals. Each is as productive as 10–20 traditional workers. These roles command premium salaries, but they are scarce.
2. **Skilled Manual and Trade Workers (20–25%)**: Electricians, plumbers, machinists, high-end construction workers. These roles and roles like them cannot be fully automated, and their wages surge because society needs them to function. A plumber with AI-augmented diagnostics earns more than many corporate senior managers used to.

3. **The Displaced Majority (60%+)**: Former white-collar workers in finance, HR, marketing, consulting, and legal struggle to adapt. Many retrain into lower skilled jobs, moving into manual labor drives even stronger unionization of non-skilled (or wrong-skilled) workers.

Job function projections by the third phase show that 60–70% of today's white-collar roles are permanently eliminated. McKinsey, Goldman Sachs, and World Economic Forum studies converge on this point: the majority of repetitive, process-heavy jobs will vanish.

- **Accounting and Finance**: 80% of routine roles gone. Only strategic CFO-level and niche financial advisory survive.
- **Legal**: 70% of paralegal and case-prep roles gone. Litigation and negotiation remain, but slimmed down.
- **HR**: 80% reduced, transformed into AI-driven accountability hubs rather than process administrators. Humans retain ultimate control over hiring strategies and decisions.
- **Marketing**: 70% fewer roles. Content, targeting, and optimization are fully AI-native except for a few strategists and copywriters.
- **Consulting & Project Management**: 90% gone. AI First pods replace entire firms.

By contrast, manual jobs grow exponentially in prestige and pay, supported by new types and structures of unionization. Society flips its prestige pyramid: **"dirty hands" jobs become the new white-collar dream.**

Micro Case Study: The Prestige Flip¶

A young man in 2040 chooses to attend a robotics-enhanced electrician trade school rather than Harvard. Within 5 years, he earns $250,000 annually running a small AI-augmented electrical contracting firm. His cousin, who pursued an MBA, is underemployed, making $70,000 as a compliance officer for a regional nonprofit. Families brag about their kids "in the trades" rather than "in the office."

Education and Universities in the Long Term: Survival of the Practical

The long-term is catastrophic for traditional higher education. By 2040, **upwards of 50% of universities in the U.S. have either closed or merged.** Globally, the story is the same. Only those that embraced AI First early and adjust their strategy survive.

Universities that thrive embed AI into every curriculum. Students graduate with dual fluency: their field of study and AI First mastery. Programs become modular, shorter, cheaper, and deeply practical, often partnering at scale with employers, big and small, for over 50% of immediate job placement upon graduation (3-month segments).

Meanwhile, trade schools explode in popularity and prestige, with many trade schools existing as **short-term programs inside universities**. Enrollment doubles or triples as students see clearer ROI in practical skills augmented by AI than in four-year degrees. Liberal arts survive, but only as foundational "thinking" disciplines—critical reasoning, philosophy, ethics—that complement AI-driven technical mastery.

Government subsidies shift from traditional universities to vocational and applied AI First programs. Employers directly sponsor training academies, collapsing the gap between "school" and "work."

Government and Policy in Phase 3

Governments in the long term face the hardest challenge in modern history: how to stabilize societies where fewer workers are needed, profits soar, and inequality explodes.

Corporate Taxation Rises Sharply: Within seven (7) years, corporate tax rates in advanced economies climb significantly. Super Companies generating trillions of profits are taxed heavily — effective rates increase while labor costs as a percentage of GDP decrease, as the income tax from white-collar employees must be replaced. Governments justify this increase as taxation of the "AI dividend."

Universal Basic Income Pilots: After a decade of debate, UBI becomes reality in several nations. Monthly stipends provide displaced workers with a baseline income. This prevents social collapse, but does not solve cultural identity crises, as millions struggle with the loss of purpose that comes from no longer working. There will be many debates and issues about incentive perversion, incentivizing people not to work. What were the "welfare" and "safety net" discussions of previous eras become similar discussions rebranded as Universal Basic Income. Some nations move forward others do not, but UBI becomes a global political football.

Immigration and Talent Wars: Nations fight for the AI elite—the 10–15% who can wield AI First capabilities are global rock stars. Not only engineers, but executives, marketers, operations and logistics professionals that are true AI First leaders command incredible wage rates in the market.

Immigration policies prioritize these individuals, creating new global hubs of AI talent. Simultaneously, **many nations face unrest** as they fail to provide enough meaningful jobs for displaced workers. Many nations restrict flow of unskilled workers and migrants, as those unskilled workers are truly taking the now high-paying, low-skill, recently unionized jobs that are being filled by the current disenfranchised white-collar class. Around the globe, all political viewpoints begin to take a **domestic employment first** lens to immigration issues, as the politically connected class are the ones who have been disenfranchised out of employment opportunities that immigration now threatens.

Phase 3 Is Not All Sunshine and Roses

Phase 3 is not a utopia. Just as AI supercharges productivity and prosperity, it also reshapes the landscape of global conflict and the negative aspects of competition. History shows that wars are rarely fought simply for survival; they are fought for power, resources, and economic dominance. AI doesn't eliminate this dynamic. It amplifies it.

Conflicts in this era will look very different from the blood-soaked wars of the past. Human casualties may decline, but infrastructure hubs—AI data centers, energy grids, communication satellites, and autonomous systems—become the new casualties. Disabling 20% of a rival's AI processing power could cripple their economy as much as destroying a factory did in the 19th century or bombing oil fields did in the 20th.

Because these conflicts are perceived as "cleaner" (fewer immediate human deaths), governments and state-sponsored actors may be willing to engage in more frequent attacks. Cyberattacks, drone swarms, and sabotage of digital infrastructure become normalized tools of international conflict. The result is an environment in which aggression *increases*, not decreases.

Resource-rich nations will invest massively in AI defense and counterintelligence, just as they once invested in nuclear arsenals. Budgets for AI defense could reach levels similar to Cold War-era military spending—trillions of dollars annually across the globe. Strategic alliances will shift rapidly: countries with AI dominance will wield disproportionate power, while AI laggards will find themselves economically and militarily vulnerable.

The historical parallels are striking. During the Industrial Revolution, nations raced to dominate steel, coal, and railroads, leading to colonial expansion and global conflict. In the Cold War, nuclear capability—not human armies—was the true currency of power, leading to decades of proxy wars and brinkmanship. In Phase 3, **energy and AI capability become the new strategic high ground.** Wars will be fought less over land and more over processing power, bandwidth, energy resources and algorithmic supremacy.

This dynamic also raises a troubling paradox. A society enjoying unparalleled prosperity at home could simultaneously feel fragile abroad. Citizens may be living longer, healthier lives, but their governments are forced into constant defensive postures, racing to protect critical AI infrastructure from adversaries.

In short, Phase 3 brings abundance, but it also introduces new forms of conflict that test the stability of global order. Nations that master AI may not wage traditional wars, but the struggle for dominance will persist—

only it will be fought in data centers, power grids, and orbiting satellites rather than trenches.

The Global Power Shift

AI is not only reordering all of the organizations that make up society. It is reordering nations.

The global balance of power is up for grabs. For the first time, it is not armies, nor nukes, nor trade alliances that determine dominance. It is computing, data, energy and **speed to AI First**. The country that wins AI doesn't just get stronger—it dictates the rules of global commerce, security, and culture.

If the companies and organizations within United States embraces AI First fully, it retains leadership. If it hesitates, China—already deploying AI in industry, surveillance, and military systems on a national scale— seizes advantage. Europe, fragmented by regulation, risks becoming inconsequential. Smaller nations like Singapore, Israel, or the UAE, if they go all-in on AI First policies, could **punch far above their weight** and become disproportionate powers.

The timeline is short. The next several years—not decades—will determine this balance. A nation that loses even five years in AI adoption effectively surrenders its industries, its military edge, and its cultural influence.

Phase 3 Is Not the End But a Beginning

Phase 3 is not the end of history—it is the beginning of a **new chapter**. For the first time, humanity can achieve balance between productivity and quality of life. Yes, challenges remain, but, hopefully, society will learn to channel disruption into renewal, not collapse. What emerges is a world where abundance replaces scarcity, where organizations and labor exist in a mutually beneficial harmony and where people finally have the freedom to choose how to live their lives. The AI First world is not just faster and more profitable—it is more human.

This optimism is not naïve. Just as past revolutions—industrial, digital, nuclear—produced periods of turbulence before stabilizing, the AI revolution will also be required to find equilibrium after **massive and unprecedented** disruption.

The difference is the speed of the disruption and the power of the upside: the productivity and prosperity gains are so massive that even after accounting for conflict, disruption, and uncertainty, societies emerge richer, healthier, and freer than before.

The path forward will not be smooth. Humanity has never had tools this powerful, and if we learn to wield them wisely, the rewards will stretch across generations. For the first time in centuries, the promise that as the future expands, everyone rises with it, feels not just aspirational, but achievable.

What makes this moment different from any in history is that the gains are not confined to a single class or geography. Entire populations— from rural towns to megacities—benefit in tangible, visible ways. Families feel the difference in their daily lives, not in abstract statistics. Global connectivity means innovations spread instantly, closing gaps that once took centuries to bridge. The optimism of Phase 3 of the AI First transformation on global society is rooted in something real: that humanity finally has the chance to live not in constant survival mode, but in a state of continuous progress.

Conclusion: The Coming AI Reckoning

The story of AI is not the story of a tool. **AI is the story of a civilizational pivot.** A pivot that that changes humanity unlike anything before. Wheels, steam, electricity, the internet—each of these changed the arc of history. But none of them hit with the force and speed of AI. This is the first disruption when the adoption curve is measured not in decades, but in days, and the disruption will flirt with destruction.

The short-term or phase 1 of the AI transformation is **when the shock hits hardest**. White-collar jobs, once thought untouchable, vanish at

breathtaking speed. Companies that embrace AI First see profits spike 100%+ while competitors stall and die. In record time.

Social prestige is reversed as tradespeople and AI-native entrepreneurs rise, while MBAs and consultants see their value collapse. **Governments scramble** with stopgap measures, but nothing stems the tide. The first lesson is searingly clear: in the short term, AI is not "on the horizon." It is here. And it is relentless.

The medium-term or phase 2 is a time of restructuring. The deep state of business—the middle managers, PMOs, and internal and external management consultants—gets flushed out. Organizations flatten. Accountability moves down to pods and individuals. Companies that hesitated are gutted by AI First upstarts who achieve in months what legacy firms couldn't in years. Unions rise again, this time as true partners with the organizations they work within. Governments experiment with new policies: retraining, subsidies, safety nets. But **the churn is constant.** The second lesson is clear: in the medium-term, survival depends not on size, but on adaptability.

The long-term or phase 3 (7+ years) is **the payoff—or the collapse.** If societies manage the turbulence, abundance follows. Food production triples. Lifespans expand. Corporate profitability surges, and super companies worth $50 trillion + dominate industries, and large aspects of society itself. Work shrinks as a percentage of human life. Leisure, creativity, and family become central.

But if societies fail to navigate the disruption, the opposite happens: unrest, fractured democracies, authoritarian crackdowns, and mass dislocation. This lesson is undeniable: the long-term is heaven or hell—and which path we take depends entirely on how leaders handle the next decade.

What This Means for Leaders

Leaders—of companies, governments, universities—**must abandon the fantasy of gradual change.** There is no "slow adaptation" of AI. It's now or never. Being a **true** AI First organization is not optional: it is required. The entrepreneurial leaders will drive this, and make it happen, or the organization will simply lose relevance.

If you are a CEO, business owner, university president, or leader of any organization, your job is to **personally** lead from the front, to model AI First behavior, to flatten your organization, and to force urgency. If you are a policymaker, your role is to accelerate adoption while cushioning disruption—to tax windfall profits wisely, to fund reskilling, to stabilize unrest without choking innovation. If you are an individual, your survival depends on whether you become AI First yourself. Not "aware of AI." Not "dabbling in AI." But mastering it, embedding it, living it.

This is non-negotiable Your existence depends on it.

Where Do We Go from Here

The truth is hard, but liberating: AI is unstoppable. AI First is happening. And it is happening now. No government regulation, no corporate lobby, no academic resistance can halt it. If one nation slows, another surges. If one company hesitates, another dominates.

But how humanity *integrates* AI—that choice is ours. Will we weaponize it for control, or unleash it for abundance? Will we cling to outdated structures, or reinvent work, education, and society for a world of exponential growth?

The stakes could not be higher. The AI revolution will either be remembered as the era when humanity fractured under its own fear—or as the dawn of an age when prosperity, longevity, and creativity flourished beyond imagination.

This moment is **the** line in the sand. AI is not a "tool." **It is the new operating system of every organization that makes up our**

civilization. The wheel, coinage, steam, electricity, computing—each was a chapter. AI is the rewrite.

Leaders must stop treating AI as "nice to have" and immediately pivot all-in to AI First. Workers must stop waiting for someone else to tell them what to do, and grab the opportunity to lead the pack by mastering AI **now**. Governments must stop imagining they can slow it down without killing their economies. They can't.

The stakes are, for the first time in human history, literally everything – **all aspects of our lives will be affected.** The choice is binary. **AI First—or AI Finished.**

Author's Bio

Fred Voccola is a seasoned technology entrepreneur, philanthropist, CEO and board director who merges visionary innovation with large-scale operational acumen to transform organizations, cultivate industry disrupting technologies, deliver exponential shareholder returns and positively impact lives.

Currently, Fred serves as Chairman and CEO of Simpro, a multi billion dollar global AI powered operating platform for commercial and residential trade companies which serves over 500,000 people around the world.

Prior to Simpro, Fred was Co-founder and CEO of Kaseya, where he spearheaded the company's evolution into a global leader in AI-powered cybersecurity and IT management software for small to mid-sized businesses. Under Fred's leadership, Kaseya grew to over $1.5 billion in annual revenue, employing over 5,000 people around the world, and becoming one of the most valuable privately held software companies in the world.

Before his tenure at Kaseya, Fred was co-founder and president of Identify Software (acquired by NYSE: BMC Software), co-founder and CEO of Trust Technology Corp (acquired by FGI Global), and president and general manager at Yodle (acquired by Web.com: NASDAQ: Web).

In addition to serving as Chairman of Simpro, and Vice Chairman of Kaseya, Fred serves as Chairman of Upshop, the leading provider of AI powered solutions for the grocery industry. Fred also serves on the board of other technology companies, including Planet DDS, Lexipol, and Inhabit.

A recognized authority on AI, cybersecurity, business transformation, crisis management and organizational culture, Fred is an active member of the *Forbes* Technology Council, the *Fast Company* Executive Board and the *Newsweek* Expert Forum. He regularly shares his insights with national media outlets such as *FOX Business News* and *Bloomberg*.

Fred is also deeply committed to philanthropy. He founded and chairs the Cooper Voccola Family Foundation, a nonprofit dedicated to supporting conservative American-focused organizations and animal welfare initiatives. Beneficiaries include the America First Policy Institute (AFPI), Disabled American Veterans (DAV), Paralyzed Veterans of America (PVA), Leadership Institute, Judicial Watch and the Christian Appalachian Project, among others.

Additionally, Fred services on the boards of Hackensack Meridian health care system, the Miami Zoo, and the Monmouth County SPCA.